The Tapestry of Language Learning

The Individual in the Communicative Classroom

Robin C. Scarcella
University of California, Irvine

Rebecca L. Oxford
University of Alabama

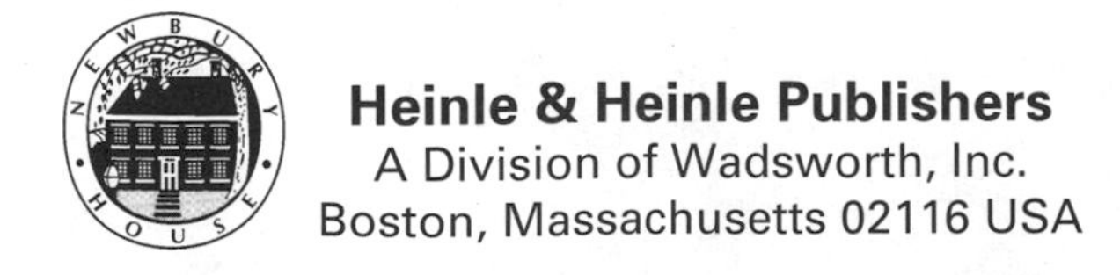

Heinle & Heinle Publishers
A Division of Wadsworth, Inc.
Boston, Massachusetts 02116 USA

Vice President and Publisher: Stanley J. Galek
Editorial Director: David C. Lee
Project Coordinator: Anita L. Raducanu/A+ Publishing Services
Assistant Editor: Kenneth Mattsson
Copy Editor: Ellen J. Kisslinger
Editorial Production Manager: Elizabeth Holthaus
Assistant Manufacturing Coordinator: Jerry Christopher
Internal Design: Bonnie McGrath
Cover Design: Hannus Design Associates

CREDITS
Illustration: p. 68, Len Shalansky
Texts: p. 23, Slobin, D.I. (1973). Cognitive prerequisites for the development of grammar. In C. Fillmore & D.I. Slobin (Eds.), *Studies of child language development* (pp. 175-208). NY: Holt, Rinehart & Winston; pp. 24-25, Vygotsky, L.S. (1978). *Mind in society: The development of higher psychological process.* M. Cole, V. John-Steiner, S. Scribner, & E. Souberman (Eds. & Trans.). Cambridge, MA: Harvard University Press; p. 102, Stevick, E. (1963). *A workbook in language teaching* (pp. 62-63). NY: Abington Press; pp. 103, 159, 161, Krashen, S.D., & Terrell, T. (1983). *The Natural Approach: Language acquisition in the classroom* (pp. 113-114, 125), Elmsford, NY: Pergamon Press; pp. 104, 109, Richard-Amato, P. A. (1988). *Making it happen: Interaction in the second language classroom: From theory to practice.* NY: Longman; pp. 128-129, Lapp, R.E. (1984). The process approach to writing: Toward a curriculum for international students. *University of Hawaii Working Papers in ESL;* pp. 154-155, Chaudron, C., & Richards, J. (1986). The effect of discourse markers on the comprehension of lectures, Oxford: Oxford University Press; p. 159, Aronson, E., Blaney, N., Stephan, C., Sikes, J., & Snapper, M. (1978). *The jigsaw classroom.* Beverly Hills, CA: Sage; pp. 160-161, Christison, M.A., & Bassano, S., (1987). *Look who's talking* (pp. 3, 7), San Francisco: Alemany; p. 168, Nunan, D. (1988). *Syllabus design* (pp. 132, 142-143), Oxford: Oxford University Press

Manufactured in the United States of America.

ISBN: 0-8384-2359-0

Heinle & Heinle Publishers is a division of Wadsworth, Inc.

10 9 8 7 6

CONTENTS

ACKNOWLEDGMENTS

This volume — and the Tapestry Approach in general — began at the 1990 international convention of Teachers of English to Speakers of Other Languages in San Francisco. Sipping coffee with David Lee, the new Editorial Director for College ESL at Heinle & Heinle, Rebecca Oxford lamented the absence of effective ESL teaching approaches that combine communicative, thematic, task-based learning with a concern for students' individual differences (learning styles, strategies, motivations, age, and developmental needs). Rebecca sketched out on paper napkins some preliminary ideas about the "ideal" ESL instructional approach that would unite all these essential pieces. David and Rebecca drew boxes showing how this approach could be implemented through a system of interlocking instructional materials.

In the spring of 1990, Heinle & Heinle commissioned Rebecca to write a position paper detailing the parameters of such an approach. Seventeen reviewers commented on the paper. Among these were dedicated ESL teachers, experienced researchers, and second language development theorists. The reviewers were enthusiastic. As a result, the Tapestry Approach was launched.

In August, 1990, Robin Scarcella joined the Tapestry team as Co-Editor with Rebecca for the entire set of instructional materials. Robin and Rebecca then wrote this volume, *The Tapestry of Language Learning: The Individual in the Communicative Classroom*. While writing this book, Rebecca and Robin worked with David in assembling a group of "area coordinators" who would assist in developing instructional materials consistent with the Tapestry Approach. To date the coordinators are: Patricia Byrd (grammar), Darlene Larson (syllabus), Sandra McKay (writing), Robert Oprandy (speaking and listening), Thomas Scovel (culture), Marguerite Ann Snow (themes and tasks), and Merrill Swain (assessment).

To gain information concerning the current status of ESL teaching, David and his colleagues at Heinle & Heinle conducted numerous focus groups across the nation and began collecting systematic survey data on the needs and emphases of ESL programs. In addition, David set up pilot sites for Tapestry at about 40 ESL institutes throughout the United States. These resources provided Robin and Rebecca with rich information especially pertinent to the needs of university-level ESL students. During its development *The Tapestry of Language Learning* benefited greatly from the comments and suggestions made by ESL administrators, teachers, and students.

We are particularly grateful to all the people who provided formal or informal comments on the chapters in this book and on Rebecca's original position paper: Paul Abraham, Jo Ann Aebersold, Sarah Benesch, William Biddle, Christine Billmyer, Gay Brookes, Debbie Busch, Patricia Byrd, Maria Cantarero, Marianne Celce-Murcia, Andrew Cohen, Mary Ann Carney Datesman, Fraida Dubin, Marie Eichler, Liz England, Susan Gass, Dennis Godfrey, Mary Hammond, Linda Hillman, Barbara Hoekje, Gary James, Donna Johnson, Diane Larsen-Freeman, Darlene Larson, Daphne Mackey,

Virginia Maurer, Sandra McKay, Carol Numrich, Robert Oprandy, Teresa Pica, Eileen Prince, Thomas Scovel, Maggi Sokolik, Earl Stevick, Merrill Swain, John Swales, and Victoria Talbott. We want to thank our students, who used or critiqued the pre-publication version of *The Tapestry of Language Learning* and provided us with insights: Pat Feller, Tatyiana Haijig, Maria Lopez, and Diana Murillo. We regret if we have accidentally missed anyone who gave us valuable ideas during the development stage.

We are very grateful to Charlie Heinle and Stan Galek of Heinle & Heinle, whose vision of ESL instruction merged so clearly with our own. Without their support, the Tapestry Approach and this particular book would certainly not have come to fruition.

On a day-to-day basis, it was David Lee's unflagging enthusiasm, keen intellect, and enduring patience that led to the completion of *The Tapestry of Language Learning.* His assistants, especially Kenneth Mattsson, were always at hand to help this book along.

We are forever indebted to Anita Raducanu for her expert work on the editing and production of the book. Her cool head, her eye for detail, and her ability to maintain creative excellence over a 3,000-mile geographic span were great boons to the authors.

Ellen Kisslinger was very helpful in copyediting the book and in giving the ESL teacher's perspective as part of the final editing process.

Finally we want to thank the men in our lives — husbands, son, step-sons, and fathers.

Robin C. Scarcella
Irvine, California

Rebecca L. Oxford
Tuscaloosa, Alabama

INTRODUCTION

CREATION OF THE TAPESTRY 

Beautiful tapestries have been woven throughout the world for thousands of years. The oldest examples appeared in Egypt around 1400 B.C. During the Middle Ages in Europe, tapestries hung on the walls of churches and castles. We still see them nowadays in elegant, modern homes and historical buildings. Learning a language is very much like weaving a tapestry.

Both language learning and weaving involve developmental processes. In developing their second language ability, language learners weave various threads — vocabulary, grammatical structures, and discourse features — to create proficiency in the four skills — reading, writing, speaking, and listening. Similarly, in developing their tapestries, skilled weavers work colored yarns into shapes and patterns.

Language learning serves various purposes. Some students acquire language to learn more about new cultures, while others acquire language to achieve financial or academic objectives. The greater the learner's need to develop language skill, the clearer the learner's reason for learning the language, and the stronger the learner's effort, the more developed generally becomes the learner's overall communicative competence. Tapestries, too, have multiple purposes. Originally tapestries functioned to cover window openings in castles to keep out the cold winter air, and later they came to be viewed as objects of grace and artistic beauty.

The learner creates the second language much as a weaver creates the tapestry. Ultimately, the learner decides when the product — the degree of communicative competence — is adequate and what its size, shape, and texture are to be. Others may help along the way, but in the long run, the learner's enthusiasm and desire to learn shape the quality of both the process and the product of language learning. Likewise, it is the weaver who creates the tapestry no matter how many others assist by providing advice, patterns, and tools. Like the learner, the weaver is in charge and determines the final product.

The learner's needs and purposes are fundamental to the development of the learner's language just as the weaver's needs and purposes — represented by the *loom* — are essential to the weaving of a tapestry. Without a solid and steady loom, the tapestry is likely to be loose, coarse, and raveled. Moreover, weaving on such a precarious loom is difficult.

The student's language learning task is made easier by the assistance of the teacher, who serves as a guide and companion as well as a motivator, counselor, and analyst of needs. The teacher helps the learner to overcome obstacles, suggests strategies for acquiring the language more efficiently, and provides the learner with exposure to and interaction with the necessary input. The teacher also provides encouragement to help the learner to attain communicative goals. Like the language teacher, the weaver's mentor assists by providing patterns for interesting designs, ideas for blending colors, and ways for strengthening the tapestry.

The successful teacher understands the multitude of factors that affect the learner's developing communicative competence. Developmental factors affect the universal nature of language learning. Certain stages predictably occur before other stages, and particular error types regularly appear in roughly the same order, creating an *interlanguage* as part of language development. Learners tend to pay attention to the salient aspects of the language and acquire those parts of language first. In a similar way, developmental factors also affect the nature of weaving. For instance, when weavers are first learning to weave, they tend to follow easy patterns before attempting complex ones.

In addition to the developmental processes just noted, environmental factors such as classroom interaction and input affect language development. In weaving, environmental factors represent the *warp*. Plain, uncolored yarn makes up this warp. These uncolored fibers are stretched vertically between the loom's upper and lower beams and are the foundation upon which the rich tapestry is woven.

Cognitive, affective, and social characteristics of the learner also shape language development. These characteristics, including (among others) learning styles, strategies, and motivation, result in the main individual differences in language development. In weaving, these characteristics represent the *weft,* colored yarns that are woven from side to side. The yarns may pass over and under the warp yarns or be wrapped around each warp yarn. The weft yarns are pushed close together, so you see only the colorful design and none of the plain warp. The design of the tapestry is created by changing the color of the weft yarns.

In language learning, pedagogical practices also guide the learner's emerging communicative competence. No single practice can serve the needs of all learners. The practices followed in a particular situation must be sensitive to the needs, development, and background of those learners. In weaving, these practices are called patterns, the drawings the weaver follows that show the shapes and colors of the tapestry. This book suggests patterns that help language learners weave the plain and colored yarns into shapes and designs and into beautiful scenes; that is, into fully developed communicative competence.

ORGANIZATION OF THIS BOOK

Part One provides an overview of the Tapestry Approach. Chapter One *(Overview of the Tapestry Approach)* summarizes the roles of teacher and student in the Tapestry Approach and describes the principles guiding instructional materials and testing. Unlike the Silent Way and the Natural Approach, the Tapestry Approach does not provide teachers with a set of fixed goals or rules concerning how to teach or how students should learn. This is because we consider teachers active, intelligent participants in their students' learning, and we consider students central in their own learning process. In the Tapestry Approach, teaching is a dynamic, interactional process in which instructors constantly shape their teaching to the developing needs of their students, and learners actively negotiate the instruction.

Part Two describes the learners and their language development. Chapter Two *(Developmental Factors)* summarizes characteristics of the learners (such as age, gender, and ethnicity) that cannot be changed by the teacher. In addition, the chapter discusses developmental factors that affect the learner's emerging communicative competence. In Chapter Three *(Language-Promoting Interaction),* we display the warp, the plain vertical yarns, such as input and interaction. We discuss the interactions that are explicitly designed to facilitate second language development, as well as Vygotskyan notions of the types of assistance that teachers and peers can provide students to help them learn English effectively. Chapter Four *(Characteristics of Individual Learners)* discusses learner characteristics such as styles, strategies, and motivation. Here, the tapestry of language learning bursts into full color with weft yarns. Chapter Five *(Communicative Competence)* depicts the overall tapestry, which represents the development of communicative competence.

Part Three examines each of the major and subsidiary language skills. These include reading, writing, listening, and speaking as well as grammar, vocabulary, and culture. The development of these interlocked language skills is the subject of Chapter Six *(Integrating Language Skills).* Tapestry teachers do not attempt to integrate all skills equally. Rather, they integrate them carefully through thematic and task-based instruction that best facilitates the development of the language skills students need. Chapter Seven *(Reading)* outlines the Tapestry Approach to reading instruction, emphasizing the importance of meaning, extensive reading, strategy development, and direct instruction. Chapter Eight *(Writing)* presents a process approach to writing explicitly adapted to the needs of ESL students. Chapter Nine *(Listening)* describes the Tapestry Approach to listening instruction, while Chapter Ten *(Speaking)* addresses specific activities useful for speaking and pronunciation skills. Chapter Eleven *(Grammar)* presents a balanced view in which both communicative tasks and explicit instruction are used to develop grammar in the context of meaningful communication. The final chapter, Chapter Twelve *(Culture),* focuses on the role of culture in the Tapestry Approach and emphasizes the importance of avoiding stereotypes and understanding cross-cultural differences.

Clearly, metaphors can only go so far, and we do not wish to stretch the tapestry metaphor beyond its limits. Metaphors merely provide imperfect portraits of realities. And, as Ortega y Gasset explains, "the person portrayed and the portrait are two entirely different things" *(The Dehumanization of Art,* 1949). Certainly, the metaphor may oversimplify the process of learning a second language; the myriad of factors interacting to affect language development are as complex as the human being. The categories themselves overlap, representing the complexity of the human mind and the newness of the field. However, despite these reservations, the tapestry metaphor serves a useful purpose: helping teachers remember major principles governing language acquisition and offering flexible guidelines for language instruction.

In sum, Part One presents the Tapestry Approach in its entirety. The chapters in Part Two provide a strong theoretical foundation for this approach as well as for the practical chapters in Part Three that follow. The total picture presented is that of the tapestry of language learning, a tapestry created and controlled by the learner with input from many sources, including the teacher, authentic materials, texts, and multiple media. This book shows how the language learning process and the resulting communicative competence can be made as powerful, enjoyable, and useful as possible.

PART I

THE APPROACH: THE WHOLE TAPESTRY

OVERVIEW OF THE TAPESTRY APPROACH

1

PREVIEW QUESTIONS

1. What is thematic, task-based instruction? What structural or philosophical changes in your program are necessary in order to use this type of instruction?
2. What roles do effective ESL teachers play, and how do these roles vary as a function of the teaching context? In what ways would the roles of the teacher be different in beginning and advanced ESL classes?
3. How can teachers encourage students to become learners who control their own language learning?
4. In what ways can instructional materials be adapted to meet the needs of individual learners?
5. What is the role of individual student assessment in the ESL classroom?

In order to make a tapestry, the weaver combines vertical and horizontal strands to make an aesthetically pleasing picture or design. Similarly, in order to learn a language, the learner combines multiple factors. There is interaction between the student's individual characteristics (for instance, learning styles and motivation) and external influences (such as teaching practices and instructional materials). When such interaction is tightly woven, communicative competence emerges.

ORGANIZATION OF THIS CHAPTER

This chapter concerns the weaving of the tapestry of language learning. Here we present an overview of the Tapestry Approach. First, we discuss the role of teachers and learners. Next, we outline the major principles guiding the development of Tapestry instructional materials and summarize the key types of Tapestry instruction. Then, we describe the content taught in Tapestry classrooms. Finally, we discuss the theoretical framework underlying Tapestry assessment.

THE ROLES OF TEACHER AND LEARNER

In the Tapestry Approach, teaching is a dynamic process involving teachers and students in meaningful, collaborative efforts. Teachers carefully tailor their instruction to the needs of individual students. Instruction arouses and maintains the interest of all students so that they are motivated to become successful, self-directed learners. Because the Tapestry Approach fosters motivation and learner autonomy, we must reconceptualize the roles of teacher and learner.

Teacher Characteristics

This section describes the two main characteristics of Tapestry teachers.

Caring. In Tapestry classrooms, teachers are, above all, caring. The act of caring has certain distinguishing features (Barth 1990, Gilligan 1982). Caring actions grow out of a concern for "the welfare, protection or enhancement of the cared for" (Noddings 1984, p. 23) as well as for oneself. Caring involves helping someone grow and become self-actualized (Mayeroff 1971).

Caring for students involves stepping out of one's personal frame of reference and considering the students' needs and expectations. It begins with an attitude of openness and receptivity. Teachers are aware of who their students are, what their strengths and weaknesses as learners are, and what is conducive to their language development. Teachers know how to respond to student needs and are aware of their own teaching abilities. Caring also includes some kind of action on behalf of the students. These actions include assuming instructional responsibility and acting responsively, especially at critical times. A teacher does not just decide, "I can't help the student now. I'd rather be doing something else." Responsive teacher behavior develops when teachers and students collaborate to overcome teaching and learning difficulties in a committed way (Gilligan 1982).

Responsive Tapestry teachers contribute to the development of nurturing classroom communities. These communities are essential because they foster caring, growth-inducing relationships that enhance the quality of lives. These communities develop when students and teachers meet together in the pursuit of common causes. In such communities, students and teachers experience a sense of membership, influence one another, have personal needs fulfilled, and share a satisfying connection with those around them.

Professionalism. Yet Tapestry teachers are more than caring. They are also professional. Richards (1990) argues that the assumption underlying most methods is that the teacher cannot be trusted to teach well. The Tapestry Approach involves a different way of looking at teaching, one in which teachers are viewed as professionals involved in reflecting upon their own teaching as well as the behaviors of their learners. Tapestry teachers are flexible and willing to alter plans depending on the kinds of language assistance individual students need. Teachers take a global look at all aspects of their students. For example, in addition to examining the learner's language performance, teachers analyze the learner's emotional reaction to learning tasks. Underlying the teacher's analysis are solid theory (see Chapters Two–Five) and an understanding of the language skills being taught (see Chapters Six–Twelve), as well as a careful consideration of what happens inside learners as they interact in their classrooms. Tapestry teachers recognize that learner characteristics and reactions to activities often change throughout a lesson.

Thus, the teacher's role varies. Teachers are information-gatherers, decision-makers, motivators, facilitators, input providers, counselors, friends, providers of feedback, and promoters of multiculturalism — depending on the context in which they teach.

Teacher Roles

Information-Gatherer. In response to their students' ever-changing needs, teachers constantly collect information about learners, analyze their language behavior, and observe ongoing interactions.

Decision-Maker. Teachers make decisions on a moment-to-moment basis. Their knowledge of learning theory and educational practice allows them to plan flexible learning experiences and to respond sensitively to learners of differing language ability levels and varying backgrounds, interests, and needs. While providing the necessary linguistic and emotional support, teachers encourage students to use their abilities to the utmost.

Motivator. Teachers motivate students to acquire English. They arouse and maintain their students' interest by constantly assessing the needs, interests, and goals of their students and tailoring their instruction accordingly. They provide stimulating, interesting lessons that respond to the emotional, cognitive, and linguistic needs of the learners.

Facilitator of Group Dynamics. Teachers have strong skills in group dynamics that help them to provide efficient classroom routines and smooth transitions. They organize instructional tasks logically and understand how to use different types of grouping (including individual, pair, small group, and large group work) to encourage specific types of learning.

Provider of Large Quantities of Authentic English Input and Opportunities to Use This Input. Teachers provide students with extensive exposure to English through readings, lectures, movies, films, audiotapes, and so on. They invite native speakers to class and arrange field trips for students so that students encounter a variety of native speakers. Teachers also arrange rich opportunities for learners to communicate with peers, native speakers, and themselves.

Counselor and Friend. Teachers know when to serve as counselors and friends. They provide emotional support just when it is required and help learners feel secure and confident about second language learning. They recognize psychological problems that may hinder their students' progress acquiring English and help students overcome these difficulties.

Provider of Feedback. Teachers monitor students' learning progress regularly. The feedback that they provide learners is timely and constructive. Students value the incentives that teachers regularly provide.

Promoter of a Multicultural Perspective. Teachers expect their students to take a multicultural perspective. They encourage students to be tolerant of cultural conflicts, to respect those of diverse cultures, and to avoid stereotyping others.

In sum, the Tapestry Approach depends on caring, professional teachers, who understand second language development, know effective teaching techniques, and make appropriate use of curriculum and materials. Tapestry teachers constantly update their training by attending professional conferences and workshops and reading relevant journals and books. (See the description of ESL and foreign language journals listed at the end of this chapter.) Yet what the teacher does is only part of the picture. The role of learners is also an important consideration in the Tapestry Approach.

The Learner

Learners are active in the Tapestry Approach. They have considerable control over their own learning, and they help select the specific themes and tasks of instruction. In addition, they provide teachers with valuable details about their learning processes.

There may be some conflict between the teacher's view of learning and the learners'. For example, learners from some cultures may expect to be passive recipients of information. In the Tapestry Approach, the teacher helps learners to understand why they must be active participants and why so much emphasis is placed on seeking information from learners regarding their attitudes, learning styles and strategies, preferences about interaction modes and learning tasks, and beliefs about effective teaching and learning.

In this section, we have considered the roles of the teacher and student. We are now ready to summarize the key principles guiding Tapestry instructional materials.

KEY PRINCIPLES OF TAPESTRY INSTRUCTIONAL MATERIALS

In the Tapestry Approach, materials serve as a valuable source of language input, but they are not the only one. They are supplemented with a wide variety of authentic, communicative tasks that provide students with increased exposure to and interaction with native English speakers. Based on empirical study, Tapestry materials are carefully matched to the skills, abilities, goals, backgrounds, and interests of students. A broad array of materials prepared by a team of experienced researchers, material developers, and practitioners is available. The materials allow teachers and students the flexibility to choose the pedagogical tasks that best suit particular goals.

Unlike the Silent Way and the Natural Approach, which present materials to be used in a precise way, the Tapestry Approach encourages teachers to adapt materials to the evolving needs of their students. The creation of these materials is guided by the principles listed below.

- Materials provide opportunities for communicative and authentic language use through thematic, task-based instruction.
- Materials accord with individual learners' differences, including proficiency levels, learning styles and strategies, cultures, needs, interests, and goals.
- Materials integrate language skills.
- Materials provide learners with extensive exposure to authentic language and numerous opportunities to use this language.
- Materials provide learners with a variety of supports that help students understand and use authentic language.
- Materials stimulate learner-centered (as opposed to teacher-centered) activity.
- Materials promote learner self-direction.
- Materials are highly motivating.

Each of these principles is discussed below.

Theme- and Task-Based Instruction

Tapestry materials emphasize acquiring English through instruction that encourages task-based learning centered upon themes. Underlying this principle is the notion of depth of learning — the notion that if students are actively engaged in meaningful, related theme-based tasks, they gain repeated exposure to language that helps them to process the language.

Theme-Based Instruction. Content materials are chosen primarily for their meaning as related to relevant, interesting themes. All other considerations (grammar, vocabulary, and pronunciation) are secondary. In theme-based instruction, topics provide the content for the ESL class.

> From these topics, the ESL teacher extracts language activities which follow naturally from the content material. Thus, a unit on "Advertising" might engage the students in a variety of activities such as designing and administering a marketing survey, plotting a graph of the results of the survey, and comparing and contrasting consumer attitudes.
>
> (Snow 1991, p. 7)

Task-Based Instruction. Within a given theme, tasks are constructed that call for students to utilize different learning strategies and that foster different aspects of communicative competence. (Refer to Chapter Four for a discussion of strategies and Chapter Five for a description of communicative competence.) Tasks encourage communicative interaction, both with learners and native speakers. In addition, they have *real world relevance;* that is, they require students to do in the classroom what they must do outside of the classroom. Tasks such as ranking what camping equipment students should take on a trip might be fun for some students, but such tasks are irrelevant to students who never plan to camp and cannot use camping vocabulary.

Individual Learner Differences

All aspects of Tapestry materials underscore the importance of individual differences in language proficiency, learning styles and strategies, cultures, needs, interests, and goals.

Language Proficiency. Tapestry materials are responsive to students of different English proficiency levels. The materials are roughly graded by the difficulty level of the instructional tasks. Content and genre contribute to task difficulty. The easiest content for ESL students to handle is related to their everyday activities — their family and their neighborhood. Culturally familiar topics are also easier to process than culturally unfamiliar topics. Props such as photos, slides, handouts, and objects help ESL students successfully process information presented to them during tasks.

The difficulty level of tasks is also determined by the cognitive demands on the learner to accomplish the task, the number of steps involved in completing the task, the amount of information the learner is expected to process, the difficulty of the instructions, and the amount of time given to complete the task (Oprandy 1991). Other factors affecting task difficulty include the number and quality of available supports — such as contextual and emotional aid, the processing difficulty, and the degree of stress. Long (1985) also points out other nonlinguistic variables that contribute to task difficulty, including the number of parties involved in a conversation, the pace and duration of a conversation, and the intellectual challenges posed by interlocutors.

Learning Styles and Strategies. Tapestry materials are responsive to differences in students' broad learning styles. Instructional materials and tasks generate interaction that provides communication opportunities for learners of all styles. In the Tapestry Approach, both global and analytic styles are utilized and promoted, and opportunities to learn from auditory, visual, and hands-on (tactile and kinesthetic) experiences are provided. Instructional materials encourage students to develop flexibility in their style and also demonstrate the optimal use of different learning strategies and behaviors for different tasks. (See Chapter Four.)

Cultures. Tapestry materials reflect the cultural diversity of ESL classrooms. They give students specific information that will help reduce their difficulty interacting with native speakers of English. They strike a healthy balance between the necessity of teaching the target culture and validating the students' native cultures. The importance of knowing the learners' cultures is often forgotten in the rush to help students adjust to their new environment.

Learner Needs, Interests, and Goals. The real world relevance of Tapestry materials is determined through analyses of the learners' needs, interests, and goals. Goals constitute the students' general aims or purposes for language learning, as opposed to specific objectives (Shavelson and Stern 1981). The educational goals of Tapestry materials are readily ascertained by students and teachers alike.

In the Tapestry Approach, task-related goals are further specified as objectives according to the learners' proficiency levels, needs, and interests. The objectives are systematically revised in response to the teachers' formal and informal surveys of students. This type of model allows for recycling, since needs analyses lead directly to a reconsideration of educational objectives, materials, and activities. Sample tasks and a teaching objective follow:

Tasks:	Role-play situations involving talk between strangers. Community contact assignment in which students are asked to start conversations with two strangers.
Objective:	Learner will be able to open a conversation with a native English-speaking stranger.
Language:	Greetings, talk associated with the weather and the immediate environment.

(See Nunan 1985, 1988, 1989, and Richards 1990 for further suggestions.)

Integration of Skills

An integrated-skills approach is reflected in all Tapestry materials. In these materials, language is viewed as a meaning system. While this system is composed of many different strands (such as grammar and pronunciation), the strands are not treated independent of the whole. Every skill relates to other skills. Touching any skill in the system affects other skills because of their related nature.

Skills are brought to bear upon each task or lesson in an integrated fashion. While the purpose of a lesson may be to develop a specific skill (such as writing a letter of complaint describing the condition of a dormitory or an apartment), the content is explored through tasks that draw upon all language skills that meet that purpose (including listening to the complaints of the other residents).

Authentic Language

The language used in Tapestry materials is as authentic as possible. The use of simplified language for instructional purpose is minimized. Taped talks, meetings or interviews, radio excerpts, overheard conversations, and other authentic sources are included for listening materials. Readings come from newspapers, directions for travel, menus, flyers, college catalogs, license plates, memos, letters, press releases, and so on.

Authentic language — particularly when keyed to subjects that students are concerned about — is highly motivating to students. When learners begin to use the language in natural ways, just as their English-speaking peers do, they realize that English is not just a series of word lists or grammar forms, but a living language for communication.

Language Assistance

To help students understand and use authentic language, many types of language assistance are provided by the materials. The types of supports, which are outlined in Chapter Three, include visuals of all types that enhance student comprehension, and strategies that help students express meaning just when they need to do so.

Language assistance does not necessarily involve using a *silent period,* in which students only listen and do not produce the sounds of the language. Some educators maintain that *all* learners must experience a silent period, and language instructional methodologies have been based on this assumption. However, empirical studies provide at best only partial and dubiously reliable evidence for this assumption. Therefore, the Tapestry Approach does not mandate a silent period for all students. In line with the Tapestry concept of individual differences, we encourage students to speak at their own pace, regardless of whether that pace involves a silent period.

Learner-Centered Activity

Learner-centered activity is the primary focus of Tapestry materials, and teacher-centered or explanatory instruction is kept to a minimum. The materials encourage student-generated communication. Learner-centered activity varies at different levels in the curriculum as a response to such variables as the task, proficiency level of the learner, and learner needs.

Learner Self-Direction

Learner-centered activities lead to learner self-direction, an important goal of Tapestry classrooms. To become truly competent in the second language, ESL students must be able to communicate effectively without assistance. To help learners gain autonomy, Tapestry materials help students set their own goals and assess their own progress. In addition, they encourage learners to interact outside of class, read for pleasure, and establish a regular self-study program involving Tapestry workbooks and reference materials.

Motivation

One way that Tapestry materials motivate learners is by appealing to individual needs, interests, and goals. To appeal to diverse students, the focus of every Tapestry task is "... an operation of some kind which the student might actually want to perform" in English (Johnson and Morrow 1981, p. 60). A second way that the materials motivate students is by allowing them to make choices. There is a wide variety of tasks from which to choose. Finally, the materials motivate individuals by appealing to whole persons. "Whole-person learning takes into consideration not only the cognitive but also the emotional and physical dimensions of the learners" (Oprandy 1991, p. 16). Tapestry materials contain activities specifically designed to create a climate that facilitates language development.

The principles outlined above guide the creation of Tapestry materials and are consistent with the types of instruction teachers provide students.

TYPES OF TAPESTRY INSTRUCTION

In this section, we discuss four types of Tapestry instruction: incidental learning; student-centered, planned, indirect instruction; teacher-centered, direct instruction; and student self-directed study.

In the 1980s, consensus in language teaching seemed to be strong for *incidental learning.* In this type of learning, students immerse themselves in the target culture. The best language learning approaches were considered natural ones that reproduced the conditions of child first language learning, in which incidental learning plays a sizeable role. *Direct teacher-centered instruction,* in which teachers explicitly teach students the rules of language use through teacher-fronted instruction, seemed to have little support at all. The Tapestry Approach embraces a more recent view of language teaching based on considerable research (summarized in Chapters Two through Twelve). In this perspective, the primary focus of all language instruction is *planned, indirect, student-centered instruction.* In this type of instruction, the teacher immerses learners in meaningful, communicative situations, involving natural input and requiring use of this input. To maximize the students' abilities and capitalize on their interests and goals, instruction is carefully orchestrated. Students are provided with multiple types of assistance to help them improve their ability to communicate. Tapestry teachers recognize that learners can and do acquire much language through incidental learning — such as regular, self-selected, sustained pleasure reading and conversations with native speakers. Yet this type of learning, what we call learning through osmosis, only takes place when learners are given adequate assistance to help them process the input. (Refer to Chapters Three and Four.) Teacher-centered, direct instruction also plays a definite role in the Tapestry Approach. However, this type of instruction occupies far less class time than planned, indirect, student-centered instruction, since it does not provide learners with extensive exposure to English input and practice using this input. All these types of learning are augmented by *student self-directed study,* an essential component that allows students to expand their skills on their own.

CONTENT TAUGHT IN TAPESTRY CLASSROOMS

It is distressing that many ESL materials and instructors attempt to teach language as though it can be dissected into skill areas, broken up into a number of habits, defined in behavioral terms, and taught in lock-step fashion, sequentially presented in terms of perceived linguistic difficulty level. This view of teaching is reminiscent of the factory model of schooling in which students are seen as passive recipients of language, empty vessels ready to be filled, incapable of learning more than one aspect of the language at a time.

Although in this volume we isolate such language skills as reading, writing, listening, and speaking, we do this only for organizational convenience. The Tapestry Approach suggests that optimal conditions for language development exist when the skills are integrated and meaning is central. The content of instruction is dynamic, changing as a direct response to the learners' needs, interests, and goals. Content is jointly shaped by teachers and students as they collaborate in caring, nurturing, language-promoting communities. Here is a description of the content taught in Tapestry classrooms.

Language Pertaining to Theme-Based Tasks

Tasks in theme-based instruction cut across many areas and entail the use of all skills in communicative ways (Brumfit 1984, Edelsky 1986, Enright and McCloskey 1988). Instructors teach those aspects of language that are needed to complete the tasks. All aspects of communicative competence are stressed when appropriate. Note that the instructors do not "contextualize." That is, they do not first start with language forms and only later embed them in context through tasks.

It is also necessary to teach isolated skills or language components that help students to carry out specific tasks. For example, teachers may provide learners with punctuation lessons so that their students can write effective letters to pen-pals.

Strategies

Specific strategies are taught to learners that help the learners successfully complete tasks. Many suggestions for teaching students to use better learning strategies are given in Oxford's (1990) volume. Since her research indicates that strategies are best presented in the context of meaningful instruction, we suggest that strategies be task-related.

Language Learning Concepts

Language learning concepts are also important. As Cohen (1990) suggests, such concepts are essential in helping learners to develop a realistic idea of their own capacity to learn English, providing students with guidance pertaining to how to learn, creating an awareness in students of their own roles and those of others in the learning-teaching process, creating enthusiasm for language tasks, and helping learners to develop a sense of responsibility for the social, cognitive, and psychological aspects of classroom communities.

Just as the content of the Tapestry Approach has required a rethinking of traditional ESL methods, a different aspect of the Tapestry Approach that calls for reconceptualization is assessment. By assessment, we refer to the means of assessing and monitoring student progress in language learning.

THEORETICAL FRAMEWORK UNDERLYING ASSESSMENT

Effective weavers regularly seek guidance and advice from others and monitor their own progress when they are weaving. If they find that the pattern needs to be modified, they modify it. Only poor weavers wait until they have finished their tapestries to assess their work's utility and beauty. At that point, assessment is almost useless. If weavers are unhappy with their finished products, they have to unravel their tapestries and start all over in order to take advantage of the assessment results. They may use some of the information from their final assessment when they create new tapestries, but, in many cases, the new tapestries that they make require entirely different types of assessment criteria.

Like good weavers, good language learners routinely monitor their own progress. This has a positive effect on their language development, since it provides them with constant feedback concerning the changes that they need to make to learn more efficiently. The Tapestry Approach helps students learn effective monitoring skills that allow them to set their own meaningful goals, specify their objectives from these general goals, and assess their progress in meeting these goals. In this section we outline the theoretical framework underlying this approach to assessment. We then describe practical ways of assessing student progress.

Theoretical Framework for Assessment

In the Tapestry Approach, tests are viewed as a form of language assistance. (See Chapter Three.) Their primary purpose is to help learners improve their English. Thus, in the Tapestry Approach, students learn not just by doing class activities, but also by taking tests. Tests provide interesting, relevant information that exposes them to the types of language they must know and the types of tasks they need to undertake outside their language courses.

Tests help teachers improve their instruction in several ways. They motivate instructors to become more effective, help teachers tailor their instruction to the needs of individual learners, and provide valuable feedback to teachers concerning the success (and failure) of specific language learning tasks and materials.

Many measurements are used to assess the students' learning progress. The final examination may seem important to some teachers, but this exam often tells us little about what students have actually learned and rarely assesses the learners' best performance. This is because students need multiple opportunities to demonstrate their finest language abilities. On the day of a given test, students might come to class sick, in love, in the midst of family quarrels, or homesick. As a result of these situations, they sometimes perform lower than they normally would. Another reason for multiple measurements is related to learning styles and preferences. (See Chapter Four.) Students learn and demonstrate what they have learned in different ways. "By using a variety of measurement tools, an instructor can provide outlets for students' different learning styles" (Pica, Barnes, and Finger 1990, p. 143).

Like Swain (1984), we argue that teachers need to bias for the best whenever they test student performance; that is, they need to elicit their students' best performance on language tests. Unfortunately, many tests appear to elicit the students' worst work. For instance, sit-down writing exams tend to bias against certain types of learners (older students, auditory or hands-on learners, students who fall apart under the pressure of time, and learners who have no experience taking such exams). If teachers are really interested in measuring their students' progress in developing writing skills, then they need to take a look at a variety of writing samples collected by each student in a writing portfolio. Tests should provide learners with feedback concerning all four components of communicative competence. Whenever possible, Tapestry teachers employ direct assessment that provides a truer, more realistic, less stilted measure of language than indirect (artificial) testing.

The Tapestry Approach favors criterion-referenced assessment, which compares a given student with a pre-established standard or criterion, typically reflecting the objectives of the lesson. Checklists (either formal or informal) are an obvious example of criterion-referenced measurement, but just about any kind of task or activity can be used for a criterion-referenced instrument, just as long as the items are based on specific, measurable objectives defined in advance. Language learning portfolios can and should be used in a criterion-referenced way. These portfolios contain an ongoing record of the students' needs analysis information, objectives, measurements of progress in attaining objectives, and peer and teacher responses to student work. Just as physicians pass their patient records on to other physicians, Tapestry teachers can pass their student language learning portfolios on to other instructors who teach their students.

Criterion-referenced assessment does not focus on ranking students in a normative way, but instead emphasizes what students can actually do with the language. In criterion-referenced assessment, a single letter grade (though one might be given for bookkeeping purposes) is less significant than the specific details of which communicative language abilities the student has successfully demonstrated.

Ways to Assess Language

Modalities of assessment are many and varied; in fact, they are as wide-ranging as classroom activities. Paper-and-pencil assessments are the most familiar to many teachers. These can be short tests, essays, research papers, or any other format involving the use of reading and writing. Paper-and-pencil assessments do not have to measure just recognition and recall of factual knowledge, but can and should assess comprehension, application, synthesis, and evaluation (higher-order thinking skills). To call forth basic recognition and recall, "what is. . .?" is a sufficient question. For higher-order thinking skills to be aroused, the teacher can ask students to compare and contrast, explain, reframe from a different perspective, challenge, justify, evaluate, and so on. The level of performance demanded is directly associated with the type of question posed by the teacher.

Oral assessment can be done in many different ways: in person, or audiotaped or videotaped; through one-to-one interviews or in a small group or in a large group; through analysis of discourse; through a participation frequency checklist; in an individual presentation.

Demonstration is yet another kind of assessment. Students can use language as an integral part of models, posters, graphs, dioramas, diagrams, original productions (plays, skits, poems), photography displays, sculpture displays, and so on. Multimedia demonstrations linking verbal and nonverbal sound, sight, and movement are especially effective, both as regular classroom activities and as assessment tools.

Thus, assessment is not restricted in any way to the old paper-and-pencil mode. Creativity in assessment techniques is essential in the Tapestry classroom.

Other Assessment Techniques

Additional assessment techniques are also useful to Tapestry teachers and students. For instance, informal opinion questionnaires and interviews can help teachers find out students' attitudes about what they are learning, what they find easy or difficult, and what they like or dislike. Student diaries are useful for helping students express their feelings about their own progress. These diaries can be either unguided or patterned on guidelines set by the teacher. Such diaries can be transformed into dialog journals if the teacher responds to each journal and thus creates a student-teacher dialog. Diaries and journals can be graded in relation to language use, or they can be employed simply for purposes of communicating and assessing feelings, without a grade attached. For suggestions on using diaries and journals, see Oxford (1990).

CONCLUSION

This chapter has presented a new way of looking at teachers and learners. In addition, it has summarized the main principles guiding the instructional materials, the key types of Tapestry instruction, the content that is taught in Tapestry classrooms, and the theoretical framework underlying Tapestry assessment. Our hope is that the tapestry we have presented here will be useful, and that the ESL students who create their own tapestries will be pleased with their tapestries' brilliant colors and intricate designs. Perhaps you and your students will add your own multihued sections, borders, embroideries, and appliqués to the tapestry shown here.

ACTIVITIES AND DISCUSSION QUESTIONS

1. Of all the roles of Tapestry teachers summarized in this chapter, which ones are new to you? (Consider the roles of decision-maker, information-gatherer, motivator, organizer, provider of input, friend, and counselor.) Which roles have you already played in your classrooms, and which ones would you like to try? Why?

2. What principles guide the creation of Tapestry instructional materials? Which of these principles can also be used to guide Tapestry instruction?

3. What problems might you encounter in using the Tapestry Approach? List all the solutions that you can think of. Get help from a friend or colleague. Are there any actions that you can take now to overcome problems that hinder the implementation of Tapestry? Set up a specific plan for overcoming any obstacles.

4. How can you keep informed of recent trends in ESL teaching? With a colleague or a friend, write a list of local teaching organizations that you could join.

5. What types of assessment can teachers use to elicit their students' best second language performance?

SUGGESTED READINGS

- *Applied Linguistics.* Articles of interest to ESL and foreign language teachers.
- *English Language Teaching Journal.* Practical views and ideas for ESL and EFL teachers.
- *Foreign Language Annals.* Research and views of interest to foreign language teachers.
- *Language Learning.* Research and theory useful for understanding the complex process of language learning.
- *Studies in Second Language Acquisition.* Scholarly research on second language acquisition.
- *TESOL Quarterly.* Research on aspects of ESL instruction and learning.
- *TESOL Journal.* Highly practical reports about ESL curricula, materials, and activities.

Most of the above are available at any major university or college library.

PART II

LEARNERS AND THEIR LANGUAGE DEVELOPMENT: WEAVERS AND THEIR WEAVING

DEVELOPMENTAL FACTORS

2

PREVIEW QUESTIONS

1. How much control do teachers have over their ESL learners' emerging grammatical proficiency in the second language? Are teachers responsible for the students' progress in acquiring grammatical structures? Why or why not?
2. What processes internal to the learner might affect the learner's ability to acquire a second language? Consider such factors as age and gender.
3. Are children or adults more capable of acquiring a high level of proficiency in a second language?
4. Do maturational constraints prevent adults from acquiring native-like proficiency in a second language?
5. Do all learners acquire the grammatical structures in the same way? Why or why not?

Developmental factors shape the nature of language learning. These factors must be considered in ESL instruction. Simply put, ESL students cannot acquire what they are developmentally incapable of acquiring. If, for example, students are not ready to acquire causative structures, such as *I made my brother wash the dishes,* they will be unable at that time to do so — regardless of their teachers' best efforts to present these structures.

Just as developmental factors affect second language development, so too they affect weaving. When weavers have not yet acquired the prerequisite skills and competencies to complete an elaborate tapestry, they are unable to do so. Even when they are given beautiful yarn, if they do not know how to weave a pattern, their tapestries cannot yet take shape.

Both ESL learners and weavers actively and creatively go about their work — weavers, making tapestries and ESL students, producing English. Both produce interesting patterns without necessarily receiving explicit instruction. The following examples are illustrative of the types of creative patterns ESL learners use:

Example 2.1
I should to read English all the time. (Burt and Kiparsky 1972, p. xiii)

Example 2.2
Why won't you let me to go? (Burt and Kiparsky 1972, p. xix)

As seen in these examples, ESL learner language does not result from imitation. Rather, it is shaped by developmental factors that govern language acquisition.

ORGANIZATION OF THIS CHAPTER

This chapter has three parts. First, we describe commonalities in the ways in which learners acquire their second language. Then, we suggest developmental explanations that account for these commonalities. Finally, we argue that effective ESL classrooms support the learners' creative construction in talk and print and allow the learners opportunities to experiment with the language as real communicators.

COMMONALITIES IN THE WAYS IN WHICH LEARNERS ACQUIRE THEIR SECOND LANGUAGE

Although second language development is not a uniform phenomenon, learners go about the task of acquiring language in remarkably similar ways. For instance, they often go through identical stages in the acquisition of specific grammatical structures (see below). They also acquire these grammatical structures in similar sequences — such that some features of the language (like the modal auxiliary *can)* are acquired before other features of the language (like the modal auxiliaries *could, would,* and *should).*

Stages in the Acquisition of Grammatical Structures

Considerable first language acquisition research indicates that there is a more or less fixed set of *stages* of language development through which children pass on their way to becoming competent adult first language speakers (see, for example, Klima and Bellugi 1966). There are striking similarities in the stages through which second language learners and first language learners pass. The example below provides a clear illustration of the sequential stages that learners pass through on their way to acquiring the negative structure, *I didn't want to go.*

Stage One:	No. I no want go.
Stage Two:	I don't wanna go.
Stage Three:	I didn't want to go.

In Stage One, learners use the word *no* before the verb *want.* In Stage Two, learners use the word *don't* before the verb *want.* In this stage, learners have not actually acquired auxiliaries such as *do.* Rather, they use the auxiliary *don't* with the verb *wanna* as a memorized whole. In the third stage, learners have acquired the auxiliary *do* and are able to form the past tense of this verb correctly, according to native English norms.

The Natural Order in the Acquisition of Grammatical Morphemes

Adult second language learners, like child first language learners, also seem to manifest similar ways of acquiring grammatical features. In fact, the vast bulk of the literature indicates that these learners follow a more or less invariant order in the acquisition of morphemes. Here, we define the term *morpheme* as the smallest unit of meaningful language. (Morphemes include the *-ing* ending on the word *running* as well as the third-person singular ending *-s* on the word *runs.)*

In a series of studies pertaining to children acquiring a second language, Dulay and Burt (1974) provided evidence that children from different language backgrounds do not use their first language as the source for developing hypotheses about the second language. Instead, these researchers argue, children use universal, developmentally determined processes. Dulay and Burt examined the acquisition of English morphemes by Chinese- and Spanish-speaking children, ages 6 to 8. Their methodology consisted of collecting speech samples of the subjects' English language production and comparing the relative amount of error found in the use of 11 different grammatical morphemes — including the present progressive *(-ing)*, plural *(-s)*, and past tense marker *(-ed)*. This set of grammatical morphemes was chosen because there had been previous studies concerning the order of these particular grammatical features for children acquiring English as a first language (Brown 1973).

Following Dulay and Burt (1974), Bailey, Madden, and Krashen (1974) used the same research methodology in an investigation of the morphological development of adult learners of English as a second language. Like Dulay and Burt, these researchers found that regardless of the learner's first language, the subjects displayed the same order of acquisition of morphemes.

Regardless of the learner's first language, type of language instruction, and input, all learners seem to acquire many features of the language in a similar order. They learn simple sentence structures such as *I left the building* before complex ones such as *I left the two-story building that is on the corner of Mission and Geary.* They learn simple speech acts such as *Open the window* before complex ones such as *Would you mind opening the window?*

The results of these natural order studies, however, are far from conclusive. In fact, in the 1980s the concept of natural orders in second language development was virtually under attack. For example, researchers pointed out that morphemes were difficult to identify reliably and were often analyzed out of context. Moreover, recent research has shown that specific morphemes might occur accurately in the speech of an ESL learner in one context but inaccurately in the speech of the same learner in a different context. Huebner (1983) also found that an increasing accuracy of one form may be related to a decreasing accuracy of a different form in a specific context. Like Huebner, Tarone (1988) has also investigated the role of function and the linguistic environment. She suggests that the *function* performed by a given morpheme in different sorts of discourse can lead to variability in second language performance. A large number of interlocutor variables have been shown to result in variation in the morpheme order. Such interlocutor variables include the interlocutors' native languages, status, goals, ages, socioeconomic levels, and first language and second language proficiency levels. (For an excellent review of the criticism of natural order studies, see Larsen-Freeman and Long 1991; see also Hatch 1983.)

Even though a consistent natural order might not exist (Eisenstein 1989, Ellis 1987, 1988, Tarone 1988), the cumulative conclusion of nearly all researchers today is that the acquisition of the second language does not involve wholesale transference of morphemes from the first language, but rather involves what is variously called the *creative construction process* (Dulay and Burt 1974), *developmental processes* (Ellis 1986), or the *language acquisition device* (Chomsky 1965).

Dulay, Burt, and Krashen (1982) define *creative construction* as "the subconscious process by which language learners gradually organize the language they hear, according to the rules they construct to understand and generate sentences" (p. 276). Like child first language learners, adult second language learners creatively construct their new language. Justification for this belief comes from similarity in error types.

Similarity of Error Types in the "Interlanguage"

The errors that learners make reveal remarkable similarities in second language acquisition. In a breakthrough study, Corder (1967) found that second language learners produced errors that were both systematic and creative in nature. Corder's work gave rise to the field called *error analysis,* which examined systematic errors in order to determine the underlying rule-governed behaviors of learners. (See also George 1972 and Richards 1974. For an excellent review of the literature, refer to Robinett and Schachter 1983.) Numerous researchers produced taxonomies of ESL learner errors. One category of errors was termed *acoustic approximations,* which were hypothesized to occur when learners were forced to communicate before they had acquired the necessary competence and approximated words based on what they thought they had heard. Examples of acoustic approximations, sometimes referred to as Archie Bunkerisms, follow:

> *Example 2.3*
> ESL student, writing an essay:
>
> This essay discusses many aspects of truth. *Firstable,* it examines factual truth.
>
> *Example 2.4*
> ESL student, trying to convince his ESL teacher that he has completed his pleasure reading assignment:
>
> I read the book, *Catch Her in the Right.* (instead of *Catcher in the Rye)*

The field of error analysis showed that although some errors are due to transfer from the learner's native language, many errors are produced that have nothing to do with the learner's first language; rather, they reflect the learner's creative capability of using language. The examples of errors made by non-native English speakers below are illustrative:

> *Example 2.5*
>
> *In a Czechoslovakian tourist agency:* Take one of our horse-driven city tours — we guarantee no miscarriages.
>
> *Example 2.6*
>
> *Outside a Hong Kong tailor shop:* Ladies may have a fit upstairs.
>
> *Example 2.7*
>
> *In a Bucharest hotel lobby:* The lift is being fixed for the next day. During that time we regret that you will be unbearable.

Noting such creativity, Selinker (1972) coined the term *interlanguage* to refer to the learner's developmentally changing, systematic knowledge of the language. Other researchers also examined the creativity and systematicity of the language used by second language learners. (Refer to Corder's 1967 discussion of *transitional competence,* Nemser's 1971 discussion of *approximative systems.)* Selinker claimed that interlanguage systems are unique in that they belong neither to the source language nor the target language. Interlanguages are dynamic; that is, they are constantly changing as the learner acquires new features of the language. Each new feature acquired by the learner necessitates adjustments in the learner's developing competence. Some of the rules that the learner acquires may be permanent or relatively stabilized, whereas other rules may be in a state of flux. (See also Selinker and Lamendella 1981 and Selinker forthcoming.)

All the literature points to the striking similarities in the ways in which learners acquire many aspects of their second language. As Hatch (1983) cogently explains, "while there is a good degree of argument about the degree of systematicity in interlanguage, many researchers believe that the move from the beginning stages of language learning to later fluency follows a sequence that is not random" (p. 105).

EXPLANATIONS FOR COMMONALITIES IN ADULT SECOND LANGUAGE DEVELOPMENT

In this section, we examine several developmental factors that explain these similarities. These factors include linguistic properties, Slobin's Operating Principles, and maturational constraints. We argue that these factors have a strong effect on the learner's acquisition of the second language. While the aging process may prevent many adult learners from acquiring native-like pronunciation and native-like inflectional morphology (such as the *-s* ending on the word *paints),* we are encouraged that adults are capable of acquiring advanced levels of English proficiency successfully. Our view is that the most effective language classroom is one that supports the learner's efforts to use language creatively. Before discussing this view, let us first consider the explanations.

Universal Linguistic Properties

Regularities of language development can be partially explained in terms of purely linguistic properties. To understand these properties, it is useful to clarify the distinction between *competence* and *performance.* Chomsky (1965) states that *competence* consists of the mental representation of linguistic rules that constitute the speaker-hearer's internalized grammar. *Performance,* on the other hand, consists of the learner's actual production. This production is affected by memory and attention lapses and is characterized by false starts, changes of plan, and slips of the tongue. Performance, therefore, is not a perfect reflection of competence. We sometimes like to think of competence as Plato thought of reality, which we cannot see, and performance as Plato thought of reality's shadow, which we can see.

In discussing competence, Chomsky argues that without a set of innate principles, children cannot attain grammatical competence in their first language. Some structures occur so infrequently in the input that it is impossible for children to obtain sufficient exposure to them. Chomsky suggests that innate principles that constitute Universal Grammar help children to discover the rules of their first language with restricted input. For Chomsky, Universal Grammar limits the form that the grammars of individual languages take.

Cook (1985), summarizing the Chomskyan position, defines Universal Grammar as properties that are inherent in the human mind. It consists not of a set of particular rules, but rather a set of general principles that apply to all languages. Universal Grammar does not constrain the forms of the grammars languages take directly, by providing children with prefabricated rules that can be incorporated in grammar. Instead, it sets *parameters* that must then be fixed in response to the particular input data to which children are exposed (Chomsky 1981a). In constraining the kind of grammar that children can develop, parameters delimit the number of possibilities that children need to investigate. However, children still need input data to fix the parameters. When they select the appropriate input, they are able to accurately fix the parameters. (Appropriate input for language development is discussed in Chapter Three.)

Children's knowledge of their language is made up of *core rules*— determined by the Universal Grammar (the *core)*— and *peripheral rules*— learned without the help of the Universal Grammar (the *periphery).* Core rules consist of, among others, those rules governing the movements of words within sentences as well as rules that determine how pronoun references are to be interpreted. Peripheral rules are language-specific ones, such as preposition-stranding in English, that exist in few other languages. English is characterized by a somewhat unusual relative clause pattern that may lack a relative pronoun, but does have a stranded preposition that marks an indirect object (for example, *Give me the pen I write with).* Core rules are normally acquired earlier than peripheral ones. Hence, learners acquire simple (core) patterns such as *I want the book* before they acquire language-specific (peripheral) patterns in sentences such as *I want the paper that I write on.* (Refer to Figure 2.1.)

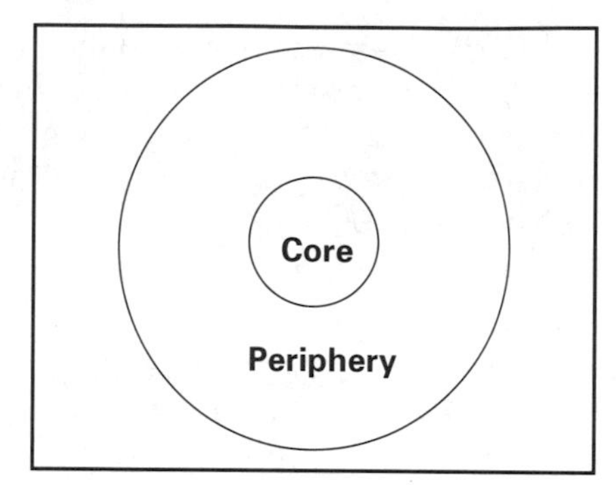

Figure 2.1 The Learner's Core and Periphery Grammar

Related to concepts of core and periphery is Chomsky's (1981b) theory of *markedness.* Core rules are *unmarked;* that is, they are consistent with the general patterns of language. For example, in English most past tense verbs end in *-ed.* Thus, *painted* is unmarked. Periphery rules are *marked;* that is, they stand out in some way. For instance, the word *ate* is marked since it does not follow the rule: *to form the past tense, add an -ed on the end of verbs.* It should be noted that marked and unmarked rules are not discrete units. Rather, they should be viewed as opposite extremes of a continuum. This is because rules can be more or less marked. Children and adult second language learners are likely to learn unmarked rules before marked ones. (For a useful summary of the second language studies, refer to Eckman, Bell, and Nelson 1984.)

Universals can also be divided into two types: *absolutes* and *tendencies. Absolutes* have no exceptions. An example of an *absolute* would be the fact that *all* languages that have verb-subject-object word order also have prepositions. *Tendencies,* on the other hand, occur when there is a high probability or tendency of a language structure occurring, but there are also exceptions. An example of a *tendency* is the fact that *most* languages with subject-object-verb word order have prepositions, but there are also exceptions. *Absolutes* are generally acquired by language learners before *tendencies.* (See Ellis 1986 for an excellent review of universals.)

There is considerable discussion about the role of Universal Grammar in adult second language acquisition. Universal Grammar may unfold developmentally, on a maturational schedule, as suggested by Felix (1984). If this is true, the principles of Universal Grammar are themselves subject to innately developmental processes. On the other hand, Universal Grammar may develop piecemeal as a result of the input to which learners are exposed at different developmental states (White 1985).

Adults do as well, if not better, than children in many aspects of the language, but there is mounting evidence that it is difficult, if not impossible, for adults to achieve native-like proficiency in a second language. (See, for example, Long 1991, Scovel 1988, and Singleton 1989.) We assume that the principles of Universal Grammar are available to adults and are relevant to second language acquisition. However, they may be less accessible to adults because of maturational constraints related to aging (see below), linguistic constraints, and the fact that second language acquisition involves two languages — the target language and the learner's native language. For second language acquisition, the problem is to determine to what extent already identified universal constraints or parameters are true for second language learning situations and to what degree they differ from those identified for first language acquisition.[2]

Slobin's Operating Principles

Similarities in the acquisition of linguistic structures may also be due to sources other than Universal Grammar. Slobin (1973), for instance, proposes that *universal operational constraints* underlie the ways in which young children acquire their first language. He cites several commonalities governing the ways children acquire a number of different first languages and, based on these, posits some operating principles, "a sort of general heuristic . . .which the child brings to bear on the task of organizing and storing language" (1973, p. 191). Second language researchers such as Andersen (1989) argue that second language learners, as well as first language learners, adhere to these operating principles. The principles are listed in the box below.

Slobin's Operational Principles

Learners. . .

- **Pay attention to the ends of words.**
Learners normally pay attention to suffixes that appear at the end of words (such as the *-ing* on *running).*

- **Pay attention to the order of words and morphemes.**
Learners typically preserve the order of the target language. They may leave out words that proficient speakers would include, but they do not reorder them.

- **Avoid rearrangements.**
Learners tend to preserve the subject/verb order in question formations. Thus, it is common to hear learners use such questions as *Where you are going? Why he is doing that?*

- **Avoid exceptions.**
Once learners learn a common pattern of the language, they maintain this pattern and avoid exceptions. This explains why learners who have acquired the past tense marker, *-ed,* sometimes avoid using irregular verbs. As a result, they use such verbs as *comed, goed,* and *bringed.*

- **Mark semantic relations clearly and overtly.**
Learners tend to mark the meanings of words clearly. This may be why they frequently acquire the word *putted* before they acquire the correct form *put. Putted* is much more clearly marked.

Maturational Constraints on Second Language Learning

Several researchers have attempted to explain similarities in the acquisition of grammatical structures in terms of maturational constraints on learning. Age is the most commonly cited determiner of success or failure in second language learning. Krashen, Long, and Scarcella (1982) argue that three generalizations explain the role of age, rate, and eventual attainment in second language development:

1. adults proceed more rapidly through the initial stages of syntactic and morphological development than children, but not through the later stages;
2. older children acquire faster than younger children; and
3. acquirers who begin second languages in early childhood through natural exposure achieve higher proficiency than those beginning as adults.

Their basic position is that adults do better in initial learning, but younger is better in the long run. It appears that the aging process itself may affect one's ability to pronounce the language fluently with native-like pronunciation and to use inflectional features of the language (such as the *-s* ending on the word *hits)* accurately. (See also Long 1991.)

The lack of generally guaranteed success is the most striking characteristic of adult second language acquisition. Adult ESL learners do not inevitably achieve perfect mastery of the language. Many fail to reach native-like proficiency in a second language. As Bley-Vroman (1986) puts it, "[second language] development ceases, and even serious conscious efforts to change are often fruitless" (p. 22). Selinker (1972) called this phenomenon *fossilization,* the permanent cessation of second language development. (See also Selinker forthcoming.) For Selinker, most adults stop acquiring a second language before acquiring native-like proficiency. In children, there is no fossilization; all children normally pass through all developmental stages on their way to becoming competent language users. Those who do not acquire the language fluently are the rare exception. Thus, while children are apparently endowed with innate propensities for acquiring language, adult second language learners do not seem to have the same innate propensity to learn language.

Vygotsky's Notion of the Zone of Proximal Development

Vygotsky (1978) also offers an explanation of commonalities in language development. He suggests that the learner's language performance actually exceeds what the learner is capable of doing with the language alone. In so doing, he proposes the notion of the Zone of Proximal Development, the distance between the learner's individual competence and the capacity to perform with assistance. In his words, this zone constitutes:

> *the distance between the actual developmental level as determined by individual problem-solving and the level of potential development as determined through problem-solving under adult guidance or in collaboration with more capable peers.* The Zone of Proximal Development defines those functions that have not yet matured, but are in the process of maturation; functions that will mature tomorrow, but are currently in an embryonic state. These functions could be termed the *buds* or *flowers* of development rather than the *fruits* of development. (p. 86; emphasis his)

For Vygotsky, teaching is only effective when it "awakens and rouses to life those functions which are in a stage of maturing, which are in the Zone of Proximal Development" (Vygotsky 1956, p. 278). Although Vygotsky's work mainly concerns child first language learning, it can easily be applied to adult second language acquisition as well. Tharp and Gallimore (1988) propose the following stages in the learner's progression through the Zone of Proximal Development.

Progression through the Zone of Proximal Development

Stage One
Assistance provided by more capable others (teachers, experts, peers, coaches)

<u>Example</u>

Teacher: Which one do you want — the big piece of cake or the little one?

Student: *(pointing)*

Teacher: Okay. You can have this one. This big one over here.

Student: Yeah. Big one. Big one.

Stage Two
Assistance provided by self

<u>Example</u>

Student: *(talking to self)* Now let's see what do I say in a wedding line. Um, *Congratulations*, that's right, *Congratulations*.

Stage Three
Internalization, automatization

<u>Example</u>

Student: *(without help from others or him or herself)* Hi, Max. Can you give me some help with my essay tonight?

In the first stage, learners are only able to communicate with assistance. They may have limited understanding of others' messages, and, as a consequence, before using English independently by themselves without the help of others, they may first rely on more capable speakers of the language. With the help of their interlocutors' gestures, questions, and simplified English, they gradually come to understand their interlocutors' English and to communicate. Assistance to learners comes in many forms. "Sometimes, the adult directs attention. At other times, the adult holds important information in memory. At still other times, the adult offers simple encouragement" (Griffin and Cole 1984, p. 47). (Refer to ChapterThree, pp. 27-31, for a detailed description of the types of assistance available to ESL learners.) At the end of Stage One, the assistors steadily decline their responsibility for helping ESL learners to communicate. Learners who were silent now begin to communicate actively.

In Stage Two, ESL learners are able to use English without the assistance of others. However, this does not mean that they have fully acquired English. Rather, they employ self-instruction. Control of English is passed from more competent English speakers to the learners themselves. They begin to guide their own use of English through self-directed speech (talking to themselves) and to assist themselves in many different ways. For example, they ask themselves what to say in specific circumstances. They question their own knowledge of the language and push themselves to communicate more accurately.

In Stage Three, the learner's speech is automatic — devoid of self-regulation. Learners can convey their messages in English fluently and smoothly. At this point, self-regulation is disruptive. The learner's competence is fully developed.

Our Explanation for Commonalities in Adult Second Language Acquisition

Our own view is consistent with that of Vygotsky. We believe that developmental factors have a profound effect on second language development and must be considered carefully. We also believe that second language learners pass through sequenced stages as a result of a predisposition to process English input in specific ways. Grammatical structures are acquired in somewhat predictable orders. Creativity is a characteristic of all language development.

TAPESTRY PRINCIPLES CONCERNING DEVELOPMENTAL FACTORS

The discussion above leads us to propose the following principles for language instruction.

PRINCIPLES

1. Effective teachers support the learner's creative construction in talk and print.
2. When acquiring a second language, learners initially require a variety of supports, including: constructive feedback, encouragement, advice on language use. As learners gain more proficiency in the second language, they need to rely upon fewer supports.

CONCLUSION

In this chapter we have dealt with issues regarding second language acquisition and developmental trends. We have recognized that no one variable can explain commonalities in the ways in which ESL learners acquire the grammatical structures of their new language. The Tapestry Approach presupposes an innate language-specific endowment that enables learners to create novel sentences in their second language. In other words, we believe that all learners have the innate capability of acquiring a second language. Most likely, this innate language-specific endowment, in combination with many factors (including developmental ones), underlies the commonalities in the errors and creative structures that students produce. We also recognize that maturational constraints may limit the adult learner's ability to acquire native-like proficiency in a second language.

In effective language classrooms, students move through the various stages of the Zone of Proximal Development. In such classrooms, students are encouraged to experiment with their new language. Errors in these classrooms are considered a creative aspect of second language development, indicators of the learners' proficiency.

ACTIVITIES AND DISCUSSION QUESTIONS

1. In child first language acquisition, developmental errors like *all gone sticky, comed,* and *goed* are eventually replaced with the correct forms. Consider below the errors that young children make in acquiring their first language:

   > A five year old:
   > *But when he was in here he was "afrain," but then he lost his "fraidness."*
   >
   > A second grader:
   > *He was flying over the "south-west-east thing" (weather vane).*
   >
   > (Lindfors 1987, p. 6)

   Do adult second language learners make similar errors? If you believe that they do, do you also think that they inevitably replace such developmental and creative errors with the correct forms?

2. Chomsky's (1981a) Government Binding Theory allows an important role for both a Universal Grammar and the first and second languages. This theory claims that all human beings are constrained or limited in what they can do because of biological traits that are innate to our species. In terms of language, this means that all human babies are endowed with the capacity to acquire language. Do you think that adult second language learners have this same capacity? Why?

3. Linguistic features of the target language vary in terms of how difficult they are to acquire. What are some of the factors that determine this difficulty? (In answering this question, it might be useful to consider universal linguistic properties and Slobin's Operating Principles.)

4. Vygotsky's (1986) work suggests that many learner characteristics (such as attitudes, motivation, intentions, beliefs, and emotions) are themselves variable since they are constantly changing throughout the course of interaction and interacting with other variables. For Vygotsky, learner characteristics can only be understood as interaction actually unfolds. What practical implications does Vygotsky's work have for ESL instruction?

5. While it is true that second language learners acquire their new language in remarkably similar ways, it is also true that there are great differences in the way learners acquire their new language. Recent second language research has shifted attention from the *invariance* and universality of second language performance of a limited number of grammatical structures to *variation* in L2 performance of a wide number of linguistic structures. How can you account for this variation?

6. In what specific ways can ESL teachers support their students' creative construction in talk and print?

NOTES

1. However, development is influenced not only by Universal Grammar, but also by other non-linguistic factors such as memory capacity and cognitive abilities.
2. In addition, researchers are interested in knowing whether the second language learner goes about setting or resetting the parameters of grammar.

SUGGESTED READINGS

• Ellis, R. 1986. *Understanding Second Language Acquisition.* Oxford: Oxford University Press. This volume provides a general treatment of the roles of maturational constraints and Universal Grammar in second language acquisition. It also considers how other variables (such as motivation and instruction) interact with developmental ones to affect ultimate levels of achievement in a second language.

• Gass, S.M., and Schachter, J. (eds.). 1989. *Linguistic Perspectives on Second Language Acquisition.* Cambridge: Cambridge University Press. This book attempts to place second language research within a theoretical framework. Many of the contributors examine Universal Grammar within the context of second language learning. Of particular interest is a chapter by Bley-Vroman, who examines whether adult ESL learners have access to the Universal Grammar. Other empirical studies assume the Government Binding Theory of language outlined by Chomsky.

• Larsen-Freeman, D., and Long, M.H. 1991. *An Introduction to Second Language Acquisition Research.* London: Longman. This comprehensive and readable volume examines major topics in second language acquisition, including current theories of second language acquisition, maturational constraints governing second language development, and explanations for success and failure. Each chapter contains an extensive bibliography and suggestions for further reading.

• Rutherford, W., and Sharwood Smith, M. (eds.). 1988. *Grammar and Second Language Teaching: A Book of Readings.* Rowley, MA: Newbury House/Harper and Row. This important anthology explores the relationship between pedagogical grammar and second language acquisition. The contributors address theoretical, empirical, and pedagogical issues involved in grammatical development in a second language.

LANGUAGE-PROMOTING INTERACTION

3

PREVIEW QUESTIONS

1. Can learners acquire English without interacting with English speakers? Consider those who attempt to learn English by watching television or listening to the radio. These learners may not use the English they hear. To what extent will these learners acquire English?
2. Does one need to have superior English language proficiency to help ESL learners develop their English skills? Why or why not?
3. How can teachers support their ESL students' efforts to communicate with peers when the students lack the proficiency to converse by themselves?
4. When teachers speak to ESL learners, they sometimes "simplify" their speech. (For example, they speak more slowly and use simpler sentence structures.) Will the speech simplifications teachers make help their students to acquire English more efficiently? Why or why not?
5. Why do some learners fail to acquire English even when they are exposed to large quantities of English input and have ample opportunities to interact with native English speakers?

This chapter displays the *warp* of language learning. The plain vertical yarns that make up the warp constitute the background of the tapestry. Without a strong warp, weavers are unable to finish their tapestries. The vertical yarns are represented in language learning by input, output, and interaction. Together, these elements constitute the immediate linguistic context in which language develops.

Innate mechanisms do not work alone. If they did, students could learn English by themselves, without interacting with others. But students do not learn English alone. Their previous and ongoing experiences provide data for the innate mechanisms discussed in the previous chapter. These experiences help students to make sense of their linguistic input and communicative encounters.

In this chapter, we consider the *context of language learning,* consisting of the hundreds of goal-oriented interactions that constitute everyday life. This consideration allows us to put forth a new view of language teaching. According to this view, what most facilitates second language instruction is neither providing learners with *input* (the language that learners read and hear) nor encouraging learner *output* (the spoken and written language that learners produce). Rather, what best aids language instruction is a combination of various types of *language assistance.* This assistance encourages learners to stretch their linguistic abilities just when they need to do so. It occurs in the context of *language-promoting interaction,* which we define as interaction that facilitates language development. If the immediate linguistic context is facilitative, we conclude, it is so not because it encourages a particular type of English input or output, but rather because it assists students precisely when they require this assistance.[1]

ORGANIZATION OF THIS CHAPTER

Our view of language-promoting interaction is largely grounded in the research of Vygotsky (1956) and his followers in the United States (most specifically, Tharp and Gallimore 1988). Although Vygotskyan work has been applied in education (see, for example, Goldenberg 1991), the Tapestry Approach is the first to incorporate it systematically in ESL instruction. A direct application of Vygotskyan research in the Tapestry Approach is the emphasis on supporting learners' efforts to communicate. In the Tapestry Approach, teachers provide students with a broad range of assistance that helps the students stretch their linguistic abilities in language-promoting interaction.

In the section that follows, we provide a detailed description of the characteristics of language-promoting interaction. We then discuss hypotheses concerning the role of input, interaction, and output in language teaching. We conclude by arguing that, in contrast to these earlier hypotheses, our own hypothesis pertaining to language-promoting interaction has richer, broader implications for language pedagogy.

LANGUAGE-PROMOTING INTERACTION

In providing effective ESL instruction, Tapestry teachers provide language assistance in *language-promoting interaction.* This interaction takes place when learners receive help in communicating what they are incapable of communicating without assistance. Example 3.1 below is illustrative of such interaction.

Example 3.1

Student: So then I climbed hill and went across park to um um to the big house.

Teacher: Do you mean the White House? *(smiles)*

Student: Yeah. White House in you know Washington, D.C. Not so big. Not rich. Not elegant.

Teacher: Why do you think the main government building — the most important building of the U.S. — is not elegant? Do you think it should be more impressive — impress people?

Student: No. American people want small building. They impress with regular house for people of people.

In this exchange, the teacher helps the student to sustain the interaction by providing responsive comments that encourage him or her to communicate. The teacher smiles, suggests new vocabulary items, and is instrumental in keeping the interaction going. The assistance the teacher provides the student enables him or her to use English better than in the past. This in turn facilitates his or her English language acquisition.

Vygotsky's Notion of Assistance

Vygotsky's concept of language assistance has, until recently, been little known in the United States and has certainly been absent from all of the major models of second or foreign language instruction discussed in the literature. It is truly strange that Vygotsky, the Russian psychologist whose key theme is language and communication, has not been more influential in the field of second language teaching in the United States. Only very recently have experts begun to cite Vygotsky as an important theorist whose work potentially affects instructional practices in the language classroom.

One of the factors that makes the Tapestry Approach so unique is the inclusion of Vygotsky's profoundly rich ideas at the very heart of the approach. The Vygotskyan concept of the Zone of Proximal Development suggests that language learning occurs when production is stretched through required skillful *assistance* at points in the learner's Zone of Proximal Development. As discussed in Chapter Two, the distance between the learner's individual capacity and the capacity to produce language with assistance constitutes the Zone of Proximal Development. This zone is likely to be different for various students in any given class, based on many individual characteristics of learners. It is here that Vygotsky's contribution to the Tapestry Approach links up with another main strand of the approach: individual differences as described in Chapter Four. These student characteristics include, among others, motivation, self-esteem, anxiety level, risk-taking ability, learning styles, and learning strategies; and these differences are sometimes very major, relating both to cultural background and to individual personalities. Such differences among our learners directly influence the Vygotskyan Zone of Proximal Development for any particular learner. Thus, Vygotsky's concept and our own research on individual differences merge to form a coherent theme within the Tapestry Approach: *that students are highly distinct individuals even within the same classroom context and that, in many instances, they need different kinds of assistance from the teacher in order to perform most effectively.* In other words, "one size does *not* fit all." We must concern ourselves with not just the similarities among our students, but also with the many differences among them, if we as teachers want to provide the most useful aid in the language development process. Thus, the amount and kind of assistance that is required varies. The assistance might be of a wide variety — encouragement, information, learning strategies, specific lexical items or grammatical structures, the direction of attention. The teacher plays an important, though not exclusive, role in providing this assistance.

Types of Assistance

Recently, Tharp and Gallimore (1988, 1989), drawing on Vygotsky's research, have described various types of assistance. These researchers have proposed "a new definition of teaching, . . . teaching as assisted performance" (Tharp and Gallimore 1989, p. 23). In teacher-assisted performance, conversations are interesting and engaging. These conversations have a coherent focus and a high level of participation. Students participate in extended discussions, exploring ideas that make sense to them. The skilled teacher may clarify or instruct when necessary, but always efficiently, without wasting the students' time. The teacher knows how to draw students out, but also how and when to ease up. The teacher also knows when to step into a discussion and when to leave it. Most important, the teacher manages to keep everyone engaged in extended topical discussion by providing language-promoting assistance of varying types. (These types of assistance are outlined in Table 3.1.)

Table 3.1 Some Types of Language-Promoting Assistance

Teacher provides encouragement.

- Teacher compliments the students.
  I like the way you said that.
- Teacher encourages students to communicate.
  Tell me more.
  I'd like to hear someone else's opinion.
- Teacher encourages students to talk through nonverbal means, for example, smiling, nodding in approval.

Teacher helps students to understand the input.

- Teacher simplifies talk, for example, speaking slowly and clearly, rephrasing key ideas, repeating important words and concepts, explaining and defining words, and expanding utterances when necessary.
- Teacher checks to make sure that students understand by asking questions, using short quizzes, asking students to perform an act or point to items, respond to a lesson in writing, gesture, etc.
- Teacher trains students to ask questions when they do not understand. Such questions include, *Huh? What? I'm sorry, I didn't understand. Could you repeat that?* and *What do you mean?*
- Teacher attempts to hook into students' background knowledge and to activate relevant schemata in the students' minds. Teacher also assesses whether students have requisite background knowledge to understand the discussion. Teacher provides students with this knowledge.
- Teacher previews the material.
- Teacher illustrates words that students do not understand by showing them pictures, charts, tables, graphs, illustrations, and realia (real objects), and by acting out motions.
- Teacher uses classroom routines that are easily understood.

Teacher helps students to remember key words and ideas.

- Teacher writes key words and ideas on the blackboard. Teacher asks students questions about key words and ideas — so that the students' attention is focused on these words and ideas.

Teacher helps students to interact.

- Teacher uses the following conversational features and teaches students how to use these features:
  confirmation checks — *Is this what you are saying?*
  comprehension checks — *Do you understand what I'm saying?*
  clarification requests — *What do you mean by that?*

- Teacher uses a variety of elicitation techniques, such as questions, restatements, pauses (increased *wait time),* and invitations to expand (such as *Tell me more about that).*

- All students are encouraged to participate, and teacher uses a variety of strategies to arrange for participation for all. However, teacher does not exclusively determine who talks, and students are encouraged to influence speaking turns.

- While the teacher might pose some *known-answer* questions in which the teacher already has the answers, many of the questions have more than one answer.

- Teacher models correct forms.

- Teacher promotes equal-status group activities in which all students are encouraged to participate. (Teacher employs games, conversational dyads, and cooperative learning activities.)

Teacher provides direct teaching.

- When necessary, the teacher provides direct teaching of a skill, concept, or language feature. (For instance, the teacher might say, "Today we're going to review when to use *a* and when to use *an.*" Then, the teacher might provide an explanation for this grammatical point and provide examples.)

Teacher maintains the students' interest.

- Teacher personalizes instruction.

- Teacher focuses on thematically-related topics of interest to students.

- Students are encouraged to choose topics they like. Students have some control over topics.

- Teacher focuses primarily on meaning rather than on linguistic features.

- Teacher highlights students' culture in the classroom, the institute, the community, the nation, and the world.

Factors Influencing Assistance

The types of language-promoting assistance that teachers provide students vary as a function of a number of factors. The teacher needs to consider, among other things:

- *the goals and interests of the learners* (The goals and interests of the students must be congruent with the activity.)
- *the materials that are needed to assist the learner's successful completion of the task* (The materials must be interesting, relevant, and readily available.)
- *the linguistic demands of the task* (The task must expose students to useful, meaningful input and provide opportunities for students to use this input in situations that enable them to stretch their linguistic abilities.)
- *the interlocutors working on the task* (Interlocutors must be capable of helping one another communicate.)

Goals and Interests of Learners. When ESL learners share common goals and interests, they communicate with one another better. Tharp and Gallimore (1988) underscore the importance of goals, stating: ". . .it is only the goal-driven activity that makes the maximum contribution of each individual desirable to the entire group, thus motivating assistance by the less competent for the good of all" (p. 73). Tasks requiring students to communicate vital information, which is relevant to student interests and goals, often exert a natural pressure on students to edit and revise their writing and to practice and perfect their speech. For instance, Pica, Holliday, Lewis, and Morgenthaler (1989) found that *information gap tasks* (in which one student has the information and needs to give it to another) produce better output for language development than do other types of oral tasks, such as discussions. (See also Doughty and Pica 1985.) This is why in the Tapestry Approach, thematic and task-based instruction is designed with the goals and interests of students in mind.

Materials. The availability of appropriate materials facilitate language-promoting interaction. Teachers cannot teach their students the language of car repair by discussions held in classrooms. The students must learn this language in a car repair shop, as they work there repairing cars together. Whenever possible, Tapestry teachers bring objects from the real world into the classroom, creating *world life theaters,* replicas of settings that occur outside of the classroom. When this is not possible, teachers send their students into the real world where the students are provided with appropriate materials.

The Linguistic Demands of the Task. The linguistic demands of the task must be such that they encourage student interaction of a particular nature. The interaction must push the students to use their linguistic capabilities to maximum. This means that the linguistic demands of the task should neither be too difficult nor too easy. If the demands are too high, the students may fail to interact meaningfully at all. An example of a task that is too difficult for many ESL students is the oral report. Given this assignment, some students are tempted to memorize canned talks and simply recite their reports by rote. If they are interrupted in the course of their reports, they are unable to continue, since they lack the competence in English to do so. The linguistic demands of the task are simply too difficult for them at this time. On the other hand, the linguistic demands of the task should not be too low. Tasks that do not challenge students result in the students' boredom or their failure to learn. An example of a task with low-level linguistic demands might be the recitation of a poem that the students already know. If the students have already learned the vocabulary of the poem, they will not acquire new vocabulary by repeating the poem. Tapestry teachers recognize the importance of the linguistic demands of classroom tasks. They carefully observe the linguistic abilities of their students and the availability of supports, and they choose tasks that challenge their students, but which do not exceed the abilities of their students when the students are assisted.

Interlocutors. Language-promoting interaction occurs when learners assist one another while communicating. Where language performance is assisted by more capable others, the second language develops. The input provided to learners during instructional activities is "good only when it proceeds ahead of development. It then *awakens and rouses to life those functions which are in a stage of maturing*" (Vygotsky 1956, p. 278; italics in original; quoted in Tharp and Gallimore, p. 20). Tapestry students rely on both teacher and peer assistance.

Teacher Assistance

Opportunities for the teacher to assess the learner's actual language performance are provided when the teacher interacts with learners individually. Through interaction, the teacher can determine what we call the learner's ongoing, in-flight performance. We use the term *in-flight* to refer to the fact that the learner's communicative needs and productions are ever-changing since they are embedded in the context of interaction. What the learner produces varies as a function of a number of variables such as the learners' feelings, goals, and relationship with the interlocutor, and the topic of the conversation. All these variables fluctuate in the course of interaction. After assessing the student's in-flight communicative needs, Tapestry teachers tailor the types of assistance they provide.

Peer Assistance

Students do not need to rely solely on the teacher for assistance. They can receive valuable assistance from their peers. In the Tapestry Approach, ESL learners help one another on a variety of levels; for example, in addition to helping their peers with language, students also help their peers by providing them with information, responding to their ideas, and giving them needed encouragement. In small groups and cooperative learning activities, learners receive considerable assistance. (See Chapter Ten.)

Building and Removing the Scaffolding

The more the learners are able to communicate in English effectively, the less assistance in language-promoting interaction students require. Bruner's (1983) remarks pertaining to child first language development are relevant to second language acquisition. In his words, "One sets the game, provides a scaffold to assure that the child's ineptitudes can be rescued or rectified by appropriate intervention, and then removes the scaffold part by part as the reciprocal structure can stand on its own" (p. 60). Clearly, there should be a steadily declining place of teacher and peer responsibility for carrying on interactions with a learner and a reciprocal increase in the learner's proportion of responsibility.[2] As learners in Tapestry classes become more capable communicators, they are given tasks such as attending lectures, going to movies, and reading books. Such tasks allow them to use the English language purposefully without the assistance of a more proficient English speaker.

HYPOTHESES PERTAINING TO INPUT, INTERACTION, AND OUTPUT

Our own hypothesis is that the best input and output for language development is that which occurs in the context of language-promoting interaction. This hypothesis departs significantly from earlier ones, including: (1) the Simplified Input Hypothesis; (2) the Comprehensible Input Hypothesis; (3) the Interaction Hypothesis; and (4) the Comprehensible Output Hypothesis. Below, we discuss each hypothesis and its related criticism. We conclude that our own hypothesis has the broadest application to second language teaching. However, before turning to this discussion, it will first be useful to consider Corder's notion of *intake*.

Intake

Research on children's English language development has shown that children often "unconsciously internalize and then experiment with patterns they hear in the speech going on around them" (Farr and Daniels 1986, p. 60). In the same way, ESL students may internalize English vocabulary and grammar through exposure to written and spoken English. Yet mere exposure to English input may not necessarily facilitate English language acquisition. This is because not all input leads to language development. As Corder (1967) explains, just presenting a certain linguistic form to a learner does not necessarily qualify it for the status of *intake,* since intake is *what is processed by the learner;* it is not simply what is *available* for processing. In other words, input may or may not facilitate second language development since only a small portion of this input serves as intake. This notion is illustrated in Figure 3.1.

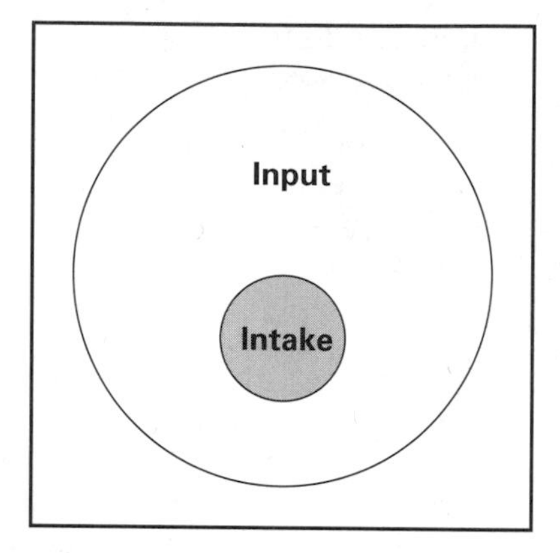

Figure 3.1 Input and Intake

The Simplified Input Hypothesis

The Simplified Input Hypothesis holds that *simplified input,* language directed to those who have limited proficiency in the language, provides a rich source of learner intake. Simplified language relies less heavily on complex syntactic structures than does language used by adult native English speakers. However, as will be seen in the discussion that follows, what was initially termed simplified input really is not so simple.

Types of Simplified Input. Following the classical research of Ferguson (1971), numerous researchers have identified three types of simplified input (referring here only to the spoken mode): (1) what is variously called *caregiver talk, baby-talk,* or *motherese* (the talk of mothers, fathers, and other caregivers to babies); (2) *teacher talk* (the talk of teachers to students); and (3) *foreigner talk* (the talk of native speakers to non-native speakers).

• *Caregiver Talk.* Many of the first studies of simplified input concerned the way middle-class mothers in the United States talk to their children. (See, for example, Snow and Ferguson 1977.) Caregiver talk is characterized by simple sentences (Newport 1976), sentences with a limited range of grammatical relations (Newport 1976, Corsaro 1979), exaggerated and slowed intonation (Garnica 1977; Sachs 1977; Snow 1972, 1977), and a high level of redundancy (Ochs-Keenan 1974). Lindfors (1987) and others also suggest that this kind of talk exhibits a high number of known-information questions (that is, questions in which the mother already knows the answer, such as *What's this?* when the mother points to a stuffed animal). Perhaps most characteristic of caregiver talk is the focus on the *here and now* (Andersen 1977, Gleason and Weintraub 1978). That is, when caregivers simplify their speech for young children, they discuss topics that are firmly anchored in the present and are frequently contextualized, often in a visual and/or tactile way, as in the following example: (The adult shows child a green ball.) *Look. Look. Green ball. Pretty green ball. Look at the pretty, green ball. Here, hold the green ball.*

Numerous studies on caregiver talk have also shown that mothers and their children jointly focus attention, construct talk, and create experiences. (See, for example Scollon 1974 and Ochs-Keenan 1974.) Caregivers cooperatively express meaning with children by expanding on their own and their children's utterances. For instance, in discussing cars, one might easily imagine a child saying, *Car,*

car, car. Car goed vroom., with the child's father replying, *That's right, son. That big yellow car is going too fast around the corner.* Ochs and Schieffelin (1984) summarize the investigations of this aspect of caregiver talk: "These studies indicate that caregivers make extensive accommodations to the child, assuming the perspective of the child in the course of engaging him or her in conversational dialogue" (pp. 280-281).

• *Teacher Talk.* Another simplified type of language or register is teacher talk. Investigations of this register grew out of studies of classroom interaction. Among others, Flanders (1970), Sinclair and Coulthard (1975), and Sinclair and Brazil (1982) developed sophisticated means of analyzing the talk of students and teachers. Systems specifically designed for language classrooms are discussed by Fanselow (1977), Allwright (1980), van Lier (1988), and Cazden (1988).

In some ways, teacher talk resembles caregiver talk. "Both registers are characterized by higher pitch, more exaggerated intonation and careful enunciation, shorter sentences and more frequent repetitions, and many more questions than the same adults would use in speaking (outside of parenting or teaching roles) to other adults" (Cazden 1988, p. 160).

Other features characteristic of teacher talk include the fact that teachers dominate the talk, usually taking up at least two-thirds of it; they initiate all interactions, often with a set of words such as *well, now,* and *so;* and they interrupt their students but do not allow themselves to be interrupted. The primary feature of the content of teacher talk is the expression of authority. Stubbs (1983) lists these ways in which teachers control student behavior and talk:

1. Attracting or showing attention.

Look! Look! Look! I want you to sit down here.

2. Controlling the amount of speech.

Teacher: Has anyone been to South America? Do you know where the Amazon is?
John: My dad and I went there. We had a great time. I really liked it.
Teacher: *(interrupting John)* Could someone tell me where the Amazon is?

3. Checking or confirming understanding.

Do you understand?

4. Summarizing.

Well, what I'm trying to say is . . .

5. Defining.

That definition isn't quite right. Can anybody define it in a different way?

6. Editing.

That's getting nearer (the answer).

7. Correcting.

(When a student has said that the meaning of "paramount" is "important.") Yes, more than that, all-important.

8. Specifying topic.

Now, we were talking about structures and all that. *(What the teacher means here is:* Let's go back to the topic of structures.)

In brief, teachers control who can talk about what to whom and for how long. By restricting the students' contributions, the teacher also restricts the range of discourse functions that students typically perform.

Recitation constitutes a major portion of much teacher talk (Duffy 1981, Durkin 1978-1979, Hoetker and Ahlbrand 1969). It consists of a series of unrelated teacher questions that require specific factual answers. As seen in Example 3.2, in *recitation questioning,* teachers ask their students for information that the teachers already know and immediately evaluate students' responses.

<u>Example 3.2</u>
Teacher: Where is Kuwait?
Student: In the Middle East.
Teacher: Good. Where is Cuba?

Only rarely are questions used to assist students to develop more complete or elaborate ideas. Goodlad's (1984) research is directly relevant here. He conducted a broadly based survey of 38 schools in 13 communities and seven regions of the United States. His researchers interviewed and observed hundreds of students and teachers in small schools and in large ones, in low-socioeconomic areas and in middle-socioeconomic ones, in rural communities and metropolitan ones, with heterogeneous cultural populations and homogeneous ones. They found a striking similarity in the instruction in all teaching situations. For the most part, teachers controlled student behavior and language. Teachers emphasized rote learning, factual test questioning, and immediate responses. They avoided questions that probed higher-level thinking skills. Only an average of seven out of 150 minutes of the school day involved a teacher responding to a student's work. There were almost no opportunities for interaction between teachers and students and among the students themselves.

Studies of teacher talk in foreign and second language classrooms have been reported by such researchers as Henzl (1979), Gaies (1977, 1981), Long (1983b), Long and Sato (1983), and Pica and Long (1986). (For an excellent review of this research, refer to Chaudron 1988.) Henzl (1979), in analyzing the language that 11 language teachers used with their students, showed that, in contrast to ordinary adult talk, teacher talk contains fewer words and subordinations per sentence and fewer verbs in the non-present tense. Long and Sato (1983) note that rather trivial, known-information questions such as *Are you a student?* and *Is the clock on the wall?* are far more frequent in language classrooms than in natural settings. The same researchers suggest that whereas teacher-generated comprehension checks (such as *Do you understand?)* are more frequent in the classroom, student-generated confirmation checks (such as *Right?)* and student-generated requests for clarification (such as *Could you repeat that?)* are less frequent (probably because the teacher dominates the conversation in the classroom).

• *Foreigner Talk.* Foreigner talk, the language used by native speakers when they address non-native speakers, is also said to be simplified. Adults speaking to second language learners automatically adjust their speech to *what they believe to be* the linguistic and cognitive levels of the learners. They use a slower rate of speaking, containing longer pauses between major speech con-stituents, along with clear articulation, a high pitch, and simple vocabulary items. Like caretaker talk, foreigner talk often focuses on concrete objects in the immediate environment, as in Example 3.3.

<u>Example 3.3</u>
Native English Speaker: Do you want the salt?
Non-native English Speaker: What?
Native English Speaker: Do you want the salt? Salt. See the salt. Do you want the salt? *(picks up salt and hands it to non-native English speaker)*

As illustrated by this example, repetitions are also characteristic of foreigner talk. More detailed descriptions of foreigner talk are provided in several studies, including those reported by Ferguson (1975), Henzl (1973, 1979), Long (1980, 1981, 1983b), Clyne (1981), and Chaudron (1982a, 1982b).

Benefits of Simplified Input. Having discussed three types of simplified registers, we turn next to a discussion of their hypothesized benefits. We conclude by arguing that the benefits of simplified input are very limited. While such input may facilitate the language development of those learners who are just beginning to acquire the language, it may hinder the language development of other learners.

In the early 1980s, numerous researchers attempted to demonstrate that simplified input facilitates second language development. Hatch (1983) provides a useful summary of the features of simplified input and their hypothesized benefits for language development.

Characteristics of Simplified Input and Hypothesized Benefits

Pronunciation

- Fewer reduced vowels and contractions
  Example: I want an apple. (Instead of: I wanna apple.)
  Benefits: Learner receives the full word form.

- Slow rate
  Benefits: Articulation is clearer and easier for the learner to understand.

- Longer pauses
  Benefits: Learner can easily hear and attend to language.

Vocabulary

- High frequency vocabulary, less slang, and fewer idioms
  Example: I see the *child.* (Instead of: I see the *kid.)*
  Benefits: Learner is more likely to understand words and recognize topic.

- Fewer pronoun forms
  Example: I see the man. The man is sitting. (Instead of: I see the man. He is sitting.)
  Benefits: Reference is clearer.

- Definitions are marked.
  Example: This is an X.
  Benefits: Definitions are salient.

- Gestures and pictures accompany lexical items.
  Benefits: Comprehensibility is increased.

- Endearment terms
  Example: Look, honey. See the ball, honey.
  Benefits: Affective boost is given to learning.

Grammar

- Short MLU (mean length of utterance)
  Example: See big green ball. (Instead of: I see the big ball that is green.)
  Benefits: It is easy for learner to process and analyze grammatical structures.

- More left dislocations of topic
  Example: Friday, Saturday, you have a nice weekend.
  Benefits: Topic is easily identified.

- More repetitions and restatements
  Example: Green ball. Green ball. Pretty big green ball.
  Benefits: Learner receives more processing time.

- More collaborative completions *(Native speaker fills in the blank.)*
  Example:
  Non-native speaker: The car went
  Native speaker: over the cliff.
  Benefits: Learner is provided with a model of syntax.

Discourse (Conversation)

- More requests for clarification
  Examples: What? Huh? What do you mean?
  Benefit: Learner is aided in his or her communication.

- Fewer interruptions
  Benefit: Learner can understand more easily.

- Salient conversation components (such as the openings and the ends of conversations)
  Example: Okay, this is the end of the interview. Good-bye.
  Benefit: Conversation flows more smoothly.

- More frames, such as *okay*
  Example: Okay, this is a green ball, okay?
  Benefit: Learner can easily identify utterances.

(Adapted from Hatch 1983, pp. 183–184.)

Criticism of the Simplified Input Hypothesis. We agree with Hatch that simplified input can provide some learners with valuable language assistance. However, we also argue that simplified input has a very limited role in second language development. There are three reasons for this. First, although it may help some learners in some situations, many learners will not benefit from receiving such input. Recall Vygotsky's view that the learner's language development is stretched through required skillful assistance at points in the learner's Zone of Proximal Development, the distance between the learner's individual capacity and the capacity to produce language with assistance. Clearly, advanced ESL learners will not benefit from simplified input since this type of input does nothing to stretch the advanced ESL learner's proficiency. Second, simplified input is not sufficient for language development. Many learners who receive this input never achieve proficiency in the second language. Third, simplified input is just one type of possible assistance. Learners need a myriad of types of assistance of varying amounts. The amount and kinds of simplified input required to foster language development depend on such variables as the learner's second language proficiency and individual characteristics.[3]

The Comprehensible Input Hypothesis

Krashen (1980) was among the first to question the facilitative effect of simplified input for all groups of learners. For Krashen (1982, 1985a, 1985b), simplified input can only help those who are in the beginning stages of language development. He suggests that the single most important factor for language development is not simplified input, but what he terms *comprehensible* input. He replaced the Simplified Input Hypothesis with a new one, the Comprehensible Input Hypothesis. According to this hypothesis, we acquire language proficiency "... by going for meaning, by focusing on what is said rather than how it is said. We are aided in this process by extralinguistic context [for instance, pictures and hand movements], and our knowledge of the world. We do not acquire by first learning about the structure of the language. We try to understand the message, and structure is thereby acquired" (Krashen 1985, p. 39).[4]

A corollary of the Comprehensible Input Hypothesis states that optimal input for language development is input that is aimed at what Krashen terms the learner's *i + 1*. For Krashen, *i + 1* consists of language that is just a little beyond the learner's current level of English language proficiency. If the input is too easy, Krashen suggests that the learner then won't learn anything new in English, but if the input is too hard for the learner to understand, Krashen claims that it will then be beyond the learner's grasp. Note that this corollary hypothesis differs from the Simplified Input Hypothesis. According to Krashen's hypothesis, optimal input for language development is that which is of a complexity level that approximately matches the learner's proficiency in the second language. In contrast, the Simplified Input Hypothesis holds that optimal input for language development is of a simplified nature; simplified input may or may not be tailored to the learner's current second language proficiency level.[5]

Another corollary hypothesis proposed by Krashen concerns communication. According to this hypothesis, optimal input for language development is not that which is tightly tailored to the learner's proficiency level, but that which results from communicating. Krashen believes that through communication learners receive input at a variety of levels; for Krashen, some of this input is beyond the students' proficiency levels while some is below their proficiency levels. However, if native English speakers communicate with non-native English speakers, Krashen believes, the native speakers frequently *hit* the non-native speaker's current proficiency level.[6]

Criticism of the Comprehensible Input Hypothesis. The hypothesis that comprehensible input aids language development is intuitively appealing. However, although the Comprehensible Input Hypothesis goes beyond the Simplified Input Hypothesis in explaining language development, this hypothesis is also limited. One major criticism is that the hypothesis is difficult to verify empirically. (See, for example, Gregg 1984, Chaudron 1985, and White 1987.) For example, just because native speakers provide ESL learners with roughly tuned input (tailored just a little beyond the ESL learners' current proficiency levels) does not necessarily mean that this input aids language development.

In line with this criticism, learners are capable of understanding relevant, authentic discourse far beyond their current English proficiency levels. In fact, we suspect that the range of input that can be used for language development is far wider than that assumed by Krashen. Vygotsky's (1956) notion of the Zone of Proximal Development is again relevant here. A Zone of Proximal Development can be considered a map of a student's sphere of readiness to acquire the second language. It is bounded at the lower end by the student's existing level of competence and at the upper end by the competence the student can acquire under favorable circumstances, such as when the student is helped by a friend who is proficient in the second language. (See Chapter Two.) Thus, the Zone of Proximal Development suggests that a wider range of input is valuable for language development. Unlike Krashen's *i+1*, the zone varies with respect to the favorable (or unfavorable circumstances) the learner encounters. We believe that Vygotsky's notion of the Zone of Proximal Development accounts more accurately for the role of input in second language development than does Krashen's notion of *i+1*.

Another criticism of this hypothesis concerns the importance of comprehensible input in language development. A number of studies have now demonstrated that comprehensible input may facilitate language development, but it does not guarantee mastery of the language. Perhaps it is a necessary but insufficient condition for language development. (See, for example, Larsen-Freeman and Long 1991. See also Schmidt 1983.)

A different criticism concerns input preferences. Krashen assumed that all input was processed more or less the same, regardless of who provided the input. However, as Beebe (1985) explains, second language learners are active participants in choosing the target language models they prefer and thus acquire, in Beebe's terms, *the right stuff* according to their own values. They have input preferences in the sense that they consciously or unconsciously choose to attend to some target language models rather than to others. They do not simply acquire a language; they actively adopt a variety of that language. A number of variables affect the learner's choice regarding this variety. Two important variables have been found to be status and solidarity. For instance, if the learner relates to his or her native English-speaking peer group more than to the teacher, then the learner will tend to acquire the variety of his or her peer group. If, on the other hand, the learner feels that people of high status are acquiring the language spoken by the teacher, the learner may tend to acquire the teacher's language regardless of the language spoken by his or her peer group.

Yet another criticism related to input preference concerns learning style. Krashen assumes that regardless of the students' individual learning styles, all ESL students process input in the same way. However, some learners are reflective and appear to require longer to process the input, while others are impulsive and appear to need much less time; impulsives often appear to deal more easily with spontaneous, natural input than reflectives. Learners who have a high tolerance of ambiguity may also find rapid, natural speech more acceptable as input than learners whose ambiguity-tolerance level is lower; the latter may appreciate more simplified input.

Researchers such as Swain (1985) and Schmidt (1983) are also quick to point out that Krashen uses the phrase *genuine communication* to refer to one-way rather than two-way communication. They argue that such one-way communication does not necessarily guarantee appropriate input for language development. When a learner does not interact, interlocutors are deprived of the learner feedback they need to make the linguistic adjustments necessary to support the learner's effort to acquire the language.

Also, in our view, natural communication does not automatically provide learners with exposure to the language that learners need to acquire. For instance, students who need to acquire engineering terms will not necessarily acquire these terms by conversing with their teachers. Such terms are not automatically used in normal classroom communication.

We argue here that comprehensible input plays an important role in second language development, but also that the notion of *input at the i+1* is oversimplified. Such input may serve as language assistance in language-promoting interaction in some situations with some learners. However, it is just one form of assistance. Optimal input for language development is clearly that which is relevant and useful to the learner. It is not necessarily provided through ordinary, informal conversation; rather, special efforts need to be taken to provide students with exposure to the specific types of authentic discourse that represent the language students need to acquire. Although such input will vary from one learner to the next, all learners will benefit from input received and used in *language-promoting interaction.*

The Interaction Hypothesis

Numerous theoretical and empirical papers have acknowledged the effect of learner interaction on second language development. (See, for instance, Schachter 1986; Hatch, Flashner, and Hunt 1986; Kasper 1985.) Van Lier (1988), for instance, argues:

> When children learn their first language, they do not first learn sounds, then words, then sentences, and then finally apply this linguistic knowledge in their interaction with the social world around them. They begin by interacting with the meaningful people in their environment, and they converse, play games and engage in rituals long before they are able to utter their first recognizable words. Their caretakers typically spend enormous amounts of time in setting up and developing these interactions, and language develops along the way. (p. 229)

Van Lier's (1988) research draws our attention to the difficulty of suggesting that second language development is enhanced when learners receive input by listening to others rather than interacting with others. Other researchers have gone even further than van Lier in suggesting the important role of the learner's language production. Long (1981) was among the first to focus on the interactional nature of conversations between native and non-native English speakers and to question the importance of comprehensible input.

In a series of articles, Long (1981, 1983a, 1983b) proposes what we term the Interaction Hypothesis, which states that the interactional nature of conversation facilitates language development. (See also Varonis and Gass 1985a, 1985b, Ellis 1988a, 1988b.)

Long and his colleagues went beyond earlier researchers in claiming that interaction does not affect all learners in the same way. Interestingly, a number of variables have been found to affect the number and types of conversational modifications that occur in conversations between native and non-native English speakers. Such variables include the age and gender of the interlocutors as well as the nature of the tasks in which they participate.[7]

Benefits of Interaction. Long (1981) argues that the conversational devices interlocutors use when interacting provide ESL students with a means of ensuring that their input is comprehensible. For instance, learners can use requests for clarification (such as, *Could you repeat that, please?* and *What?*) to get their interlocutors to clarify their messages.

Following Long, other investigators have also suggested that the learners' comprehension is increased through negotiation (see, for example, Doughty and Pica 1985; Gass and Varonis 1984; Pica 1987, 1988a, 1988b; Pica, Doughty, and Young 1986; Pica, Young, and Doughty 1987; Varonis and Gass 1982, 1985a, 1985b). These researchers use the term *negotiate* to refer to exchanges between learners and their interlocutors as they attempt to resolve communication breakdowns and to work toward mutual comprehension. The amount of comprehensible input learners receive is a consequence of negotiation since it enables interlocutors to evaluate and re-evaluate their addressee's ability to understand and to be understood (Gass and Varonis 1985).

Interaction also helps students to attend to the ongoing exchange. As numerous researchers have pointed out, it helps learners to pay attention to language forms and messages. This in turn enhances language development. (For research on the role of negotiation and attention, see, for example, Schmidt 1990; see also Doughty and Pica 1985; Gass and Varonis 1984, 1985; Pica 1987, 1988a, 1988b; Pica, Doughty, and Young 1986; Pica, Young, and Doughty 1987; Varonis and Gass 1982, 1985a, 1985b.)

In addition, interaction gives learners opportunities to repair their own utterances. Such repairs are thought to facilitate second language development. For instance, in a recent study, Gass and Varonis (1989) demonstrate that learners make frequent repairs to their utterances and, as a result of these repairs, they incorporate standard language forms into their own speech. These standard language forms may appear immediately as well as after considerable delay. Undoubtedly, the ability to carry out self-repair and to elicit repair from one's conversational partner is an essential skill for second language learners.[8]

Ellis (1988b) further suggests that a characteristic of interaction associated with rapid language development is "talk about topics related to ongoing activity in which both the participants are engaged" (p. 87). When learners are actively involved in sustained purposeful interaction related to their own personal interests they are exposed to meaningful input. Research on caregiver talk is consistent with Ellis' view, suggesting that conversation provides children with *relevant* input. For instance, Cross (1977), in her study of linguistically advanced children, found that a high proportion of mothers' utterances were directly contingent upon what the child had said; mothers seemed to tune into and build on what their children were telling them. This suggests that the optimal input for language development is that which is thematically related and relevant to the learner.[9]

Finally, conversational devices enable native speakers to ensure that their non-native speaking interlocutors understand their messages. Comprehension checks (moves by which one speaker tries to determine whether the other speaker has understood a message, as in *Do you understand?)* and confirmation checks (moves by which one speaker seeks confirmation of the other's preceding utterance through repetition) are examples of such devices.

Criticism of the Interaction Hypothesis. The Interaction Hypothesis makes a significant contribution to our knowledge of language development and has important implications for language teaching. Input alone does not facilitate language development. Learners must *do* something with their input if it is to become intake. The conversational activities in which learners engage can personalize the input and make it more readily available to be processed as intake. Not only do the conversational activities potentially provide data for language development, but they also provide students with valuable information concerning the roles, events, preferences, and beliefs of native English speakers. Moreover, they provide learners with information concerning who may direct certain kinds of information to whom under what circumstances. Conversational features (such as *huh?* and *what?)* help students to control the com-prehensibility of the input they receive. Such features support the learners' efforts to communicate.

However, despite these strengths, the Interaction Hypothesis is also problematic. Most specifically, it fails to explain *when* conversational features are useful in second language development. In our view, these features assist language development only when they are *required* to help learners stretch their linguistic abilities in communication. The amount and kinds of such modifications that facilitate language development depend on many variables including the learner's linguistic proficiency and other individual characteristics. We also consider conversational features just one type of possible assistance. Again, although this hypothesis is a vast improvement over earlier ones, in our view, learners need a myriad of types of assistance of varying amounts. Conversational features are helpful to learners, but they are not enough to ensure language development.

The Comprehensible Output Hypothesis

Building on the work of Long and others, Swain (1985) was concerned with the relationship of both input and output as mediated through aspects of the learner's second language proficiency. Like Long, she questioned the value of Krashen's Comprehensible Input Hypothesis. Swain's Comprehensible Output Hypothesis states that what is needed for language development is not simply comprehensible input, but what Swain calls *comprehensible output,* that is, required language production that is just one step beyond the learner's current proficiency level. Within her framework, comprehensible output is the aspect of language use that is essential for language development. Without it, learners do not have the opportunity to actively test and refine their knowledge of the target language. (See also Schachter 1984, 1986.) Additionally, as Swain suggests, in production, the learner is pushed from semantic processing to syntactic. This is because listening is more receiver-oriented than production. In comprehending the language, it is possible that a learner does not understand the syntax of an utterance that he or she has understood; in production, the learner is forced to impose some syntactic structure on the utterance.

Criticism of the Comprehensible Output Hypothesis. The Comprehensible Output Hypothesis makes a valuable contribution to our knowledge of language development and goes far beyond the Comprehensible Input Hypothesis. However, even this hypothesis is somewhat limited, since both comprehensible input and output appear to support language acquisition, but neither fully explains language development in classroom settings. Comprehensible output is just one form of assistance. There are many other rich sources of assistance that are not accounted for by the Comprehensible Output Hypothesis. (Refer to Table 3.1.)

THE LANGUAGE-PROMOTING INTERACTION HYPOTHESIS

The Language-Promoting Interaction Hypothesis states that teachers can best help students acquire language by providing students with numerous language supports in the context of language-promoting interaction. As stated earlier, in such interaction, learners receive assistance in communicating what they cannot communicate alone. The types of supports teachers provide students vary with respect to such variables as the students' attention, individual characteristics, and second language proficiency. Types of potential language supports include, but are not limited to, simplified input, comprehensible input, interactional features, and comprehensible output.

Our approach to language instruction contrasts with other approaches that provide students with only limited assistance. For example, comprehension approaches to language teaching miss the mark in that students do not *use* the input that they receive. Output approaches, on the other hand, fall short of success because students produce language without sufficient input. Neither sets of approaches provide students with the broad range of language assistance that they need.

Although assistance is normally given in the context of language-promoting interaction, the reader should not think that such assistance only helps learners develop speaking and listening skills. Such assistance is invaluable in helping learners express themselves in writing and increase their reading proficiency. Examples of supports that help students to write better include brainstorming strategies and editorial suggestions. Examples of supports that facilitate the learners' ability to read include preview questions (which help the students anticipate the meaning of a reading passage) and discussion questions (which help the students remember the ideas in a reading). (See Chapters Seven and Eight.) Although the research on input, interaction, and output focuses on oral communication almost exclusively, the findings also have implications for reading and writing. Simply put, when students' efforts to read and write are supported through the assistance of a more knowledgeable other, literacy skills develop.

The assistance occurs in the context of language-promoting interaction. Contexts that promote language development do not occur randomly. Contexts in which language promoting interactions happen — in which language development occurs — must be carefully orchestrated.

TAPESTRY PRINCIPLES CONCERNING INPUT, OUTPUT, AND INTERACTION

The discussion above leads to the following set of related principles regarding input and interaction.

PRINCIPLES

1. Tapestry teachers employ instructional tasks that facilitate language-promoting interaction by providing students with a wide variety of types of language assistance.
2. Optimal interaction for second language development is responsive to the students' ever-changing needs, interests, goals, and understanding. Tapestry teachers provide students with language that is responsive to their students' productions in-flight, that is, their learners' productions that are embedded in interaction.
3. Students require experience using English in real, meaningful communication. This entails using the input they receive to convey meaning.

CONCLUSION

What constitutes a favorable linguistic environment for one student will be different for another student and will vary throughout an ESL lesson. Seize the moment. Respond sensitively to the students. If the linguistic context is facilitative it is so, not because it provides simplified or finely or roughly tuned input or output. Rather, a facilitative context might be better viewed as a rich and intricate one — much like our concept of *tapestry.*

ACTIVITIES AND DISCUSSION QUESTIONS

1. What types of assistance could you provide advanced ESL learners that would help them understand an academic lecture on earthquakes?
2. In many ESL programs in the United States, ESL students from one cultural background greatly outnumber students from other cultural backgrounds. When ESL students interact with students from the same cultural background and the same proficiency level, they sometimes pick up each other's partially acquired, frequently incorrect English grammar. What are some ways to provide these students with sufficient quantities of English input and opportunities to use this input? Would it be better to put these students in a classroom taught by a teacher who encouraged group work and cooperative learning, or in a tightly controlled classroom where the teacher directed most of the activities?
3. What are three sources of English input you can provide your students after your ESL class has ended? Examples of sources include television shows, radio programs, and newspaper columns. (If you are not currently teaching, imagine you are teaching a specific group of students at the adult education level.)
4. What conversational strategies could you teach adult learners that would allow them to control the amount and comprehensibility of the input they receive?
5. Who would provide the best input for second language development to these ESL students?
   a. a Mexican engineer who has intermediate-level English speaking skills;
   b. a Japanese university student who has just arrived in the United States and does not speak any English;
   c. a Romanian university student who is a nearly fluent English speaker;
   d. a Korean dentist who exhibits advanced English speaking skills.

NOTES

1. Our notion of language-promoting interactions is not original to us. We have adapted Tharp and Gallimore's (1988) concept of *instructional conversations* to conversations for language development. Their concept has been influenced by Vygotsky's (1956) idea of *assisted* performance.
2. This is Bruner's (1983) *handover* principle.
3. The limited role that comprehensible input plays in second language development is also reflected in the research of those who have examined simplified input across cultures. These researchers have found that simplified input does not necessarily play a central role in language development. After all, children from diverse cultures all learn languages in comparable time periods. Two studies, undertaken by Ochs (1989) and Heath (1982), particularly illustrate the wide diversity of input children receive. Ochs (1989) explains that "in certain societies more than others, caregivers are expected to make rather dramatic accommodation to young children's cognitive immaturity . . . In American white middle-class society, caregivers [mothers and fathers] simplify their speech in addressing young children. In other societies, such as traditional Western Samoan society and Kaluli (Papua New Guinea) society, caregivers do not simplify their speech to the extent characteristic of the American middle class" (p. 23). Despite the Samoan

children's lack of exposure to simplified input, they acquire the Samoan language quickly and efficiently. Along similar lines, Heath (1982) reports that black mothers in certain regions in South Carolina do not provide their children with simplified input. Nevertheless, these black children acquire the complex English language spoken by their mothers. These results might suffice to at least question the necessity of providing language learners with simplified input. They suggest that many groups of learners do acquire language without the benefit of simplified, watered-down input. (Larsen-Freeman and Long 1991 hold a slightly different view.)

4. Krashen (1985a, 1985b) draws on first and second language research to support his hypothesis. For example, he points out that researchers such as Clark and Clark (1977) argue that in the process of *making children understand,* mothers provide language teaching lessons. They provide utterances that their children can understand with the help of context, and they expand on what their children have said by using words for different aspects of the contexts. (For instance, they might show their children two cars and say, *Do you want the red car or the blue car?)* Mothers also give incidental clues as to how utterances can be divided up into words, phrases or clauses (for example, by putting new words in familiar frames like *There's a . . .).* Such language lessons appear to increase the children's comprehension of their mothers' messages.

5. Krashen (1985a) states:

> The best input is not grammatically sequenced. Rather, if the acquirer understands the input presented, and enough of it is made available, $i+1$, the structures will be automatically sequenced. . . . The acquirers will receive comprehensible input containing structures just a little beyond them *if they are in situations involving genuine communication,* and these structures will be constantly provided and automatically reviewed. They need not worry about missing the past tense forever (or at least until next year). With natural, comprehensible input, the hypothesis predicts that they will hear the past tense again and again (pp. 38-39, emphasis ours).

6. To support this particular hypothesis, Krashen draws on the literature on caregiver talk and teacher talk. He argues that child first language researchers (such as Bruner 1983, Cross 1977, and Moerk 1983) have provided evidence that caregivers roughly tune their language to that of their children. By *roughly tune,* Krashen means that caregivers provide input that is a little more complex than that of their children. (Note that he does not define the term *complex.)* He cites Cross' (1977) classic article as evidence for this hypothesis. Cross proposed that when caregiver talk is tailored to a child's linguistic proficiency level, language development is facilitated. She noted that, as a child grows older, the nature of caregiver talk changes such that it becomes more advanced linguistically and includes fewer caregiver features than it did when the child was younger. Cross' findings, then, suggest that simplified input may facilitate the language development of children who are in the beginning stages of language development, but may impede the language development of children in the advanced stages. Cross' observation led to her analysis of the conversations of 16 mother-child pairs. The children in Cross' study were advanced linguistically, and Cross wanted to explain the children's rapid language development. She found that the mothers' mean length of utterances directed to the children was closely associated with the children's rate of language development.

   Krashen also claims that research on teacher talk provides evidence that is consistent with his hypothesis, since teacher talk apparently provides students with input that approximates the students' language proficiency. In analyzing the ESL lessons given to students of four different proficiency levels, Gaies (1977), for instance, found that the English that teachers use when talking to ESL students varies as a function of the proficiency level of the learners. In measuring the complexity of the recorded speech, Gaies examined six criteria: words per T-unit, clauses per T-unit, words per clause, adjectival clauses per 100 T-units, adverb clauses per 100 T-units and noun clauses per 100 T-units. (A T-unit is a sentence-like unit.) The results of his study suggest that, for every criterion, the complexity of the teachers' language increased as a function of the proficiency level of the students. Other researchers, such as Hakansson (1986), also examined teacher talk used with adult second language learners and found evidence that teacher talk is adjusted to the expected language proficiency levels of the learners.

7. For instance, Scarcella and Higa (1981) found that adult native English speakers modified their input to provide a larger number of simplified interactions with non-native English-speaking children than they did with non-native English-speaking adolescents. However, they also found that non-native English-speaking adolescents were more capable of modifying their conversations to enhance communication. Cathcart-Strong (1986) compared interactions between non-native English-speaking children and native English-speaking children. She found that adults responded to more non-native English-speaking topic initiations than did the native English-speaking children.

   Gender also plays a role. Varonis and Gass (1985), looking at the effect of gender on conversational modifications, found that, with Japanese learners of English, ". . . men took greater advantage of the opportunities to use the conversation in a way that allowed them to produce a greater amount of comprehensible output, whereas women utilized the conversation to obtain a greater amount of comprehensible input" (p. 349). In a similar study of gender, Pica, Holliday, Lewis, and Morgenthaler (1989) found that gender affects the amount of comprehensible input learners provide one another.

8. Studies on group work indicate that some learners notice others' errors and incorporate these errors into their own language productions while engaging in group work, and other students do not. Over the long run, however, students who have contact with only one native speaker, their teacher, attain a comprehensible but often non-fluent variety of the second language. (For a recent review of these studies, refer to Larsen-Freeman and Long 1991.)

9. Schachter (1986) also argues that interaction enables learners to receive what she refers to as *negative input,* that is, corrective feedback that indicates that the learner's output deviates from that of native speakers. Chaudron (1977), too, suggests that during interaction ". . . the ways in which the learners' utterances are rejected or reformulated can contribute to the individual's rate and manner of learning" (p. 29).

   Krashen (1985a) takes a different view. Turning to research in child first language development, he argues that when learners communicate, corrective feedback plays a limited or negative role in language development. He points out that research indicates that caregivers only correct children's language forms when there is some communicative purpose, as when the communication fails or the child tells a lie. For example, if a child drops his or her ice cream on the couch and the mother cleans it up, the child might say, *All gone sticky.* In this case, the mother would not correct the child's language. If, on the other hand, the child smashes his or her Halloween make-up into the carpet and says, *All gone sticky,* the mother is likely to correct the child — saying, *No, the mess is not gone. It's still here.* Krashen also argues that corrective feedback can intimidate some learners and discourage them from making further attempts to communicate. (For a recent review of the role of corrective feedback in second language development, see Chaudron 1988.)

SUGGESTED READINGS

- Gass, S.S., and Madden, C. (eds.). 1985. *Input in Second Language Acquisition.* Rowley, MA: Newbury House. This edited volume brings together a selection of papers presented at the Xth University of Michigan Conference on Applied Linguistics. Twenty-three papers are divided into four areas: language acquisition in an instructional setting, aspects of interaction, the interrelationship of input, intake, and output, and methodological and theoretical issues relating to language input. A final chapter by Larsen-Freeman reviews past studies and suggests future directions for research.

- Day, R.R. (ed.). 1986. *Talking to Learn: Conversation in Second Language Acquisition.* Rowley, MA: Newbury House. The empirical studies in this volume examine the role of conversation in second language development and pedagogy. Section One presents theoretical background. Section Two includes papers that consider teacher and teacher-student interaction in language classrooms. The next section considers the nature of the conversation that occurs in small groups of students within the classroom. The final section includes studies that examine the conversations of learners with one another and native speakers outside of classrooms.

- Krashen, S.D. 1985. *The Input Hypothesis: Issues and Implications.* New York: Longman. In this cogent volume, Krashen discusses the various corollaries of his input hypothesis, the research that supports these corollaries, and the role of comprehensible input in his theory of second language development. The volume gives a comprehensive and persuasive account of his comprehensible input hypothesis. Topics covered include the role of affective factors, individual variation, and age differences. The book also includes practical suggestions for language pedagogy that are consistent with Krashen's theory.

- Tharp, R.G., and Gallimore, R. 1988. *Rousing Minds to Life: Teaching, Learning and Schooling in Social Context.* Cambridge: Cambridge University Press. Although not specifically intended for second language educators, this volume is directly relevant for this audience. It presents the interactionist theory of development that has emerged from Vygotsky's ideas and discusses their application in teaching and learning contexts. The volume also contains an excellent discussion of the various means of assisting learners' cognitive development and proposes detailed theories of schooling and literacy. The authors provide numerous examples from over ten years of a research project involving the Kamehameha Elementary Education Program (KEEP), a program that serves many elementary students of diverse cultures and first language backgrounds.

- White, L. 1989. *Universal Grammar and Second Language Acquisition.* Amsterdam/Philadelphia: John Benjamins Publishing Company. This book explores the relationship between linguistic universals and second language acquisition. It provides an accurate and readable description of the research on this topic. Especially useful are White's overview of Government and Binding Theory and discussion of learnability theories.

CHARACTERISTICS OF INDIVIDUAL LEARNERS

4

PREVIEW QUESTIONS

1. What are the roles played by motivation and attitudes in learning a second language?
2. Why is anxiety frequently a major factor in developing skill in a new language?
3. How do self-esteem, ambiguity tolerance, and risk-taking interact in second language learning?
4. How do cooperation and competition operate in language classrooms?
5. What are language learning styles and strategies, and why are they crucial?

Many of the most obvious and most varied strands of the tapestry of language learning are formed by students' own individual characteristics, such as motivation, attitudes, anxiety, self-esteem, tolerance of ambiguity, risk-taking, cooperation, competition, learning styles, and learning strategies. These aspects comprise the *weft* of the tapestry. The weft consists of brightly colored yarns woven horizontally, passing over and under the vertical warp yarns or wrapped around each warp yarn. The colorful weft yarns are the ones that show. They create the beautiful design that catches the eye and conveys the story of language learning.

In the ESL classroom, we must pay close attention to the characteristics of our students. For instance, to provide optimal instruction, it is important to know students' preferred learning styles and their motivations for studying ESL. This knowledge will help us design and tailor the activities we conduct in the classroom. Without such knowledge our instruction might miss the mark.

ORGANIZATION OF THIS CHAPTER

In this chapter we discuss the weft strands — individual student differences — one by one and show how they relate to each other. We begin with motivation and attitudes, go next to anxiety, move to the triple combination of self-esteem, tolerance of ambiguity, and risk-taking, shift to competition and cooperation, and conclude with learning styles and strategies.

MOTIVATION AND ATTITUDES

Gardner (1985) has shown through statistical path-analysis techniques that motivation strongly influences the degree to which learners take advantage of opportunities to use the language.

Regardless of whether we believe motivation to be the single primary factor, one of several equally important factors, or an intermediary factor, it is impossible to dismiss the importance of motivation in language learning.

Motivation decides the extent of active, personal engagement in learning. A recent study (Oxford and Nyikos 1989) shows that the degree of motivation is the most powerful influence on how and when students use language learning strategies, the techniques learners employ to take charge of and improve their own progress.

Motivation is directly affected by whether language instruction is relevant to the learning style preferences of students. For instance, analytic students (whose tendency is to break down material and look for details) are often more motivated by grammar-based activities and less motivated by communicative, free-flowing activities. The opposite can be said of global students, who prefer to look for main ideas and are not focused so much on details (Oxford, Ehrman, and Lavine 1990).

Despite its undeniable importance, exactly how motivation works in language learning is not completely understood. Most researchers have not even defined motivation clearly. To redress this problem, let us adopt the following definition of motivation (by Crookes and Schmidt 1989).

Definition of Motivation

Motivation has both external, behavioral characteristics and an internal, attitudinal structure. Three behavioral features of motivation are: decision, persistence, and activity level. The learner *decides* to choose, pay attention to, and engage in one activity but not others; *persists* over an extended time and returns to the activity after any interruptions; and maintains a high *activity level*. The internal structure of motivation is just as important and includes these four attitudinal factors: interest, relevance, expectancy, and outcomes.

1. *Interest* in the subject or process, based on existing attitudes, experience, and background knowledge on the part of the learner;
2. *Relevance*, which involves the perception that personal needs such as achievement, affiliation with other people, and power are being met;
3. *Expectancy* of success or failure; and
4. *Outcomes*, that is, the extrinsic or intrinsic rewards felt by the learner.

If any of these factors — behavioral or attitudinal — is missing or negative, overall motivation of the learner is weakened. For instance, a language teacher who overcorrects the student can lower the expectancy of success and thus reduce the student's willingness to pay attention or persist in learning the language. If language classroom activities are perceived as uninteresting or irrelevant, the learner might decide, with a greater or lesser degree of conscious choice, to tune out or to reduce the level of involvement. Clearly, the attitudes of the learner directly affect the behaviors, and both aspects are integral to the concept of motivation.

Many Approaches to Motivation

All the major researchers have taken a social-psychological slant toward understanding the role of motivation in language learning. A social-psychological slant involves concern about the individual person in the context of a group, usually the target culture, that is, the society that uses the language which the student is learning.

Gardner and his colleagues (see, for example, Gardner 1985; Gardner, Lalonde, Moorcroft, and Evers 1985; Gardner and Lambert 1959, 1972) for many years championed *integrative motivation*, the desire to learn a language so as to integrate oneself with the target culture, as preferable to *instrumental motivation,* the desire to learn the language in order to get a better job or meet a language requirement. According to this formulation, if Miko wants to get to know U.S. citizens and fit into American culture, she will learn English more effectively than if her goal is just to get a better job that requires facility in English.

The desire to become integrated with the target culture relates strongly to Speech Accommodation Theory (Giles and Byrne 1982, Beebe 1988). In this theory, the learner's degree of identification with the "in-group" (the group that speaks the target language and is therefore advantaged socially and communicatively) is a crucial factor. We can liken Giles' and Byrne's in-group identification to what Gardner calls integrative motivation. The more closely identified the learner feels to the in-group (that is, the more the learner intentionally integrates with that group), the more the learner's speech will accommodate to the in-group's speech, and hence the more proficient and appropriate the learner's language performance will be. Schumann's Acculturation Model (1978, 1986) likewise concerns many aspects of integrative motivation, though the model uses other terms.

However, many researchers including Oller (1981), Au (1988), Horwitz (1990), Oxford, Talbott, and Halleck (1989), and Crookes and Schmidt (1989) disagree with the primacy of integrative motivation in language learning. Basically they argue that different kinds of motivation — integrative or instrumental — may be important to language learning success, depending on the circumstances.

For instance, Horwitz (1990) pointed to research showing that instrumental motivation was more predictive than integrative motivation for language learning success in the Philippines, while integrative motivation was a stronger influence than instrumental motivation in English-speaking Canadian populations. People in the Philippines wanted English for advancement (for example, career and economic), according to the research, but the Canadians in the studies learned French for purposes of becoming closer to — integrated with — the French-speaking Canadian population.

Oxford, Talbott, and Halleck (1989) found that many successful ESL learners in an American university program were instrumentally motivated by career concerns rather than by a burning desire to get to know U.S. citizens and U.S. culture.

We might add that many kinds of language learning motivations have not even been researched yet. Instrumental and integrative (and a more recent offshoot called assimilative) motivation are not the only brands of language learning motivation that exist. For instance, many people, hard as it is to believe sometimes, learn languages for fun, not for profit or for social purposes. Other language learners view their goal to be simply *communicating* with native speakers, rather than integrating with them or assimilating totally into their society. Still other motivations probably exist as well. A thorough examination of many types of motivation still needs to be accomplished, and various perspectives — not just the rich perspective of social psychology, but also other perspectives including that of humanistic psychology — should be applied to enlarge our understanding.

Facing new evidence from other researchers, Gardner has recently softened his emphasis on integrative motivation by saying, "the *source* of the motivating impetus is relatively unimportant provided that motivation is aroused" (1985, p. 169; emphasis ours). Thus, the arguments about instrumental vs. integrative motivation that have dominated the research literature might be less important than the absolute degree of motivation possessed by the individual learner.

General Comments on Motivation and Attitudes

Unquestionably, motivation and attitudes are very important in language learning success. High motivation (based on positive attitudes) might spur learners to interact with native speakers of the language (Schumann 1986), which in turn increases the amount of input that learners receive (Krashen 1982). Motivation often leads learners to use a variety of learning strategies that can facilitate greater skill in language learning (Oxford and Nyikos 1989).

Motivation encourages greater overall effort on the part of language learners and typically results in greater success in terms of global language proficiency (see, for example, Clément, Major, Gardner, and Smythe 1977; Gardner 1985) and competence in specific language skills such as listening, reading, and speaking (Tucker, Hamayan, and Genesee 1976; Genesee 1978). Strong motivation and positive attitudes also help learners maintain their language skills after classroom instruction is over (Gardner, Lalonde, Moorcroft, and Evers 1985; Oxford and Crookall 1988). Of course, the role of motivation in language learning research and in classroom practice is tempered by developmental factors such as age differences and variations in the stages of language acquisition. (See Chapter Two for details.)

Because motivation is so very important in language learning, instructional activities and materials must be exciting, stimulating, and interesting to learners. Moreover, we as teachers must pay special attention to the attitudes students bring to language learning. We must help reverse any negative attitudes (including cultural stereotyping) students may have and must try to inculcate positive attitudes toward the target culture, the language, and the language learning process.

ANXIETY

In language learning, motivation and attitudes are related to anxiety defined as "a state of apprehension, a vague fear" (Scovel 1978, p. 134). Such apprehension or fear can cause motivation to plummet and attitudes to drift toward the negative. In a downward spiral, low motivation can then lead to poorer performance, which then results in still greater anxiety.

State vs. Trait

Anxiety sometimes arises in response to a particular situation or event (situational or state anxiety), but occasionally it is a permanent character trait, as in a person who is predisposed to be fearful of many things (trait anxiety). The kind of anxiety we ordinarily see in the language classroom is situational or state anxiety rather than trait anxiety. Most language learners who are anxious are not displaying a generalized personality characteristic, but are instead reacting to certain aspects of the language learning situation (Horwitz 1990). A recent book (Horwitz and Young 1990) is devoted to situational anxiety in the language classroom.

Can Anxiety Ever Be Helpful?

Some experts say that anxiety can be helpful rather than harmful. The "good" kind of anxiety is called *facilitating anxiety,* which can be useful in keeping students alert and on their toes (Scovel 1978, Brown 1987). The "bad" kind of anxiety is known as *debilitating anxiety,* because it harms learners' performance in many ways, both indirectly through worry and self-doubt and directly by reducing participation and creating overt avoidance of the language.

Horwitz (1990) notes that what some researchers call *facilitating anxiety* is only helpful for very simple learning tasks, but not for more complicated learning such as language learning. By implication, there might be no such thing as facilitating anxiety for language learners.

For this reason — and also because the term *anxiety* as commonly used carries only negative connotations — we prefer to use the term *anxiety* to refer only to debilitating anxiety. We believe that while a certain amount of positive tension is helpful to language learners, any degree of true anxiety is detrimental in the language classroom.

Performance Anxiety

Many kinds of language activities can generate performance anxiety, depending on the student. Speaking in front of others is often the most anxiety-provoking of all. Many of us have observed students who exhibit extreme anxiety when they are required to use the new language in such activities as oral reports, skits, role-plays, or speaking-and-listening tests. Students prone to anxiety when speaking include introverts who do not enjoy interacting with others spontaneously or who dislike performing in front of others. Visual learners — students who are very strongly oriented to the printed word and whose oral-aural skills are considerably weaker than their visual skills — also display anxiety when asked to speak without a visual prompt.

But speaking is not the only skill that triggers anxiety. For some students, writing or listening can also create fear, depending on the students' learning style preferences and skill level. Even reading, which has the advantage of a permanent, written stimulus to which students can return repeatedly, can be anxiety-provoking — especially to individuals who have difficulty reading efficiently or well in their native language due to a learning disability or lack of appropriate reading strategies.

Traditional, Teacher-Centered Structure

Here is a dramatic but realistic description of what sometimes happens in a traditional, teacher-centered classroom:

> It is all too easy for a foreign [or second] language classroom to create inhibitions and anxiety. It is not uncommon to find a teaching situation where, for example: the learners remain constantly aware of their own state of ignorance before a teacher who possesses all relevant knowledge; they are expected to speak or act only in response to immediate stimuli or instructions from the teacher (or tape, etc.); whatever they say or do is scrutinized in detail, with every shortcoming being made a focus for comment. In such circumstances, the learners occupy a permanent position of inferiority before a critical audience, with little opportunity for asserting their own individuality. They are unlikely to feel drawn out to communicate with those around them or to develop positive attitudes toward the learning environment. On the contrary, many learners will prefer to keep a "low profile," in the hope that they will not be called upon to participate openly.
>
> (Littlewood 1981, p. 93)

In the description above, anxiety stems from the traditional social structure of the classroom, which is still all too often powerfully teacher-centered at the expense of student-student communication. In such a classroom, learners do not feel free to interact with each other spontaneously. They also feel they will receive punishment (personal notice or criticism) for making mistakes, although mistakes are a normal and predictable part of language learning, as demonstrated in Chapter Two. In such an environment, learners feel severe anxiety, which involves fear of looking or acting stupid or fear of negative comparisons with others who might perform better.

Other Sources of Anxiety

Anxiety can come from other sources, too. This painful feeling can arise from a fear of, or from the actual experience of, "losing oneself" in the target culture. This occurs especially in *culture shock*, which is "a form of anxiety that results from the loss of commonly perceived and understood signs and symbols of social intercourse" (Adler 1987, p. 25). Language learners who are living in the target culture, such as ESL learners in the United States, frequently experience culture shock, at least initially. Learners undergoing this form of anxiety typically experience one or more of the following symptoms: emotional regression, panic, anger, self-pity, indecision, sadness, alienation, "reduced personality," and physical illness. However, if handled effectively, culture shock can become a cross-cultural learning opportunity involving increased cultural awareness, increased self-awareness, and reintegration of personality. As teachers dealing with ESL students, we need to be aware of the signs of culture shock and must be prepared to open and maintain supportive dialog with any student who feels this type of anxiety.

Anxiety can also occur when, for any number of reasons, students feel the language learning process is an annoying, irrelevant, or hopeless waste of time. This happens when students do not want to study the language and are coerced into doing so to meet parental, institutional, or societal expectations. It occurs when students are not interested in the language and see no instrumental reason to learn it for academic or career purposes. It happens when students are totally uninterested in relating to the culture. And it especially arises when the needs of the learner — either the student's goals or learning style — are ignored by the teacher.

Diagnosing Anxiety

We can diagnose anxiety through a number of surveys and other instruments. However, sometimes anxiety is observable with the naked eye and discoverable through personal discussion with students. We must be aware, though, that behaviors vary across cultures, and what might seem like anxious behavior in U.S. culture might be calm, normal behavior in another culture.

We offer some clear signs of anxiety in the language classroom:

1. General avoidance: "Forgetting" the answer, showing carelessness, cutting class, coming late, arriving unprepared.
2. Physical actions: Squirming, fidgeting, playing with hair or clothing, nervously touching objects, stuttering or stammering, displaying jittery behavior, being unable to reproduce the sounds or intonation of the target language even after repeated practice.
3. Physical symptoms: Complaining about a headache, experiencing tight muscles, feeling unexplained pain or tension in any part of the body.

In diagnosing anxiety, try to distinguish signs of anxiety from common differences in cultural values. Read about cultural customs, attitudes, and beliefs, and ask students to explain when you do not know for sure.

Reducing Anxiety

Oxford (1990), Lavine and Oxford (1990), and Horwitz (1990) list a number of ways to reduce anxiety in the language classroom:

1. Awareness: Be aware of the possibility of language learning anxiety. This awareness diminishes teacherly impatience with nervous students who seem unwilling or unable to participate freely. Consider their possible anxiety level and try to lower it, rather than raising it through criticism.
2. Positive climate: Create a positive learning environment by not disparaging students in front of others, by learning students' names, by using an encouraging rather than threatening style of questioning, by avoiding overcorrection, by avoiding sarcasm and intimidation, by testing fairly what the learners know rather than giving "trick questions," and by addressing the learning styles of all students in the class.
3. Self-talk: Help students to help themselves through *positive self-talk* as opposed to *negative self-talk* in order to reprogram their thinking. For instance, if you hear a student saying, "I'm sure I'm going to fail this test!" or "I can't speak this language!" or "I'm not a good language learner!", you can aid the learner in *reframing* this kind of negative idea. For example, you can encourage

the student to say, "If I study hard, I know I can pass this test," or "I am learning every day how to speak this language better," or "I *am* a good language learner!"

4. Cooperative or group learning: Use pair work, group work, or cooperative learning activities, which take the onus off the individual student to perform in front of the whole class and which allow greater student-student interaction.

5. Diaries and dialog journals: Use language learning diaries, which allow students to express their fears and anxieties freely and to obtain the emotional support of their peers and teachers in a interactional format. For descriptions of these diaries, see Oxford (1990), Rubin (1981), and Bailey (1983). Similarly, dialog journals — notebooks in which each student and his or her teacher write to each other on a regular basis in a natural dialog — provide an opportunity for students to share their feelings and for the teacher to respond supportively (Staton 1984).

6. Rewards: Reward students for a job well done through verbal praise. Let successful students have, as a reward, the opportunity to choose the next activity or decide on the location of the next field trip. Assist them in developing their own intrinsic reward system.

7. Behavioral contracting: Have the student sign a contract with the teacher outlining very specific performance expectations in a step-by-step way, so that the student knows what to do and how to do it. This often reduces anxiety. See Oxford (1990) for formats for deciding on personal, short-term and long-term learning objectives and for monitoring progress toward these objectives.

8. Relaxation: Teach students how to use relaxation techniques, such as progressively tensing and relaxing each of the major muscle groups or imagining a calm, beautiful vista. These techniques are frequently used in clinical psychology to reduce tension and induce a sense of well-being.

9. Student support groups: Create language learning support groups for students outside of class. These can serve as places to share learning strategies, practice the language together, prepare for tests and projects, and provide emotional support. Horwitz (1990) gives an example of such a support group for language learning.

Not every one of these anxiety-reduction techniques will work equally well with all students. For example, while enthusiastic praise might be valuable to many students, learners from certain cultures might not relate well to such praise, especially if given in front of other people. Although many learners benefit from practicing positive self-talk, it might be awkward or artificial for some other learners. The skilled teacher will want to vary the techniques according to the needs of individual students.

SELF-ESTEEM, TOLERANCE OF AMBIGUITY, AND RISK-TAKING

The next set of learner characteristics includes self-esteem, tolerance of ambiguity, and risk-taking ability. These are important and highly related factors that influence the success of language learners.

Self-Esteem

Student self-esteem is very important in the language classroom. We define self-esteem as a self-judgment of worth or value, based on feelings of *efficacy* — a sense of interacting effectively with one's own environment (White 1959). Low self-esteem is obvious in statements like, "I sure feel stupid!" High self-esteem is found in comments such as, "I feel so good about what I just did!" Self-esteem influences motivation and attitudes, and vice versa.

Just like anxiety, self-esteem can be a trait (a global personality characteristic) or a state (related to a particular situation). Global self-esteem arises when the person is at a mental age of eight. It is based on two factors: (1) self-perceptions of competence in various broad areas, such as academics, athletics, social interaction, physical appearance, and conduct, and (2) a personal assessment of the importance of each of these areas.

For instance, if the student is doing well in sports and if athletic ability is viewed as important, then global self-esteem is enhanced. If a different student is a failure in sports but does not rate athletic ability as personally important, global self-esteem is maintained despite this failure. A problem arises if the student does not do well in an area that he or she considers very significant; that is when global self-esteem can be hurt.

Teachers can help students feel generally good about themselves — that is, boost students' global self-esteem — by helping them succeed in all the broad areas that are important in the students' lives. That is, of course, a very tall order. A less ambitious plan to enhance global self-esteem is to help students do well in a number of areas and to assist them in discounting, when feasible, the perceived importance of those areas in which they do not shine (Harter 1986).

Learners with high global self-esteem maintain positive evaluations of themselves by assessing themselves and the world in a rosy way, even if that assessment is not always accurate (McCombs 1987). In other words, to feel really good about oneself on a consistent basis, a little bit of positive self-delusion might be better than brutal self-honesty!

Situational self-esteem is much more specific. It relates to a specific situation, event, or activity type. A person can feel good about himself or herself globally or generally yet at the same time experience low self-esteem in a particular situation or environment. For example, a learner can feel decreased situational self-esteem in a language class that is especially stressful or failure-inducing, or in a specific skill that is a source of perceived failure.

Again, just as in global self-esteem, the student must consider the focus (event, situation, task, skill) important if situational self-esteem is to be either helped or hindered. For instance, situational self-esteem can sink if an ESL student is not doing well in writing and if writing is considered crucial for future progress. But if writing is not an important goal for this learner, then situational self-esteem will be maintained in spite of any difficulties with writing.

Not surprisingly, unsuccessful language learners — those who have particular problems in the language learning situation — have lower self-esteem than successful language learners. Whether this affects their overall self-esteem or only their situational self-esteem partly depends on how important language learning is to the individuals involved.

Teachers can help students develop higher self-esteem by training them to set reasonable goals in the first place and to assess their own progress toward these goals realistically and positively. One major problem is that students are often unrealistic in what they believe they can and should accomplish in a given period of time, so their self-esteem suffers. Greater realism, along with positive reinforcement from the teacher and from the student himself or herself, goes a long way toward enhancing self-esteem.

Tolerance of Ambiguity

Self-esteem is related to other personal characteristics of learners, such as tolerance of ambiguity, that is, the acceptance of confusing situations. A student with low self-esteem might be intolerant of ambiguity in the language learning classroom. The self-esteem problem might fuel the student's intolerance of ambiguity, or the intolerance of ambiguity might make the learner feel insecure and therefore lower the situational self-esteem.

Moderate tolerance of ambiguity is probably the most desirable condition for language learners. Students who are able to tolerate moderate levels of confusion are likely to persist longer in language learning than students who are overly frightened by the ambiguities inherent in learning a new language (Chapelle 1983; Naiman, Frohlich, Stern, and Todesco 1978). Students who do not need immediate closure and who can deal with some degree of ambiguity appear to use better language learning strategies than students who require rapid closure (Oxford and Ehrman 1989, Ehrman and Oxford 1989). Learners who cannot tolerate ambiguity tend to compartmentalize or analyze things too soon and often have a difficult time dealing with confusing issues in language learning. Learners who can tolerate very high degrees of ambiguity might not pay close enough attention to sometimes seemingly contradictory rules of the new language.

Teachers can be of service by helping students learn to accept the ambiguity involved in learning a language and the students' own incomplete knowledge. This acceptance often requires overt discussion with the whole class, or else with individual students who are experiencing severe problems caused by their intolerance of ambiguity.

Risk-Taking Ability

Students who fear the frequent ambiguities of language learning often suffer reduced risk-taking ability. In language classes, it is essential to take moderate and intelligent risks, such as guessing meanings and speaking up despite the possibility of making occasional mistakes (Oxford 1990).

However, language students who are very afraid of ambiguity frequently "freeze up," allowing their inhibitions to take over completely. They become emotionally paralyzed and unwilling to take even moderate risks in the language classroom or outside (Beebe 1983), particularly in situations or tasks where they are performing in front of others. These students are stalled by actual or anticipated criticism from others or by self-criticism that they themselves supply.

Because of this, such language learners take minimal risks so as to ensure that they are not vulnerable, so that they can avoid any chinks in their self-protective armor (Stevick 1976). In the process of trying to protect themselves from being vulnerable to criticism, these students do not take the risks involved in practicing the language communicatively. When they do not have enough practice, their language development becomes seriously stunted.

We as language teachers can aid students in determining when it is safe and necessary to take a risk. For instance, in conversations it is almost always essential to take risks (for example, paraphrasing, talking around a missing word, using gestures, guessing meanings) when one does not know all the words; otherwise, the conversation might come to a premature halt. We can give students the tools, such as compensation strategies (see Oxford 1990), to take risks in appropriate ways.

The Nexus

We have talked about the interactions among self-esteem, tolerance of ambiguity, and risk-taking. Recognizing the nexus — the point of contact or linkage where these three phenomena converge — is very important for language teachers and for students as well.

Ideally in the ESL classroom we would want students with high self-esteem (both global and situational), moderate tolerance of ambiguity, and moderate but not extreme risk-taking ability. When these characteristics do not occur in a given student, the skilled teacher helps the learner to develop them. Teachers need to help students feel good about themselves in the language learning context, accept the inevitable ambiguities and temporary confusions involved in language learning, and decide how and when to take sensible risks.

COOPERATION AND COMPETITION

Still another aspect of the learner that is significant in language learning is cooperation and competition. Cooperating with others is crucial, and competition can often block progress. Cooperation comes in many forms. The learner does well to learn to cooperate with the teacher, with fellow students, and with native speakers of the language who are not connected with the classroom situation.

Cooperating with peers in the classroom is a special instance of cooperation. It involves either a cooperative task structure, in which group or team participants work together on aspects of the same task, or sometimes a cooperative reward structure, in which participants receive a common reward for their efforts. Cooperative learning groups foster a sense of *positive interdependence* and mutual support (Slavin 1983, Kagan 1986, Kohn 1987).

Many studies outside the language field have demonstrated the benefits of cooperation in the classroom: higher self-esteem; increased confidence and enjoyment; more respect for the teacher, the school, and the subject; greater and more rapid achievement; use of higher-level cognitive strategies; decreased prejudice; and increased altruism and mutual concern. (See Oxford 1990.)

In the language area, classroom cooperation has the following additional advantages: stronger motivation, increased satisfaction for teachers and students, more language practice, more feedback about language errors, and greater use of varied language functions (Sharan et al. 1985, Bejarano 1987, Gunderson and Johnson 1980, Bassano and Christison 1988, Wong Fillmore 1985, Gaies 1985, Seliger 1983). Cooperation drives many recent language teaching methods and approaches, such as Community Language Learning and the Natural Approach.

But cooperation is not always second nature to language learners, especially in the ESL setting. Reid (1987) found that ESL students typically do *not* choose to work in cooperative groups and do not know about the benefits of cooperative learning. Their native cultures sometimes fail to provide extended experiences of students working together on common projects or goals. Of course, many cultures do provide such opportunities. We need to know and understand differences in the cultural values of our students concerning cooperation.

Many societies, including our own in the United States, advocate competition as the favored lifestyle for students. Competition pits students against each other, vying for approval, grades, and advancement in the educational system. The system sometimes creates a zero-sum game, in which one student wins and another loses.

In some countries from which ESL students come, suicides and mental illness arise directly from the severe stress of academic competition. Although occasionally competition can have positive results in terms of the desire to improve performance, it often results in anxiety, inadequacy, guilt, hostility, withdrawal, and fear of failure. See especially Bailey's (1983) review of diary studies for reflections of these emotions among highly competitive language learners.

ESL teachers need to help learners see how to use cooperation rather than competition in the language classroom. They must assist learners in becoming comfortable with others, because communication depends on cooperation. The more ESL students work together, the greater their opportunities for interaction in English in the classroom setting.

In addition, ESL teachers can encourage students to find native English speakers outside of the classroom for cooperative interaction. Conversation groups, conversation partners, mixed-nationality parties, friendship teams, joint projects — all these can bring ESL students together with native English speakers. The benefits are immense, both in terms of increasing language skills and increasing cultural empathy.

LEARNING STYLES

We have discussed a wide range of student characteristics so far: motivation, attitudes, anxiety, self-esteem, tolerance of ambiguity, risk-taking, cooperation, and competition. Now we turn to another phenomenon, language learning style, that relates to many or all of these other features.

Language learning styles are the general approaches students use to learn a new language. These are the same styles they employ in learning many other subjects and solving various problems. We will discuss four central dimensions of language learning style: the analytic-global aspect, sensory preferences, intuition-sensory/sequential learning, and the orientation toward closure or openness.

Analytic-Global

One very important dimension of language learning styles is analytic-global. It contrasts focusing on the details with focusing on the main idea or big picture. This concept — the difference between a detail-oriented person and a holistic one — is incredibly important in language learning, because the two types of students react differently in the language classroom.

Analytic students tend to concentrate on grammatical details and often avoid more free-flowing communicative activities. They focus on contrastive analysis between languages, on rule-learning, and on dissecting words and sentences. Because of their concern for accurate details, analytic learners do not like to guess, use synonyms, or paraphrase when they do not know a particular word. They would rather look up the information and have it exactly right, than be content with the general communication of meaning.

In contrast, global students like socially interactive, communicative events in which they can emphasize the main idea. They find it hard to cope with what seems to them to be grammatical minutiae, and they avoid analysis of words, sentences, and rules when possible. Such students are happy with compensation strategies like guessing the meaning of a word they hear or read, and using synonyms or paraphrases if they run into a communicative roadblock in speaking or writing.

Sensory Preferences

Another very significant stylistic difference highlights sensory preferences: visual, auditory, and hands-on (a combination of kinesthetic or movement-oriented and tactile or touch-oriented). Sensory preference refers to the physical, perceptual learning channels with which the student is the most comfortable.

Visual students like to read and obtain a great deal of visual stimulation. For them, lectures, conversations, and oral directions without any visual backup can be very confusing.

Auditory students, on the other hand, are comfortable without visual input and therefore enjoy lectures, conversations, and oral directions. They are excited by classroom interactions in role-plays and similar activities. They sometimes, however, have difficulty with written work.

Hands-on students like lots of movement and enjoy working with tangible objects, collages, and flashcards. Sitting at a desk for very long is not for them; they prefer to have frequent breaks and move around the room.

Reid (1987) demonstrated that ESL students varied significantly in their sensory preferences, with people from certain cultures differentially favoring the three different modalities for learning. Students from Asian cultures, for instance, are often highly visual, with Koreans being the most visual. Many studies have found that Hispanics are frequently auditory, and Reid discovered that Japanese are very nonauditory. ESL students from a variety of cultures are hands-on learners — perhaps more than we would at first imagine. Our own culture devalues hands-on learning, but it is esteemed in some other cultures.

Intuitive/Random and Sensory/Sequential Learning

Another key aspect of learning style consists of intuitive/random learning and sensory/sequential learning. Intuitive students are able to think in abstract, large-scaled, nonsequential (random) ways. Without being instructed to do so, such students are able to distill the main principles of how the new language works and thus conceive of the underlying language system. They are often bored by concrete, step-by-step learning and would rather take daring intellectual leaps.

The opposite of such learners are the sensory/sequential students. These students are concerned with concrete facts, which they prefer to be presented in a step-by-step, organized fashion. Abstract principles and underlying language systems are not very important to sensory/sequential learners, who just want to do the task at hand and then move on to the next activity. These learners are frequently slow and steady, making progress at their own rate but achieving goals nevertheless. Randomness and lack of consistency in lesson plans are difficult for such students to handle in the language classroom.

For ESL teachers, it is sometimes hard to meet the needs of such very different kinds of learners, some who want things to be fast and random and others who prefer a slower, more organized presentation. The key is to offer a highly organized structure that allows the sensory/sequentials to be happy. This same structure must also, however, provide intuitive/random students with multiple options, enrichment activities, and other aids to help them feel at home.

Orientation to Closure

A final aspect of learning style is orientation to closure, or the degree to which the person needs to reach decisions or clarity. This dimension is very closely related to tolerance of ambiguity, which we discussed earlier. It is probably also associated with flexibility in learning styles — the ability to shift styles when necessitated by the task.

Students oriented toward closure have a strong need for clarity in all aspects of language learning. They want lesson directions and grammar rules to be spelled out and are unable to cope with much slack in the system. Not for such students are spontaneous, rollicking conversations and games in the language classroom, unless, of course, they have had adequate time to prepare their vocabulary lists and understand the rules involved in any given interaction. Students who want rapid closure are serious, hardworking learners who have developed useful metacognitive skills such as planning, organizing, and self-evaluating. They like control in their lives and in their learning. Sometimes their desire for closure and control can short-circuit their ability to participate in the open-ended communication necessary for developing fluency, as found in a study by Ehrman and Oxford (1989).

Students who have less of an orientation toward closure are sometimes known as "open learners." They take language learning far less seriously, treating it like a game to be enjoyed rather than a set of tasks to be completed and judged. Open learners frequently do not worry about class deadlines. They are more concerned with having a good time in the language classroom and soaking up what learning they can by osmosis rather than hard effort. Because of their relaxed attitude, open learners sometimes do better in developing fluency than do more closure-oriented learners (Ehrman and Oxford 1989). Keeping open to new information without forcing premature closure appears to be part of a continuous quest for meaning, according to that study. Openness can be a benefit in some situations, particularly those that require flexibility and the development of fluency, but can be a detriment in other situations, such as highly structured and traditional classroom settings.

Closure-oriented and open learners provide a good balance for each other in the language classroom. The former are the task-driven learners, and the latter know how to have fun. Each group can learn from the other. Skilled teachers sometimes consciously create cooperative groups that include both types of learners, since these learners can benefit from collaboration with each other.

Beyond the Stylistic Comfort Zone

Language learners need to make the most of their style preferences. But they also must extend themselves beyond their *stylistic comfort zone* to use techniques and behaviors that might not initially feel right to them. It is easy to see that learners cannot just use the old tried and true tactics; they need to develop others as well. For instance, an analytic learner cannot stay stuck in memorizing and analyzing vocabulary, but must push hard for a more global understanding of meaning. A global student, conversely, needs to do some analysis in order to understand the structure of the language and learn how to communicate with precision and skill. Teachers can help their students develop beyond the comfort zone dictated by their natural style preferences. They can do this by providing a wide range of classroom activities that cater to a variety of learning styles and that challenge students to try new things. The key is offering variety and change in activities within a steady, consistent, learner-centered, communicative approach.

LEARNING STRATEGIES

In contrast to general styles, language learning strategies are specific actions, behaviors, steps, or techniques — such as seeking out conversation partners, or giving oneself encouragement to tackle a difficult language task — used by students to enhance their own learning. Strategies are especially important for language learning because they are the tools for active, self-directed involvement, which is essential for developing communication ability.

Appropriate learning strategies result in improved proficiency and greater self-confidence in many instances (see Cohen 1990, Oxford and Crookall 1989, Oxford and Cohen forthcoming, Chamot and Küpper 1989, O'Malley and Chamot 1990, Wenden and Rubin 1987). It appears that skilled learners tend to select strategies that work well together in a highly orchestrated way, tailored to the requirements of the language task. Less skilled learners might use similar strategies with similar frequency, but without the careful orchestration and without appropriate targeting of the strategies to the task (Lavine and Oxford forthcoming).

Oxford (1990) has developed a system of six general kinds of language learning strategies. This system is more comprehensive than most others and consists of the following:

1. Planning/evaluating (metacognitive) strategies, such as paying attention, consciously searching for practice opportunities, planning for language tasks, self-evaluating one's progress, and monitoring errors.
2. Emotional/motivational (affective) strategies, such as anxiety reduction, self-encouragement, and self-reward.
3. Social strategies, such as asking questions, cooperating with native speakers of the language, and becoming culturally aware.
4. Memory strategies, such as grouping, imagery, rhyming, and structured reviewing.
5. Cognitive strategies, such as reasoning, analyzing, summarizing, and general practicing.
6. Compensation strategies (to compensate for limited knowledge), such as guessing meanings from the context in reading and listening and using synonyms and gestures to convey meaning when the precise expression is not known.

When left to their own devices and if not overly pressured by their environment to use a certain set of strategies, students typically use learning strategies that reflect their basic learning style (Ehrman and Oxford 1989). They can, however, learn to develop additional strategies and test the value of the ones they ordinarily use. Students are not always aware of the power of consciously using language learning strategies for making learning quicker, easier, more effective, and even more fun (Nyikos 1987). Skilled teachers help their students develop an awareness of learning strategies and enable them to use a wider range of appropriate strategies.

Strategy instruction includes demonstrating when a given strategy might be useful, as well as how to use it, how to evaluate its usefulness, and how to transfer it to other related tasks and situations. In strategy instruction, students learn more than just a set of gimmicks for getting through a language course; they develop academic techniques that help them learn the language or any other subject. Overt strategy training using all six strategy groups above is a breakthrough in ESL instruction.

TAPESTRY PRINCIPLES CONCERNING INDIVIDUAL DIFFERENCES

The discussion above leads to the following set of principles regarding individual differences.

PRINCIPLES

1. Tapestry teachers do everything possible to heighten language learning motivation. Teachers need to help reverse any negative attitudes (for example, stereotypes) that might harm student motivation.
2. By becoming aware of potential signs of anxiety, teachers can take a major step toward improving the classroom climate. After diagnosing anxious behavior, teachers must take action to reduce anxiety.
3. Tapestry teachers assist students in developing their self-esteem, particularly in the language learning situation.
4. Teachers help learners relax and not be so worried if they do not understand everything right away; and at the same time, they assist learners in knowing when to take risks, particularly in conversational settings.
5. Teachers reduce any dysfunctional competition and encourage cooperation in the classroom.
6. Teachers assess and understand their own learning and teaching styles and become aware of the styles of their students. Thereby, teachers become able to spot any style conflicts and to help learners stretch beyond their stylistic comfort zone.
7. Teachers help students identify their learning strategies and develop a wide repertoire of strategies useful for different kinds of language tasks.

CONCLUSION

In this chapter we have described a vast array of factors related to individual language learners: motivation, attitudes, anxiety, self-esteem, tolerance of ambiguity, risk-taking, cooperation, competition, learning styles, and learning strategies. The Tapestry Approach deals directly with all of these factors in an integrated, unified manner that meets the needs of the students while keeping the teacher from feeling overwhelmed.

ACTIVITIES AND DISCUSSION QUESTIONS

1. Look at the research work on motivation in language learning. What do you think about the weight given to integrative and instrumental motivation?
2. Why is anxiety such a big issue in language learning? For what kinds of students is it a major problem? Which of the anxiety reduction techniques shown in this chapter do you believe would work the most effectively, and why? Try some of these out with your students, or try them yourself the next time you become anxious about anything. What makes these techniques work? Will you need to adapt any of them to make them work better in your particular situation?
3. Take the Foreign Language Classroom Anxiety Scale (Horwitz 1990). What is your own level of language learning anxiety? Administer this scale to your students; you might need to simplify the questions for students at lower levels, or translate the questions into their native languages. How anxious are your students? What are the underlying reasons?
4. Why are self-esteem, tolerance of ambiguity, and risk-taking ability so closely linked? How might these relate to learning styles and strategies? How does one variable influence the others? Give examples from your own life or from observing your students.

SUGGESTED READINGS

• Brown, H.D. 1987. *Principles of Language Learning and Teaching* (2nd ed.) Englewood Cliffs, NJ: Prentice Hall. This is a classic in the field of foreign and second language learning. In its second edition, this book still stands as an excellent summary of research on many aspects of language instruction. Especially relevant are Brown's discussions of anxiety, self-esteem, motivation, tolerance of ambiguity, and other affective aspects of the learner. This book should be read for information on much of the seminal research in the affective domain.

• Cohen, A.D. 1990. *Second Language Learning: Insights for Learners, Teachers, and Researchers.* New York: Newbury House/Harper and Row. This is a fine book for understanding more about the second language learning process. The author is able to address three very diverse audiences that have different needs: learners, teachers, and researchers. He provides especially good treatment of language learning strategies as keyed to various language skills. The writing is clear and interesting, and the book is founded on years of research.

• Gardner, R.C. 1985. *Social Psychology and Second Language Learning: The Role of Attitudes and Motivation.* London, Ontario: Edward Arnold. This is the best summary of the issues of motivation and attitudes in language learning. Gardner views the entire area through the lens of social psychology — a highly appropriate, although not necessarily all-encompassing, focus. Other motivational perspectives (for example, drive theory, humanistic psychology) are not highlighted, but Gardner does an excellent job of discussing the social psychological perspective. This book, though prematurely out of print, is still able to be found in libraries and collections for those who want to know more about the key role played by motivation and attitudes in learning a new language.

• Horwitz, E., and Young, D.J. 1990. *Language Anxiety.* Englewood Cliffs, NJ: Prentice-Hall. This recent book is the only one that looks closely at anxiety in second and foreign language learning. It contains contributions by some of the best researchers in the area of language anxiety and offers provocative ideas at every turn. Theoretical information is teamed with practical classroom advice for teachers. Anyone concerned with students' states of mind in the language classroom would benefit from reading this book.

• Oxford, R.L. 1990. *Language Learning Strategies: What Every Teacher Should Know.* New York: Newbury House/Harper and Row. This is an easy-to-read, comprehensive explanation of the importance of learning strategies in foreign and second language instruction. Written specifically for teachers, this book explains well known cognitive and metacognitive strategies and also uncovers the less known — but equally important — affective, social, and compensation strategies. By doing more than just giving lip service to affective aspects of learning, the author treats the learner as a "whole person" and thus opens up new vistas in the learning strategy field. Based on extensive research, the book offers several learning strategy diagnostic surveys, as well as tips for teaching students to use more effective strategies.

• Stevick, E. 1976. *Memory, Meaning, and Method: Some Psychological Perspectives on Language Learning.* Rowley, MA: Newbury House. Although this book is getting old by now, it still speaks to all of us today. Stevick's voice is loud and clear on the importance of affective variables in language learning. We need to concern ourselves with how our students are feeling, not just what they are thinking (though that is important also). This book provides some very helpful guidelines. As usual, Stevick breaks a few shibboleths and offers a refreshing viewpoint on an important subject.

COMMUNICATIVE COMPETENCE

5

PREVIEW QUESTIONS

1. Some ESL students who lack grammatical proficiency in English are still able to speak English effectively — at least in a limited number of situations. Why?
2. Do all ESL students need to acquire all aspects of English (including correct pronunciation, grammar, speaking, listening, and reading skills)? Why or why not?
3. Which aspects of English can students best acquire in the confines of their ESL classrooms? Why?
4. How necessary is it to teach grammar to ESL students?
5. In what specific situations is it possible to communicate without knowing the grammar of a language?

As early as the 1970s, several language pedagogues noticed that language programs were failing to develop the students' *communicative competence*. Savignon, Paulston, and Long were among the first to observe this failure. Savignon (1971), for example, pointed out that although language instructors concerned themselves with teaching grammatical and phonological accuracy, they were unconcerned with helping students to communicate effectively in a variety of situations. Paulston (1975) also described some of the difficulties language instructors faced teaching adult learners the social rules of language. Like Savignon and Paulston, Long (1976) argued that traditional language programs presented serious obstacles to the acquisition of communicative competence. He noted that in these programs students had little opportunity to speak and that teacher-student interaction was often restricted to basic patterns, in which the teacher determined who could speak about what topic, when, and for how long. For Long, this explained why students failed to learn how to communicate effectively in their second language.

ORGANIZATION OF THIS CHAPTER

This chapter considers two fundamental issues: (1) defining communicative competence; and (2) investigating its development. In examining the first issue, we will consider research in the fields of sociolinguistics, conversational analysis, and the ethnography of communication. In considering the second, we will turn to research on second language acquisition and pedagogy.

DEFINITION OF COMMUNICATIVE COMPETENCE

Early Attempts to Define the Concept

Before the mid-1960s, competence in a language was defined narrowly in terms of grammatical knowledge. At that time, linguists were interested in identifying the grammatical constructions children of different ages use. However, in the 1960s linguists and others extended the concept of competence. Hymes was among the first to investigate such extended notions. He argued that the ability to speak competently not only entails knowing the grammar of a language, but also knowing what to say to whom, when, and in what circumstances. In Hymes' (1972) perspective, "There are rules of use without which the rules of grammar would be useless" (p. 45). For instance, one may know how to use modal auxiliaries such as *would,* but not know that such auxiliaries are not generally used when making requests of intimate friends. It is far friendlier to tell a close friend, *Open the window.* than *Would you please open the window?*

Hymes (1972, 1974, 1986) was also among the first to understand the significance of communicative competence in language development. For Hymes, researchers must be concerned with the abilities the child acquires "beyond those of producing and interpreting grammatical sentences" (1972, p. 26).

One of Hymes' major contributions to second language acquisition teaching and theory was his idea of *cultural interference,* which Hymes (1972) defines as relying on one's native culture when communicating in another. The example below illustrates such interference. Juan, from Mexico, begins his conversation with his boss, from the United States, by inquiring about his boss' family. His boss, unaccustomed to such intimate small talk with his employees, feels uncomfortable. The use of personal small talk between non-intimates, though common in Mexico, is less frequent in the United States (Scarcella 1984, forthcoming).

Example 5.1

As Hymes points out, what is regarded as communicative competence in one speech community may be regarded as something else in another. He states: "Even the ethnographies that we have, though almost never focused on speaking, show us that communities differ significantly in ways of speaking, in patterns of repertoire and switching, in the roles and meanings of speech" (p. 33). For instance, while in most West Coast communities, only one speaker talks at a time, in some areas of New York, overlaps of a syllable or more are often considered friendly, representing active participation in a conversation. While in many societies, questions demand immediate answers, among Warm Spring Indians, answers to questions can be postponed for days (Philips 1983).

A different, though related, sociolinguistic contribution to notions of linguistic competence was made by Labov (1963, 1966, 1970, 1972), who noted that "there are no single-style speakers" (1970, p. 46) since all speakers adjust their *speech style* according to the social situation and the topic of discussion. He argued that styles can be measured along a single dimension, the amount of attention paid to speech. For Labov, speakers who use the vernacular (informal) style pay only a minimal amount of attention to speech, whereas speakers who use the formal style pay maximum attention to speech.

Labov's notion of style is related to an area of communicative competence that received direct attention from researchers in the 1960s and 1970s, the examination of *patterns of repertoire* within a given speech community. The term *register* was first used by Reid (1956) to describe systematic modifications in speech tied to *contexts of use.* This notion was later more fully elaborated upon by Ellis and Ure (1969) and by Halliday, McIntosh, and Strevens (1970) who, in explaining this term, state:

> When we observe language activity in the various contexts in which it takes place, we find differences in the type of language selected as appropriate to different types of situations. There is no need to labour the point that a sports commentary, a church service and a school lesson are linguistically quite distinct. One sentence from any of these and many more such situation types would enable us to identify it correctly. We know, for example, where "an early announcement is expected" comes from and "apologies for absence were received"; these are not simply free variants of "we ought to hear soon" and "was sorry he couldn't make it." (p. 87)

It was Halliday, McIntosh, and Strevens who focused attention on "the users of language, and the uses they make of it" (p. 73).

In his discussion of *functions* of language, Halliday (1970) added a slightly different perspective to the notion of linguistic competence. He argues that only by closely observing the context of the situation are we able to understand the functions of specific grammatical structures. In his terms, function is the use to which a grammatical structure is put. It is the purpose of an utterance rather than the particular grammatical form an utterance takes. For Halliday, language performs three basic functions: ideational, interpersonal, and textual.

> 1. Language serves for the expression of *content:* that is, of the speaker's experience of the real world, including the inner world of his [or her] own consciousness. We may call this the *ideational* function.
> 2. Language serves to establish and maintain social relations. . . Through this function, which we may refer to as *interpersonal,* social groups are delimited, and the individual is identified and reinforced, since by enabling him [or her] to interact with others, language also serves in the expression and development of his [or her] own personality.

> 3. Finally, language has to provide for making links with itself and with features of the situation in which it is used. We may call this the *textual* function, since this is what enables the speaker or writer to *construct* texts, or connected passages of discourse that is situationally relevant; and enables the listener or reader to distinguish a text from a random set of sentences.
>
> (p. 143)

Ethnographers of communication also enlarged earlier concepts of competence in language through their discovery of the rules underlying conversation. For example, in a now classic paper, Sacks, Schegloff, and Jefferson (1974) described the rules of the English *repair system,* which enable speakers to fix or *repair* conversational difficulties. In conversation, interlocutors repair their utterances to ensure that intended messages are communicated and understood. The term *repair* refers to efforts by the speaker and hearer to correct trouble spots in conversation. Repairs can be used to correct one's grammar or vocabulary, but, as illustrated by Example 5.2, they may also be used to clarify one's status or intentions.

<u>Example 5.2</u>
Jean: Hello, Dr. Stanley, um, er, I mean, Jim.

In this example, Jean repairs her utterance by switching from *Dr. Stanley* to *Jim.* She does this to emphasize both friendliness and the equality of her relationship with the interlocutor. Notice how her repair is flagged by the pause fillers *um* and *er.*

Repairs may be initiated by either the speaker or the hearer. Speaker-initiated repairs are termed *self-repairs,* while hearer-initiated repairs are termed *other-repairs.* Example 5.3 below illustrates the repair system as well as the complicated transcription system developed by ethnographers of the 1970s. In this example, Sam cannot understand Lori's use of a vocabulary word. He initiates a repair with the word *What?,* but Lori does not repair her utterance adequately. Her friend, Ellen, attempts to help her.

<u>Example 5.3</u>
Lori: But y' know single beds are awfully thin tuh sleep on.
Sam: What?
Lori: Single bed//they're
Ellen: → Y'mean narrow?
Lori: They're awfully narrow, yeah.

(Schegloff, Jefferson, and Sacks 1977)

Ellen's repair is intended to clarify the meaning of Lori's message. When Lori does not explain what she means by *single bed,* Ellen offers an "other" repair, mitigated by the expression *y' mean.*

Austin (1962) and Searle (1969) further expanded earlier notions of competence in language when they described the function of speech utterances (that is, what we do with language), and provided detailed analyses of such *speech acts* as the request and the refusal. Speech acts serve a wide number of purposes. They are used to command, request, describe, define, agree, and promise. When *direct speech acts* are used, what is done in a language directly corresponds to the actual words used (as in the direct request, *Turn down the heat).* When *indirect speech acts* are used, what is done in a language only indirectly corresponds to the language used (as in the indirect request, *It's hot in here).* Non-native English speakers often have great difficulty acquiring indirect speech acts.

Along very different lines, Halliday and Hasan (1976) contributed to extended notions of competence in a language. In their analysis of written text, they investigated how writers attain *cohesion* and *coherence.* They used the term *cohesion* to refer to the linguistic features that relate sentences to one another. Such features include reference items such as "he" and "she," and conjunctives such as "first," "second," and "third." *Coherence,* as employed by Halliday and Hasan, refers to text that appropriately fits its situational context. A coherent text is appropriate with respect to such situational features as the channel (written or oral), the genre (be it a poem, narrative, or an expository essay), the topic discussed, the interests and needs of the reader and writer, the purpose of the text, the relationship between the reader and the writer, etc. For Halliday and Hasan, when a text is consistent with itself (that is, when each of the sentences is related to one another), it is cohesive; when it is consistent with its context (that is, when its organization and unity is appropriate for its audience, purpose, and goals), it is coherent. (For further discussion, see Chapter Eight.)

Bringing together these various expanded notions of communicative competence, Savignon (1983) suggests that communicative competence has these characteristics:

> 1. Communicative competence is *dynamic* rather than a static concept. It depends on the negotiation of meaning between two or more persons who share to some degree the same symbolic system. . .
>
> 2. Communicative competence applies to *both written and spoken language, as well as to many other symbolic systems.*
>
> 3. Communicative competence is *context-specific.* Communication takes place in an infinite variety of situations, and success in a particular role depends on one's understanding of the context and on prior experience of a similar kind. It requires making appropriate choices of *register* and *style* in terms of the situation and the participants.
>
> 4. There is a theoretical difference between *competence* and *performance.* Competence is defined as a *presumed underlying ability,* and performance as the overt manifestation of that ability. Competence is what one *knows.* Performance is what one *does.* Only performance is observable, however, and it is only through performance that competence can be developed, maintained and evaluated.
>
> 5. Communicative competence is *relative,* not absolute, and depends on the cooperation of all the participants involved. It makes sense, then, to speak of degrees of communicative competence.
>
> (pp. 8-9, emphasis hers)

The Canale and Swain Framework

Canale and Swain's (1980) framework (see also Canale 1983) reflects the characteristics of communicative competence outlined by Savignon as well as the various expanded notions of communicative competence previously discussed. For Canale and Swain, communicative competence minimally involves four areas of knowledge and skills. These include: (1) grammatical competence; (2) sociolinguistic competence; (3) discourse competence; and (4) strategic competence.

Grammatical competence reflects knowledge of the linguistic code itself. It includes knowledge of vocabulary and rules of word formation, pronunciation, spelling, and sentence formation. Grammatical competence is of critical importance in Canale and Swain's framework. Canale and

Swain explain, "Just as Hymes (1972) was able to say that there are rules of grammar that would be useless without rules of language use, so we feel that there are rules of language use that would be useless without rules of grammar" (p. 5). As has been pointed out repeatedly in the literature (see, for example, Larsen-Freeman 1980, Hatch 1983, and Wolfson and Judd 1983), learners who have acquired the rules and norms governing how to participate in a conversation will fail to communicate competently without grammar in all but the most limited conversational situations. For instance, learners might be able to ask for directions without too much grammatical competence by approaching a stranger with the conversational opening, *Excuse me* and may then be able to say, *I need Main Street,* a sentence that they have memorized rote. However, if they are not proficient in the grammar of the language, they may find themselves lost very quickly when their addressee responds, *Just go down to the theater and then turn left when you come to the three-story building that is being painted beige.*

Sociolinguistic competence addresses the extent to which sentences are "produced and understood appropriately" (Swain 1984, p. 189). It includes knowledge of speech acts such as directives *(Come here)* and apologies *(I'm sorry).* Such competence enables speakers to vary their language appropriately according to the addressee. It allows speakers to signal levels of politeness and formality and to establish their credibility.

Discourse competence enables writers to combine grammatical forms and meanings to achieve a unified or written text in different *genres* such as the "narrative, argumentative essay, scientific report or business letter" (Swain, p. 188). It enables speakers to start a conversation by using appropriate greetings *(Hi! How are you?)* and keep a conversation going by using appropriate pause fillers *(um, er, as I was saying).* In discussing *discourse competence,* we are going beyond the definition discussed by Canale and Swain. Whereas Canale and Swain used the term *discourse competence* to refer to the knowledge of how to combine grammatical forms and meanings to achieve a unified spoken or written text in various genres and situations, we use this term to refer to verbal, nonverbal, and paralinguistic knowledge underlying the ability to organize spoken and written texts meaningfully and appropriately. Some researchers prefer the term *conversational competence* to refer to this broader definition of discourse competence related to conversations. Following Richards and Schmidt (1983), we define *conversation* as:

> . . . more than a series of exchanges; it consists of exchanges which are initiated and interpreted according to intuitively understood and socially acquired rules and norms of conversational cooperation, which can in turn be manipulated to create a wide range of meanings beyond the level expressed directly by the utterances in the conversations themselves. (p. 122)

Strategic competence "refers to the mastery of the communication strategies that may be called into action either to enhance the effectiveness of communication or to compensate for breakdowns in communication due to limiting factors in actual communication or to insufficient competence in one or more of the other components of communicative competence" (Swain, p. 189). This important component of communicative competence allows speakers to stretch their competence so that they appear more proficient in the language than they really are. Tarone (1978) was among the first to list some of the communicative strategies learners are observed to employ. (Refer to Table 5.1.)

Table 5.1 A Typology of Communication Strategies

Paraphrase	
• Approximation	Use of a single target-language [non-native language] vocabulary item or structure, which the learner knows is not correct, but which shares enough semantic features in common with the desired item to satisfy the speaker (for example, *pipe* for *waterpipe)*
• Word Coinage	The learner makes up a new word in order to communicate a desired concept (for example, *airball* for *balloon)*
Circumlocution	The learner describes the characteristics or elements of the object or action instead of using the appropriate target language structure *(She is, uh, smoking something. I don't know what's its name. That's, uh, Persian, and we use in Turkey, a lot of).*
Transfer	
• Literal Translation	The learner translates word for word from the native language (for example, *He invites him to drink* for *They toast one another).*
• Language Switch	The learner uses the native language term without bothering to translate (for example, *balon* for *balloon, tirtil* for *caterpillar).*
• Appeal for Assistance	The learner asks for the correct term or structure (for example, *What is this?).*
• Mime	The learner uses nonverbal strategies in place of a meaning structure (for example, clapping one's hands to illustrate applause).
Avoidance	
• Topic Avoidance	The learner simply does not talk about concepts for which the vocabulary or other meaning structure is not known.
• Message Abandonment	The learner stops mid-utterance because he or she does not have the proficiency to form a particular meaning structure.

(Adapted from Tarone 1978, p. 197.)

Strategic competence is especially important to ESL learners who are just beginning to acquire English. Consider, for instance, the student who has just arrived from Japan and who has no English proficiency. This student is in trouble if his or her room catches on fire and he or she has not yet memorized some canned expressions such as *I need your help!* and *Fire!*

The more proficient learners become in their second language, the less likely they are to rely on strategic competence. For example, as learners develop more knowledge of English, they do not need to *pretend* that they understand their interlocutors. Thus, they do not need to rely on such strategies as looking interested and changing the subject, which give the impression that they understand the conversation (when they really do not).

Clearly, discourse and strategic competence overlap because many discourse features (such as attention-getters *[Hey!; Look!]* and pause fillers *[um; Let's see])* also serve as communication strategies (Tarone 1981). For example, *topic shifts* can be used as communication strategies as well as conversational features since these shifts enable speakers to avoid topics for which they lack sufficient vocabulary to discuss.

Our Own Interpretation of Canale and Swain's Framework

While we accept Canale and Swain's framework, *we expand their concept of strategic competence to include all types of compensation strategies that make up for missing knowledge.* These include guessing from the context in reading and listening as well as production strategies like paraphrasing and circumlocution in speaking and writing. *We further extend Canale and Swain's framework to include brainstorming and revising strategies in writing.* Although we have adapted Canale and Swain's schema for discussing notions of communicative competence, it is certainly not the only possible one. Even Canale and Swain have pointed out that this framework provides just a partial view of communicative competence, since it excludes nonverbal communication as well as the notion of register.

Having addressed the first issue (defining communicative competence), we turn next to the second, the acquisition of communicative competence in a first and a second language.

COMMUNICATIVE COMPETENCE AND FIRST LANGUAGE ACQUISITION

Building on the descriptive work on communicative competence previously outlined, researchers in first language development began to examine the acquisition of various aspects of communicative competence. (Dore 1975, Ervin-Tripp and Mitchell-Kernan 1977, and Ochs-Keenan 1974 are just a few.) Grimshaw and Holden (1976) were among the first to discuss the acquisition of communicative competence by first language learners. They suggest that some aspects of communicative competence, such as specific registers like *doctor talk,* are acquired as late as adolescence.

Andersen (1978, 1990), on the other hand, proposes that many speech registers are actually acquired very early, even before young children reach kindergarten. Whenever these components are acquired, social competence either precedes their development or is acquired concurrently. According to Grimshaw and Holden (1976),

> Although some learning is clearly cumulative, we know little about what constraints there may be on delayed learning, or what, if anything, can only be learned *after* particular levels of physiological, psychological, or social maturation are reached. Similarly, the mastery of many sociolinguistic skills (e.g., things as different as the accomplishment of condolences or the "civilized" termination of relationships and more specific skills such as irony and euphemism) requires a prior understanding of subtleties of relationships as well as competence with linguistic forms. (p. 35)

From Grimshaw and Holden's perspective, once enough has been learned to permit speakers to communicate and to manage social relations, energies are then expended on other activities. This notion has important implications for language teaching. It suggests that speakers will fall back on the social knowledge of their first language when they *believe* this allows them to communicate effectively. It also explains why learners transfer social knowledge. Although social rules vary greatly across cultures, many adults believe that these rules still function effectively in the second language.

Andersen (1990) suggests that there are certain universal tendencies that govern specific aspects of the development of communicative competence in a first language. In contrast to Hymes (1964), she argues that "although rules for appropriate language use may vary from culture to culture, they are usually sensitive across languages to many of the same factors, including the context and topic of discourse, and the sex, age and status of the people speaking" (p. 9).

Andersen also suggests the possibility that speakers differ with respect to their production and comprehension of registers.

> Though registers are shared by different speakers, speakers differ in the registers they may control actively or only passively. Most of us recognize and respond to many registers we never use, for example, the language of sermons. (p. 8)

Moreover, she convincingly argues that "the range of registers controlled by a given individual presumably reflects that individual's language experience" (p. 8). This suggests why adult ESL learners frequently have difficulty acquiring the various registers of English; *they simply lack language experience or input in these registers.*

In addition to looking at these different aspects of communicative competence, researchers in first language acquisition have recently become concerned with the notion of context-specific competence. Hecht (1983) has shown that children demonstrate very different linguistic competence in the area of morphology related to the context in which data is collected. Similarly, researchers like Clark (1976) and Peters (1983) have explored the importance of *scripts* (i.e., situations for which one has in memory a clear model of expectations of structures and events), of familiar play situations, and of routines in facilitating a maximal expression of competence. Peters (1983) has made the point that researchers who examine the development of competence need to look at the same context across time.

COMMUNICATIVE COMPETENCE AND SECOND LANGUAGE DEVELOPMENT

Grammatical Competence

Chapter Eleven indicates the importance of grammatical competence in second language development. To summarize, grammatical competence, strictly speaking, includes the ability to understand and use morphology and syntax. More broadly speaking, grammatical competence has come to include all aspects of language dealing with vocabulary and mechanics, as well as with morphology and syntax. Grammar is teachable, according to Pienemann (1984) and Long (1983a), although it is impossible to alter developmental sequences in the acquisition of grammar. The optimum development of grammatical competence requires that grammar be presented in meaningful, authentic language contexts rather than in isolation.

Sociolinguistic Competence

Hatch (1983) and Wolfson (1981, 1989) were primarily responsible for encouraging investigations of sociolinguistic competence. Their research centers on the way second language learners acquire the rules and norms governing the appropriate timing and realization of speech acts. In an analysis of the apologies used by speakers of English, Hebrew, and English as a second language, Cohen and Olshtain (1981), and Olshtain and Cohen (1983) compared native and non-native English speaker responses to a variety of situations that included an offense of some type. They found that English speakers use a number of expressions to apologize. For instance, they may offer a direct apology *(I apologize),* provide an explanation of their offense *(The reason that I'm so clumsy is because I'm tired),* accept responsibility *(It was all my fault),* offer a repair *(Let me pay for it),* or promise behavior change *(I will never let it happen again).* Speakers of Hebrew may use some of these types of apologies, but vary in the way they use them and in the extent of their use. In a further study of speakers of Hebrew, English, and Russian, Olshtain (1983) showed that English speakers apologize more frequently than Russian speakers, who in turn apologize more frequently than Hebrew speakers. In a more recent study, Olshtain and Cohen (1987) demonstrated that speech acts can be taught at an advanced level of English language teaching.

Discourse Competence

Among second language researchers, Tarone (1981) has also stressed the importance of observing the development of communicative competence across time in the same discourse context. She suggests examining language in casual speech situations since it is in this context that speakers display their greatest competence. We would like to suggest, however, that in order to get a *complete* picture of a speaker's communicative competence, it is important to look at his or her language use— in production and in comprehension — across a wide variety of discourse contexts.

Selinker and Douglas (1985, 1989) have made initial attempts to study aspects of language variation tied to what they have called *discourse domains.* They suggest, for example, that a given speaker may use second language pronouns correctly in one domain (such as a *life story domain),* but use them incorrectly in another (such as a *technical domain).* Performance may vary from one domain to another for a number of reasons. Each domain may entail a different cognitive load, and differences in task could also affect memory. In addition, different conversational partners and situations may cause varying degrees of anxiety (Krashen 1982). Finally, different situations call for different abilities. For example, speakers can use routines and patterns in some situations, but must use complex linguistic structures in others.

Many second language investigations pertaining to communicative competence have centered on the components discussed by Canale and Swain (1980). Considerable research has focused on discourse competence. (For an excellent review of some recent studies, refer to Day 1986.) One study, by Scarcella (1983a), suggests that there are certain developmental trends in the acquisition of conversational features such that some features (such as greetings) are acquired early on and others (such as repairs) later. Studies indicate that while universal tendencies undoubtedly exist for many aspects of conversation (for example, most languages are said to have greetings and leave takings, turn-taking systems, and repair systems), and while such tendencies help learners converse in the second language, learners do not begin acquiring a second language fully equipped with knowledge of the conversational rules and norms of the target language. Students need to acquire new conversational rules and norms in order to achieve native-like proficiency in their second language. In fact, learners often experience difficulty with such conventions. For instance, they may be unable to use effective greetings. In Example 5.4, an ESL student uses the informal greeting *hi* with the formal address term *sir.*

<u>*Example 5.4*</u>
Hi, sir. (Scarcella and Brunak 1981)

Researchers no longer focus on the development of discrete aspects of second language development or propose acquisitional hierarchies, so popular in the 1970s. Today, investigators are more interested in determining how individuals differ from one another, both in terms of their inherent potential for mastery of discourse competence and in terms of the extent to which their cultures provide models and incentives for acquiring this competence. Efforts are made to account for the beliefs, attitudes, and behaviors that are valued in the second language learner's culture and reflected in interaction. For example, ethnographers of education have found that different cultural communities employ and expect different conversational patterns. When non-native speakers use conversational features from their first language in conversing with native speakers in the second language, grave misunderstandings can occur. These misunderstandings, particularly unfortunate in classroom situations, have been well documented in the literature (see, for instance, Cazden 1988, Heath 1986, Macias 1987, and Philips 1972, 1983). Children who are not taught in their homes to value spoken interaction in public situations often have difficulty communicating in Anglo-American public schools. Philips (1972, 1983) found that patterns of participation that are normally expected in Anglo-American classrooms are unfamiliar and threatening to Warm Spring Indian children. She attributes the generally poor classroom performance of Warm Spring Indian children to differences in interactional styles demanded of them at home and at school.

In many Asian cultures (including the Korean, Japanese, and Chinese), the students accept the teacher's point of view and never challenge it (Cheng 1987; see also Romaine 1986). As Asian children, Punjabi children are said to have difficulties giving their own opinions in the classroom because they have not been enculturated to participate in discussions with adults (Gibson 1987). In Punjabi culture, children are taught to defer to adult authority. Such training, it is argued, "does not prepare Punjabi students to participate in classroom discussions where they have to express ideas different from those of their teacher" (Ogbu and Matute-Bianchi 1986, p. 77).

Most puzzling and problematic for many ESL students are the interactional styles of Anglo-American teachers. In the United States, teachers interact more freely with students than they do in many other cultures, expecting students to interrupt them if they do not understand. Consistent with this research is Sato's (1982) study of interruption behavior in classroom participation. Sato reports on Asian and non-Asian patterns of participation in student-teacher interaction. The participants in Sato's study were two groups of university students enrolled in intermediate ESL courses and their teachers. Of the 31 students, 19 were Asian. Significant differences between the Asian and non-Asian students were found with respect to the frequency of turns taken. For Sato, this provides evidence for ethnic speech styles. In our view, it also provides evidence for language transfer: in this case, using patterns of interaction from one's first language when communicating in a second.

Some of the interactional features studied by Sato are also discussed by Gumperz (1977). This research focuses on the conversations of Indian and Pakistani workers in London. Through videotaped data as well as observations, he analyzes *contextualization cues,* verbal and nonverbal interactional features (such as *well* and *okay)* that function to establish cohesion and are crucial to communicating competently. Like Sato, Gumperz discusses the role of communication in interethnic relations. He attempts to show that communication difficulties that arise in *gate-keeping* situations (such as committee meetings, job interviews, and industrial disputes in which one person has power over others) are due to differences in the perception and interpretation of *contextualization cues* (including *deictic pronouns* that "point" to places, times, or participants in a conversation from the speaker's point of view and *interjections* such as *yes* and *no)* by which listeners signal their reactions to what has been said. Research by Gumperz demonstrates how differences in the use of these cues lead to communication breakdowns.

> To the extent that cultural differences persist, there is a real clash between the communicative skills and strategies that are effective within the home and friendship circles and those that are effective in public settings where majority group conventions prevail. Minority members unaware of the relevant differences regularly find themselves misunderstood; they see their intentions misread, find it difficult to predict the reactions of others, and feel an increasing sense of powerlessness to manage their own lives.
>
> (Gumperz 1977, pp. 4-5)

Although work by Gumperz primarily concerns interethnic communication breakdowns, it has important implications for discourse competence and second language acquisition. One of his major contributions to second language research concerns language transfer. Gumperz translated some of his Indian English transcripts into informal colloquial Punjabi and preserved the rhythmic and prosodic features of the original transcripts. He found that speakers of Punjabi who listened to the tape-recorded translation readily characterized the conversation as normal, fluent talk. This suggests that Punjabi speakers transfer contextualization features from Punjabi into English and that contextualization cues may be highly susceptible to language transfer. Perhaps this is because these features tend to be "culturally-determined communicative conventions" (p. 19). Another finding of interest to language teachers is that in the Gumperz study, aspects of interactional competence seem to be acquired independently of grammatical competence. According to Gumperz:

> Since Indians and Pakistanis are not native speakers of English, one might assume that their communication problems are simply due to their lack of knowledge of the language, but the problem is more complex than that. To begin with, English has been an official medium in India and Pakistan for centuries, and many of the immigrants already had at least a reading knowledge of the language. By now, after almost a decade in Britain, almost all of them, with the exception of those who spend all their time within their local neighborhoods, have at least a functional control of English. (Gumperz 1977, p. 7)

Gumperz also points out:

> . . . difficulties do not necessarily disappear as the workers gain control of basic English grammar and vocabulary. In many cases, language teachers are quite satisfied with workers' progress in the classroom, yet on the shopfloor, foremen and supervisors find little improvement in their performance. They also found that disputes resulting in communication failures arise not only with speakers who have minimal control of English but just as frequently with those who know English well. *Clearly the problem is not simply knowledge of the language.* (pp. 7-8, emphasis ours)

Speech Accommodation Theory (Giles and Smith 1979) has contributed to our knowledge of the types of discourse difficulties discussed by Gumperz. According to Giles and Smith (1979), speakers adjust their language to become more similar or dissimilar to the speech of their interlocutors. Shifts can occur at all levels — including phonology, lexicon, content, and speech rate. Divergence occurs when speakers adjust their language so that it becomes less similar to the speech of their interlocutors, and convergence occurs when speakers adjust their language so that it becomes more similar to the speech of their interlocutors. There are social trade-offs involved in converging or diverging; we weigh the costs and the rewards and then choose the alternative that maximizes the rewards and minimizes the costs. Sometimes ethnic groups make comparisons across groups and, rather than trying to reduce differences, make attempts to accentuate differences. As Beebe (1988) explains, this is because people do not take the behaviors of others at face value. Rather, "they evaluate their motives and intentions first and then attribute the cause of their behavior" (p. 64). Scarcella (1990) demonstrates how inaccurate character assessments sometimes arise when speakers make value judgments about their interlocutors based on the conversational features rather than their actual behavior. She provides this example:

> Example 5.5
> Anousheh: Teacher, my teacher. Try come here.
> Teacher: I can't, I'm working with Billy.
> Anousheh: *(interrupting)* I need your help. (p. 5)

Like many middle-Americans, the teacher in this example assumes that *repeated* interruption is impolite (Zimmerman and West 1975). In the exchange, the teacher concludes that Anousheh is rude. However, rather than associating rudeness with the student's speech behavior, she associates rudeness with Anousheh instead. Such reasoning is unfortunate for Anousheh who comes from Iran, where interruptions may be associated with friendliness and active involvement in a conversation.

Cummins (1981) has contributed to research on the acquisition of discourse competence in very different ways than Gumperz, Giles and Smith, and Beebe. His investigations suggest that ESL students frequently acquire conversational skills in their first few years in the United States, but lack the ability to communicate in academic, *decontextualized* situations. In such situations, students cannot rely upon various nonlinguistic elements (for instance, visuals and the nonverbal gestures of their interlocutors) that help provide meaning when the linguistic features are insufficient and the learners lack the proficiency to understand the input.

Cummins suggests that the most difficult language situation is one that is cognitively demanding and context-reduced. An example of such a situation would be a university lecture. Cummins further proposes that the communicative demands of schooling and the acquisition of literacy and academic skills require more exposure to and interaction with native speakers than that which daily informal, face-to-face interaction provides.

Many teachers find appealing Cummins' hypothesis that conversational features are easily acquired. However, empirical research has not verified this hypothesis. Closer examination of the conversational features actually used by some second language learners may reveal that these learners rely on conversational features of their first language (or incomplete acquisition of target conversational features) when communicating in their second language. Indeed, preliminary research (Scarcella 1983a) as well as the research of ethnographers of education (Heath 1986, Philips 1983, Macias 1987) suggests the validity of such a claim.

Strategic Competence

Like discourse competence, strategic competence has also been the topic of much recent research. Investigators such as Yule and Tarone (1990) have attempted to identify those factors that affect the use of communication strategies. They suggest, for example, that strategic performance is affected by world knowledge. For instance, students who have some knowledge of the ways in which meetings are run in the United States are able to use this knowledge to stretch their language ability. This enables them to participate actively during meetings. They can guess when the meetings are beginning, when they are expected to participate, and when they can introduce new topics. They know when they should look interested and nod their heads in agreement and when they should glance downwards to avoid being called upon to offer opinions.

Investigators have also examined how learners make the best of their second language by using strategies as *conversational management devices.* For instance, learners can memorize greetings that can help them to start a conversation and pause fillers (such as *um* and *ya know)* that help them to hold the floor while they keep the conversation going. (For an excellent review of the literature on communication strategies, refer to Faerch and Kasper 1983; for examples of recent research, see Yule and Tarone 1990, Kellerman et al. 1990; for more information, refer to O'Malley and Chamot 1990 and Oxford 1990.)

TAPESTRY PRINCIPLES CONCERNING COMMUNICATIVE COMPETENCE

We asked earlier how communicative competence could best be acquired in ESL programs. We suggest the following principles.

PRINCIPLES

1. Tapestry teachers provide students with exposure to and interaction in the diverse registers they need to know. They bring the outside world into the classroom by using role-playing, simulation, and problem-solving activities. Activities that present students with language-rich experiences outside of their classrooms also provide students exposure to and interaction with diverse registers.
2. Whenever possible, teachers use *authentic language,* naturally occurring language that is not modified for use in language classrooms. When it is not possible to use *authentic language,* teachers use simulated, authentic materials.
3. Teachers emphasize meaning. Being able to figure out a speaker's or writer's intentions is part of being communicatively competent.
4. Teachers get students to involve themselves in real communicative activities that have a genuine purpose and encourage feedback from participants.
5. Teachers give students opportunities to express their own ideas and opinions.
6. Teachers encourage students to work in cooperative learning groups that maximize their communicative involvement, draw out shy students, and help vocal students to develop good listening skills.
7. Teachers create activities that promote the students' exposure to and use of the diverse components of communicative competence discussed earlier.

CONCLUSION

This chapter has presented a brief overview of the research on communicative competence. All the research leads to the following conclusion: those aspects of communicative competence that are taught in ESL programs should vary as a function of the particular learners. For instance, vocabulary may be more important for beginning ESL learners than grammar. However, accuracy in grammar structures may become more important as students gain proficiency in English. A number of learner variables (such as motivation, needs, interests, age, learning style, and personality characteristics) as well as situational variables (the specific domains in which the learner needs to function) will shape just what aspects of communicative competence the teacher should stress. For example, learners who are in the beginning stages of English language development may need to develop basic conversational skills that will enable them to communicate on a day-to-day basis. They may need to learn how to start a conversation and keep it going, as well as how to get their addressees to speak slower and repeat their utterances. As mentioned earlier, these students may also need exposure to and instruction in English vocabulary. Their exposure to diverse registers of English may need to be restricted at this point to those specific registers they need to use to be able to communicate effectively in their daily communication. In contrast, learners in the more advanced stages of English language development may need to encounter a greater variety of registers so that they can acquire the proficiency needed to communicate effectively in a wide range of speech domains (Lee, personal communication). As the English proficiency level increases, different components of communicative competence will require emphasis. The different components of communicative competence that the teacher emphasizes will also vary according to the students' immediate and long-term needs and interests. This is why *needs analysis* is such a critical part of the Tapestry Approach. In short, teachers will need to vary the activities and techniques they use with respect to a wide range of learner and situational variables. This, of course, is the central theme of the Tapestry Approach.

ACTIVITIES AND DISCUSSION QUESTIONS

1. In what way do individual learning differences (such as analytic or global style) affect the acquisition of sociolinguistic competence? (Refer to Chapter Four for a discussion of these differences.)
2. Why are some learners able to feign native-like production in the second language while other learners are not?
3. At what proficiency levels (beginning, intermediate, or advanced) should ESL learners be exposed to such diverse registers as *baby talk* (such as *Green ball. Pretty green ball.), doctor talk* (such as *Stick out your tongue and say "ah."),* and *academese* (the language spoken by professors of higher education such as *As I mentioned in the last lecture. . .*)? Should ESL students of beginning proficiency levels be exposed to a variety of registers? Why or why not?
4. Why do you think some ESL learners transfer the discourse features of their first languages when communicating in English?
5. Why do communication breakdowns lead to feelings of frustration and uncertainty?
6. How does a learner's exposure to input affect his or her acquisition of diverse registers?

SUGGESTED READINGS

• Coulthard, M. 1985. *An Introduction to Discourse Analysis* (2nd ed.) London: Longman. This volume brings up-to-date the influential work of the author and his colleagues at the University of Birmingham and represents the Birmingham approach to conversational analysis. It is an important reference for many teachers and students and has applications in the areas of language teaching and acquisition, stylistics, reading and writing studies, pathology, and testing. Coulthard brings together work from a range of disciplines, including linguistics, social anthropology, philosophy, and psychology. The book deals with the characterization of speaker/writer meaning and its explanation in the context of use. It also portrays the structure of social interaction. The chapters range from speech acts and conversational maxims, the ethnography of speaking, and conversational analysis to intonation, linguistics, discourse analysis, language teaching, the acquisition of discourse, and the analysis of literary discourse.

•Day, R. (ed.). 1986. *Talking to Learn: Conversation in Second Language Acquisition.* Rowley, MA: Newbury House. This important anthology makes available a range of empirical reports of second language acquisition relating to conversation among native and non-native speakers with other non-native speakers, both in the classroom and outside the classroom. While Section One presents theoretical concerns, Section Two contains chapters that focus on the nature of conversational interaction in the classroom, both content classes and ESL classes, where language minority students are attempting to acquire English. The focus on language in the classroom is continued in Section Three, but with a closer look at small-group or task activities. The papers in the final section examine the more socially-oriented conversations that language minority students have.

• Faerch, C., and Kasper, K. (eds.). 1983. *Strategies in Interlanguage Communication.* London: Longman. The editors refer to strategies in interlanguage communication as potentially conscious plans set up by the learner in order to solve problems in communication. The volume focuses on the ways learners use their interlanguage in interaction as well as the variables that influence the use of communication strategies. This volume, which focuses exclusively on speaking, is divided into three parts: definitions of communication strategies, empirical studies, and problems in analyzing communication strategies. It contains a comprehensive bibliography.

• Fine, J. (ed.). 1988. *Second Language Discourse: A Textbook of Current Research.* Norwood, NJ: Ablex. This volume attempts to relate some of the diverse theoretical approaches, methods, and findings of discourse analysis to second language teaching and learning. The chapters include both oral and written language, theoretical and applied perspectives, experimental and descriptive studies, sociolinguistic and psycholinguistic considerations, classroom and real life discourse, teaching, and evaluation.

• Larsen-Freeman, D. 1980. *Discourse Analysis in Second Language Research.* Rowley, MA: Newbury House. The contributors to this volume are pioneers in the application of discourse analysis to the second language field. With the exception of the first chapter, an extensive literature survey by Hatch and Long, each of the articles is a research report that, though preliminary, tackles interesting questions in the field of second language acquisition from the perspective of discourse analysis.

• Loveday, L. 1982. *The Sociolinguistics of Learning and Using a Non-Native Language.* Oxford: Pergamon. This book aims to provide insights into the social dimensions of assimilating, employing, and imparting a linguistics system different from that acquired natively. It includes a comprehensive review of the research in sociolinguistics related to interaction in a second language. Loveday also considers the dynamics of bilingualism and the cultural dimension of non-native language development.

• Scarcella, R., Andersen, E.S., and Krashen, S. 1990. *Developing Communicative Competence in a Second Language.* New York: Newbury House/Harper and Row. The chapters in this volume focus on various aspects of communicative competence in first and second language development. The first section provides background information concerning communicative competence. The three following sections examine discourse competence, sociolinguistic competence, and strategic competence. The final sections discuss communicative competence in the workplace and in the school.

• Wolfson, N. 1989. *Perspectives: Sociolinguistics and TESOL.* New York: Newbury House/Harper and Row. Designed to give classroom language teachers in the United States a thorough understanding of sociolinguistics and its application in ESL teaching, this volume includes current overviews of the literature on conversation, bilingual education, standard and nonstandard dialects, miscommunication, and speech acts. Heavy emphasis is placed on the ethnography of education.

PART III

LANGUAGE SKILLS: INTERWOVEN STRANDS

INTEGRATING THE LANGUAGE SKILLS

6

PREVIEW QUESTIONS

1. Why should the four language skills (listening, reading, speaking, and writing) and the subsidiary skills (for example, grammar, study skills, punctuation, pronunciation, and vocabulary) be integrated in ESL instruction?
2. What is wrong with a discrete-skills (unintegrated) approach to teaching ESL?
3. What does the research say about skill integration?
4. To what degree is skill integration going on in ESL programs now?
5. Why are content-based instruction and task-based instruction useful vehicles for integrating the language skills?

This chapter focuses on a key issue in ESL instruction: the integration of the *four main language skills* (listening, reading, speaking, and writing) and the *subsidiary language skills,* such as grammar, study skills, punctuation, pronunciation, and vocabulary, within the ESL curriculum. In actual language use — the way we really communicate — any single skill such as listening is rarely employed in isolation from other language skills like speaking or reading. This is because communication, by definition, requires the integration of both the main and the subsidiary language skills.

In our tapestry motif, we can look at language skills in two different ways. We can see these skills — both the main and the subsidiary — as interwoven in an integrated, smoothly blending fashion, or we can see them as parallel, non-interactive stripes in a plain pattern, not really touching each other and certainly not crossing over and linking. The first view is that of integrated skills, and the second is that of discrete or segregated skills. The first vision is much more realistic in relation to actual communicative use of language, and it is the direction toward which many ESL programs are going; however, the second pattern is sometimes still found in highly traditional, less communicative ESL classrooms. This chapter shows how and why it is important to integrate the language skills into a well-functioning, communicative whole.

We are presenting this skill-integration chapter *before* the chapters on each of the specific main skills and subsidiary skills for a distinct purpose. By placing this chapter ahead of the chapters on specific skills, we are demonstrating how important we believe skill integration to be in ESL instruction. While reading subsequent chapters on specific skills, always keep in mind what the current chapter says about how we should pull together and synthesize all the language skills. Skill integration should serve as a conceptual framework by which to understand the contributory role of each of the language skills.

ORGANIZATION OF THIS CHAPTER

In this chapter we first present definitions of terminology and concepts related to the integration of language skills. Second, we discuss problems with the segregated-skill approach. Third, we cite advantages of integrating the skills. Fourth, we describe content-based and task-based instruction, two significant modes of skill integration. Fifth, we summarize the empirical research on skill integration. Finally, we present Tapestry principles concerning skill integration, principles that guide our methodology and that rule how the specific skills (discussed in detail in later chapters) should be handled.

DEFINITIONS

Readers of this book might have previously encountered one or more of the following five terms, which are used rather interchangeably in second language teaching and learning: *discrete skill, isolated skill, segregated skill, single skill*, and *separate skill*. These terms all refer to an emphasis on one skill or at best two skills at a time in the language classroom.

All of these terms might fit under the often-used label of *skill-oriented*, in the sense that a classroom highlighting a given skill is intentionally oriented toward the development of only that skill. Thus, in such a classroom, the development of other language skills is merely an unexamined by-product. Sometimes the approach that treats each language skill separately is called *language-based*, because the specific skills of the language itself — rather than natural communication using the language — are the focus of study.

The opposite of all these terms is known as *integrated skills* or *skill integration*, that is, the linking of the main and subsidiary language skills for the purpose of real communication. In an instructional approach that favors integrated skills, the skills are interlocked, ideally as they are in everyday life. Practice with any given skill strengthens other skills.

PROBLEMS WITH THE SEGREGATED-SKILL APPROACH

Let us examine the segregated-skill approach in more detail because it has been a source of multiple problems in the second language teaching field. In such an approach, mastery of discrete language skills or subskills, such as listening comprehension, phonics, speaking, or punctuation, is often seen as the key to successful learning, and there is typically a separation of language learning from content learning (Mohan 1986, Cantoni-Harvey 1987, Nunan 1988, Richards 1990).

The organization of many ESL programs traditionally segregates language skills for instructional purposes, often highlighting just one skill at a time. This situation contradicts the integrated way that people use language skills in normal circumstances, and it clashes with the direction in which experts in the second language teaching field have been moving in recent years.

In our discussion, we identify two levels of segregated skills, along with their associated problems: first, total skill segregation, and second, partial segregation. These are explained next.

Total Skill Segregation

In the purest form of segregation, language is taught as an end in itself rather than a means to an end, the end being authentic interaction and communication (Dubin and Olshtain 1986). This instructional approach is clearly language-based (see definition above) rather than communication-oriented.

Many ESL programs traditionally segregate language skills for instructional purposes, often highlighting just one skill at a time. Accordingly, we frequently encounter ESL classes labeled "Intermediate Reading," "Advanced Writing," or "Basic Listening." This form of instruction — including syllabus design, curriculum arrangement, and student placement — is usually founded on pragmatic, administrative decisions rather than on a conceptually sound theory of language learning and teaching. Sometimes teachers and administrators think it is logistically simpler to present courses on writing divorced from speaking, or on listening severed from reading; and sometimes they believe it is impossible to concentrate effectively on more than one language skill at a time.

Typically labeled according to a particular skill like reading or listening, language-based classes often disintegrate into a mere examination of forms and structures. The reason is that it is, in reality, very difficult to segregate the language skills from each other in a rigorous way and still maintain any degree of communication. Isolation of the skills leads to a communication deadlock.

Strictly separate-skill classes sometimes end up concentrating on subsidiary skills like grammar and vocabulary, even though the course title refers to one of the main language skills (listening, reading, speaking, or writing). Perplexed teachers, with a mandate to teach a reading or listening course, desperately focus on very concrete items such as vocabulary expressions and grammar points. Memorization rather than understanding is the primary student process involved in these kinds of classes. For many students, motivation, interest, and class involvement plummet when the language is taught in this fragmented, noncommunicative way.

Even if it were possible to effectively and fully develop one or two skills in the absence of the other language skills, this does not ensure adequate preparation for later success in academic tasks in United States universities. A person who can read adequately but cannot speak well has a serious handicap in our academic system; some degree of ability in all skills is a virtual necessity.

Partial Skill Segregation

In many cases, an ESL course is labeled by a single skill, but (fortunately) this segregation of language skills is unsuccessful or only partial. If the teacher is truly creative, energetic, and resourceful, a course bearing a discrete-skill title might actually involve all skills. Frequently skills other than the targeted one creep in. We call this situation *partial skill segregation* — a circumstance in which the language skills appear at first glance to be isolated in instruction but are actually not separated completely.

For instance, in a class on "Intermediate Reading," the teacher usually gives some or all of the directions orally, thus forcing students to use their listening skills to catch the details of the assignment. In this class students might discuss their readings, using speaking and listening skills and a host of subsidiary skills, such as pronunciation and grammar. Students might be asked to summarize or analyze readings in written form, thus activating their writing skill. The focus remains, however, always on reading.

In slanting the course toward a single skill, the teacher does not exploit the potential of any topic from the multiple perspectives and activities of the various language skills. Teachers and students miss the vitality and depth of the subject when insufficient weight is given to all the relevant skills and when the skills are not consciously coordinated.

ADVANTAGES OF SKILL INTEGRATION

It is very important for every ESL program to provide numerous and extensive opportunities for natural communication that integrates the main and subsidiary language skills in principled ways. Let us assure our readers that we are not necessarily advocating total, instant integration of all language skills in every ESL course. In fact, we do see an occasional need for courses specifically aimed at writing development, grammar improvement, or vocabulary building, alongside the more primary integrated courses that unify the major and subsidiary skills.

In integrated-skill instruction, learners are exposed to authentic language and are involved in activities that are interesting and meaningful. Integrating the main language skills and the subsidiary language skills, at least in some courses if not in all, has many advantages:

1. Learners rapidly gain a true picture of the richness and complexity of the language as used for communication.
2. The language becomes not just an object of academic interest but a real means of interaction among people.
3. Teachers are given the power and the opportunity to track students' progress in multiple skills at the same time.
4. Skill integration allows mutually supportive growth in all the main skills and the subsidiary skills.
5. In an integrated-skill format, language instruction promotes the learning of real content, rather than the dissection of language forms.
6. The learning of authentic content through language is highly motivating to students of all ages and backgrounds.
7. The significant role of background knowledge becomes evident when language skills are integrated communicatively.

Knowing the advantages of skill integration, we now describe content-based instruction and then task-based instruction, two modes that effectively integrate all language skills.

CONTENT-BASED INSTRUCTION: A SIGNIFICANT MODE OF SKILL INTEGRATION

One of the most important modes of skill integration is called *content-based instruction,* in which students practice in a highly integrated fashion all the language skills while participating in activities or tasks that focus on important content in areas such as science, mathematics, and social studies (Brinton, Snow, and Wesche 1989). In his pioneering work on content-based language learning, Mohan (1986) argues:

> Any educational approach that considers language learning alone and ignores the learning of subject matter is inadequate to the needs of these learners . . . . What is needed is an integrative approach which relates language learning and content learning, considers language as a medium of learning, and acknowledges the role of context in communication. (p. 1)

Goals of Content-Based Language Instruction

In content-based language instruction, the language teacher's primary goal is to help students develop communicative competence, which we might define as the ability to use the language effectively, appropriately, and accurately in a variety of settings (for example, social, academic, professional) despite limitations in knowledge. (See Chapter Five for more details.) This primary goal requires the use of normal, real-life, communicative language, which in turn presupposes the integration of the four main language skills and the subsidiary language skills.

The content-based teacher's secondary goals are to introduce concepts and terminology relevant to a given subject area, to reinforce content-area information learned elsewhere, and to teach specific learning strategies for writing, reading, or general study via the means of interesting content (Short 1991, Mohan 1979, 1986). Snow, Met, and Genesee (1989) have looked at these goals in terms of *content-obligatory language*, that is, language essential to understanding content, and *content-compatible language*, that is, language which links quite naturally with a given concept or content area.

Collier (1989) recommends that content-based, integrated-skill academic instruction should take place while ESL students are mastering basic language skills, so that these students will be prepared to participate effectively in very demanding cognitive tasks now and in their future studies. This relates to earlier research by Cummins (1979) on the important distinctions between basic interpersonal communication skills (BICS) and cognitive academic language proficiency (CALP). Swales' (1991) book on genres in content-based writing also supports the thrust of Collier's recommendation.

Questions often arise as to when content-based instruction can be used. Specifically, do students need to have a basic, foundational level of language competence before content-based instruction can be introduced? The answer is that content-based instruction is valuable at *all* levels, but the nature of the content differs according to student proficiency level. For beginners, the content will concern basic interpersonal and survival aspects of the language, such as renting an apartment, taking a bus, ordering food at a restaurant, and buying simple items. This is real content, which can be organized thematically and turned into authentic language tasks. Past the beginning level, the content can become increasingly academic if desired, but of course students will continue to learn additional sociolinguistically appropriate, interpersonal expressions and structures, no matter how advanced their skills become. In other words, the learning of social content does not end, but the learning of academic content is increased in terms of the proportion of time spent as students progress in their language development.

Models of Content-Based Language Instruction

Three different models of content-based instruction exist, all of which integrate language skills as part of ongoing communication:

1. *Theme-based*, in which the language skills are fully integrated in the study of a theme (for example, economics, ecology). The theme must be of strong interest to students and must allow a wide variety of language forms and functions to be practiced. This is probably the most commonly used form of content-based instruction. It is found in many ESL books today. Theme-based instruction, one of the most useful aspects of content-based instruction, is a major part of the Tapestry Approach. Theme-based instruction works effectively because the themes are chosen for their relevance, importance, and interest to the students. These factors are central to students' motivation. (See Crookes and Schmidt 1989 for components of language learning motivation; see also Chapter Four of this book.)

2. *Adjunct,* in which language and content courses are linked through instructor and curriculum coordination. Two separate courses are conducted, but they are carefully linked. This form of content-based instruction demands close coordination, but appears to be potentially quite effective.

3. *Sheltered,* in which learners are taught the subject matter and language course work in English that is modified to the students' level of proficiency. This form of content-based instruction has worked very effectively in university settings in Canada with motivated students (Edwards,

Wesche, Krashen, Clément, and Kruidenier 1984). It is working less effectively, according to our observation, in many public-school ESL programs in California, where the initial proficiency level in the target language is not as high as for the Canadian university students. Sheltered instruction, by the way, is similar to *sheltered workshops* used for children with a wide range of learning handicaps (emotional, physical, and mental) in the field of special education.

For details on each of these three formats for content-based instruction, see Snow, Brinton, and Wesche (1989).

TASK-BASED INSTRUCTION: ANOTHER KEY MODE OF SKILL INTEGRATION

Another widely used form of skill integration is task-based instruction, involving communicative tasks in the target language. These are activities that require comprehending, producing, manipulating, or interacting in authentic language while attention is principally oriented to meaning rather than form (Nunan 1989). Tasks, according to Nunan, are typically activities that can stand alone as fundamental units, but we believe that it is valuable to link tasks together through a common theme. Otherwise, task-based instruction can sometimes be too fragmented.

Thus, we advocate the combination of task-based instruction with one of the most valuable forms of content-based instruction, theme-based. The Tapestry Approach, simply put, develops communicative competence by merging two powerful modes of skill integration — task-based and theme-based instruction — while at the same time paying close attention to the needs and characteristics of individual students and the group.

In task-based instruction, basic pair work and group work are often used (Gaies 1985, Doughty and Pica 1986); for instance, students work together to write and edit a class newspaper, develop a television commercial, conduct simulated job interviews, role-play town meetings on environmental issues, enact typical U.S. academic classroom situations that involve communication problems, play learning games, and so on. More structured cooperative learning formats such as "Numbered Heads Together," "Think-Pair-Share," "STAD," and "Jigsaw" (Johnson, Johnson, and Holubec 1986; Slavin 1981, 1983, 1989-1990) are often used in task-based instruction.

Talbott and Oxford (1991) describe a task-based "English Through Video-Making" course for university-preparatory ESL students that demonstrates the highly communicative integration of language skills occurring while students wrote, produced, directed, choreographed, and acted in their own television programs. Lavine (forthcoming) shows how skill integration occurred in a task-based language laboratory for Spanish as a foreign language, with the most interesting task being a computer dating service. Other task-based instruction, all of which integrate the language skills, is presented in Nunan (1989) and Kumaravadivelu (1989).

Task-based language learning, just like content-based instruction, is relevant at all levels of competence. The nature of the tasks varies from one level to the other, however. Tasks become increasingly complex and multifaceted at higher levels of skill development when students are more able to handle such transactions. For instance, two beginners might be asked to introduce themselves and share one item of information. At a more advanced level, students can do tasks like taking a public opinion poll at the university or at a shopping mall — which would require significantly more language and social competence.

Observation of task-based instruction indicates that this mode generates highly positive student attitudes and motivation, as long as the tasks are perceived to be interesting and relevant. As noted earlier, our experience also indicates that it is best to link tasks by means of an overarching theme; this underscores the relevance and unity of the tasks.

We have just discussed two main modes of skill integration: content-based and task-based instruction. We now turn to research involving language skill integration.

SUMMARY OF INTEGRATED-SKILL RESEARCH

We can summarize the research in the following way. First, in both first and second language development, learners naturally integrate the language skills for communicative purposes. Absolutely no research exists to support the segregation of language skills.

Second, even in ostensibly segregated-skill courses in second languages, in many instances the skills are actually integrated because it is almost impossible to communicate otherwise. This partial skill segregation has already been discussed earlier in the chapter.

Third, practice in one skill supports the development of other skills but does not provide a total substitute for practice in those other skills; in other words, reading practice is not tantamount to writing or listening practice. Each skill deserves practice within an integrated-skill framework.

Fourth, much more research is necessary about the best formats for skill integration, but content-based and task-based language instruction appear to be powerful modes for uniting the language skills while at the same time conveying knowledge and experience with communicative tasks. A combination of theme-based (one form of content-based) and task-based instruction might be the most powerful of all means for integrating the language skills.

Fifth, ESL students have specific academic needs that relate to language learning, and those needs require the integration of multiple language skills in principled ways. All skills should not necessarily be emphasized equally. The ways they are integrated depend on student needs.

TAPESTRY PRINCIPLES CONCERNING SKILL INTEGRATION

Based on the discussion above, we offer the following Tapestry principles regarding the integration of language skills.

PRINCIPLES

1. Language skills can and should be integrated in ESL classes for the purpose of providing extensive practice in real-life communication. The Tapestry Approach is founded on the concept of skill integration.

2. Titles of ESL courses should reflect the integration of skills that actually takes place when communication occurs. For example, courses might be called "Speaking and Listening," "Reading and Writing," or "Writing and Grammar." Alternatively, courses might bear titles such as "Intermediate Communication" involving all language skills. Or, using themes and tasks, courses might be called "Crisis in Our Environment," "English Through Newspaper-Writing," "Social Issues in American Life," "The American Educational System," or "Ethics in Science and Technology." Insofar as possible, Tapestry materials indicate skill integration rather than skill segregation.

3. In many ESL programs at the post-secondary and adult levels, the best combination for integrating language skills is probably theme-based and task-based instruction. The Tapestry Approach unites these two potent modes.

4. Students need to encounter integrated skill, authentic language about many themes that engage their interest and heighten their motivation. They must encounter these in the form of real-life language tasks. Tapestry teachers offer this combination of themes and tasks to their students.

CONCLUSION

This chapter has presented our conception of skill integration, that is, the integration and unification of all the language skills to support the goal of natural communication. We are not suggesting that all skills be integrated equally. Rather, we are urging teachers to consider their students' needs and integrate the skills accordingly.

This chapter serves as a foundation for subsequent discussions of the main language skills and the subsidiary skills in upcoming chapters. We will be discussing these separate skills not because we believe in or advocate skill separation, but because most of the research has been done on isolated skills. Keep in mind our integrated-skill emphasis in reading the following chapters.

ACTIVITIES AND DISCUSSION QUESTIONS

1. Why do we find so many segregated-skill course structures in university and pre-university ESL programs?
2. What are the advantages and disadvantages of segregated-skill curricula?
3. Why are experts calling for integrated-skill curricula? List at least three reasons; give examples if possible.
4. What are the two major forms of skill integration discussed in this chapter? How do they differ? How are they alike? Why might they be valuable?
5. Find at least two examples of published books or materials for ESL that highlight content-based instruction. List the ways that these books or materials integrate the skills. How might you use these publications? Would you have to make any adaptations, and if so, what kind?
6. Locate at least two examples of published ESL instructional materials or books that use task-based language learning. Make a list of ways in which these materials or books integrate the skills. Could you use these materials in any way? Would any adaptations be needed?

SUGGESTED READINGS

• Cantoni-Harvey, G. 1987. *Content-Area Language Instruction: Approaches and Strategies.* Reading, MA : Addison-Wesley. This book is a must for readers who want to know about the roots of content-area instruction and how to use this mode of skill integration in language classes. Cantoni-Harvey presents a clear case for content-based instruction.

• Mohan, B. 1986. *Content-Based Language Instruction.* Reading, MA: Addison-Wesley. Mohan is one of the founders of the content-based language instruction movement in the United States. He speaks with authority as he discusses the reasons for content-based instruction and provides guidance for teachers and administrators alike.

• Nunan, D. 1989. *Designing Tasks for the Communicative Classroom.* Cambridge: Cambridge University Press. Nunan offers a useful book on task-based language instruction. The need for communicative tasks is made evident in this readable book, and Nunan provides a set of steps for designing such tasks. This book is useful to all curriculum designers and language teachers.

READING

7

PREVIEW QUESTIONS

1. What makes reading in a second language different than reading in a first language?
2. Why do some ESL learners hate reading in English?
3. What factors help students develop their ESL reading skills?
4. What can an ESL teacher do to help students understand a difficult text that contains vocabulary words and grammatical structures that the students have not yet acquired?
5. What types of assistance can teachers provide their ESL students to help these students develop their English reading skills?

In our tapestry motif, reading is one of the four essential parts of the design. It is an important strand that is interwoven with the other three language skills — speaking, listening, and writing. (See Chapter Six.)

ORGANIZATION OF THIS CHAPTER

For the adult ESL learner, reading is a key to success in higher education. Without reading, opportunities for understanding the United States and achieving educational objectives are lost.[1] In this chapter, our primary objective is to outline those pedagogical practices that foster second language reading development. However, before turning to these practices, it will be useful first to consider the abilities underlying reading competence, as well as the relevant research.

In Figure 7.1 (see page 94), we show graphically the abilities underlying reading proficiency in the framework of Canale and Swain (1980). This framework, discussed at length in Chapter Five, is important in understanding all the key aspects of reading in a second language.

Grammatical Competence

Grammatical competence in regard to reading involves use of grammar rules to help understand what is being read. In addition, grammatical competence includes knowledge of lexicon or vocabulary, which is also essential to the reading process. Reading also demands mastery of mechanics, such as the alphabet and the punctuation of the language. All of these elements are part of what is known as grammatical competence.

Figure 7.1 Abilities underlying reading proficiency

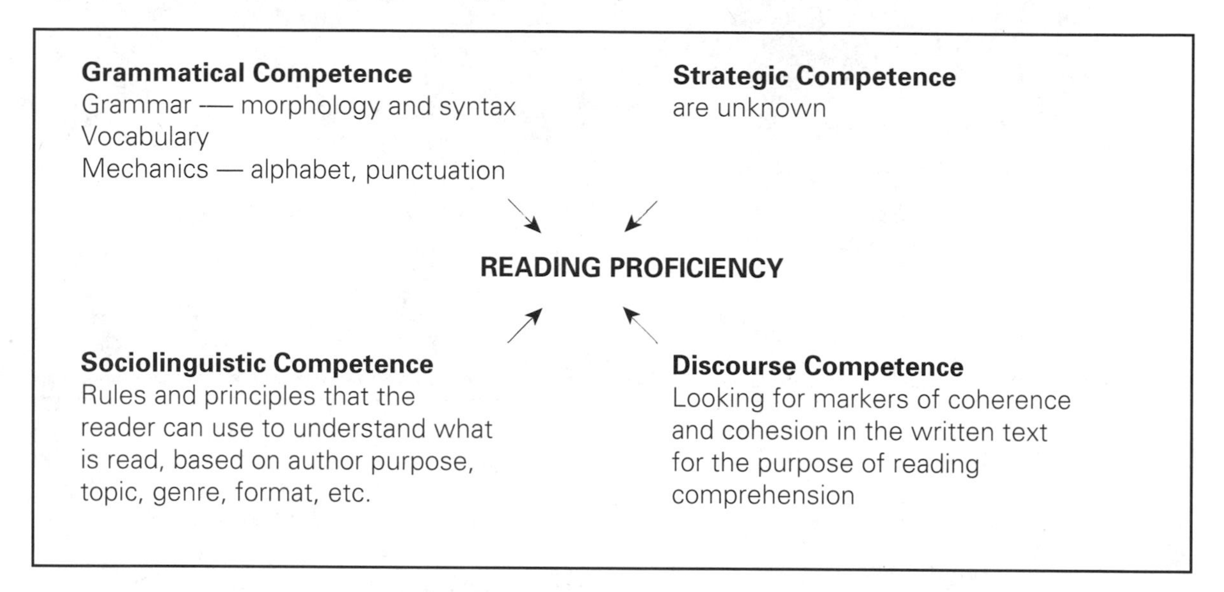

Grammatical Competence
Grammar — morphology and syntax
Vocabulary
Mechanics — alphabet, punctuation
Strategic Competence
are unknown
READING PROFICIENCY
Sociolinguistic Competence
Rules and principles that the reader can use to understand what is read, based on author purpose, topic, genre, format, etc.
Discourse Competence
Looking for markers of coherence and cohesion in the written text for the purpose of reading comprehension

Sociolinguistic Competence

To grammatical competence we add *sociolinguistic competence.* The reader needs to be able to get into the mindset of the author of the reading passage to figure out the author's purpose, genre, register, topic, and so on. A degree of sociolinguistic maturity is demanded of any reader in a new language. Teachers can assist their students in gaining these qualities, so that sociolinguistic competence can become a strong tool in the quest for meaning for second language learners.

Discourse Competence

Discourse competence is needed in addition to grammatical and sociolinguistic competence. Readers in a new language need to be able to read passages of discourse, sometimes very long ones. They need to be able to identify instances in which the writer of the passage has used cohesive devices, such as reference, ellipsis, and conjunction. Readers need to understand how and why these devices are used if they are to comprehend the meaning of the reading passage. They also must recognize markers indicating coherence in the development, balance, continuity, and completeness of a piece of writing. Teachers can help learners focus on these features of a reading text.

Strategic Competence

In reading, *strategic competence* refers to possessing a set of useful strategies for compensating for missing knowledge. All of these strategies can be boiled down to the process of guessing using any and all clues available. Clues come from the linguistic context of the sentence or the paragraph, from the reader's background knowledge, from the content, from what has been said earlier or what will be said later in the text, or from any other source the reader can find. Guessing is not only useful in reading; it is indispensable. Fortunately, it can be taught and practiced in the language classroom.

REVIEW OF THE RELEVANT RESEARCH

Considerable research provides the foundation of the Tapestry Approach to reading instruction. In this section, we consider findings from both first and second language research.

First Language Research

In the past ten years, first language reading research has enabled teachers to provide students with more enjoyable and effective reading instruction. This research has demonstrated that good readers . . .

1. read extensively.
2. skillfully integrate information in the text with what they already know. Information from the text and the knowledge possessed by the reader act together to produce meaning.
3. are flexible. How they read depends on the complexity of the text, their familiarity with the topic, and their purpose for reading.
4. are motivated. Motivation is central to learning to read. It takes a long time to learn to read well and the students' attention must somehow be sustained during this period.
5. rely on different skills interacting simultaneously. Good readers rely upon perceptual processing, phonemic processing, and internal recall of many types (grammatical, lexical, and discoursal). Phonics is helpful, but it is just one component of reading development.
6. read in situations where written language serves real functions — such as entertainment (as in novels), information (as in manuals), and direction (as on traffic signals).

We conclude from this research that the primary objective of reading teachers is making reading easy for students. Teachers can accomplish this objective by providing students with language support (such as the meaning of a new vocabulary word just at the time a learner needs it and appropriate encouragement when it is required). (See Chapter Three.)

Second Language Research

Second language researchers have also contributed to our knowledge of the process of reading in a second language. For instance, following first language investigators, ESL reading researchers have found that students seldom do much reading within the confines of their ESL classroom. Instead, they spend most of their time completing exercises that test their reading skills (Williams and Cappizzi Snipper 1990). One reason that ESL teachers may not favor reading as an activity is that, with reading, students cannot be perceived as doing anything (Enright and McCloskey 1988).

Like the first language researchers, second language investigators have also provided evidence that extensive reading contributes to reading development. (For a comprehensive review of the research, refer to Krashen 1985b.) Krashen (1982) and Krashen and Terrell (1983), no matter what the practical limitations of their Natural Approach, have succeeded in demonstrating the importance of learners' reading large amounts of meaningful, authentic, comprehensible materials, often just a notch above the learners' current level of complete comprehension. (For a detailed discussion, see Chapter Three.)

Second language reading researchers who have examined schema theory have contributed to our knowledge of the second language reading process in yet other ways. Schema theory is concerned with students' internal knowledge structures, or *schemata* (singular is *schema*). Carrell and Eisterhold (1983) and Carrell (1984) have pointed out the tremendous impact that learners' own background knowledge, captured mentally in their schemata, have on learning to read in a foreign language. (For an excellent review of the literature on schema theory and second language reading development, see Carrell, Devine, and Eskey 1988.) Schema theory, which has been around since the turn of the century, has caught hold in the foreign and second language fields because it helps explain why some language learners comprehend and remember more than do their classmates.

In a nutshell, schema theory suggests that comprehension is an interactive relationship or process involving the learners' background knowledge and the text (be it oral or written). The learner cannot comprehend anything for which he or she does not have some kind of existing knowledge structure or schema. The comprehension process involves, among other things, assimilation of new knowledge into existing schemata and accommodation of existing schemata to fit new knowledge. With reference to reading comprehension, research shows that: (1) lack of schemata or the failure to activate an appropriate schema can significantly impair comprehension; (2) appropriate content/rhetorical schema application can increase comprehension; (3) background knowledge can be just as important as language ability in terms of comprehension; and (4) comprehension is facilitated by explicitly inducing schemata through pre-reading activities.

The above findings refer only to comprehension. As might be obvious, memory will not operate effectively if comprehension is hindered; and if memory is stunted, then production skills will be limited also. Therefore, schema-related difficulties harm language learning in multiple ways.

In considering ways to strengthen and expand the learners' existing knowledge and bridge the gap between that knowledge and new input, it is important to realize that students may be at different levels of social/cognitive development. No matter which social/cognitive developmental theory one espouses — Vygotsky, Piaget, Perry, Erikson, Belenky — one must recognize that Eduardo might be more developed than José, or Erika than Li-Mihn. As a result, their background knowledge and the way they individually deal with that knowledge might be somewhat different. This factor needs to be taken into account in designing classroom reading activities so that background differences can be ameliorated (though not eliminated) through preparatory events such as pre-reading.

Less research has been done on the implications of cross-cultural differences for learning to read than on schema theory. (See Grabe 1988 for a recent summary.) Reading serves various purposes in different cultures, and cultures place different emphases and values on diverse types of reading texts. For instance, in Europe, as in the United States, there is a great emphasis on bedtime stories, and children are brought up hearing these stories (Heath 1982). This tradition is absent in many Asian cultures (Heath 1986). [2]

INSTRUCTIONAL PRACTICES

What little research exists on cultural differences draws our attention to the great diversity among learners and the need to vary our teaching practices so that we effectively serve the diverse groups of learners we find in our classes. In this section we discuss the following instructional practices: establishing objectives, motivating different types of learners, identifying reading materials that are tailored to individual needs, providing learners with large quantities of reading, improving the learners' comprehension of these materials, developing specific reading skills and strategies, and integrating reading with the other language skills.

Establishing Objectives

Although the general goals may vary from one group of learners to the next along with the level of the learner's skills, in general the objectives of any ESL reading course must include the following:

1. motivating learners and making reading an enjoyable experience for all students;
2. providing students with the culturally relevant information needed to understand texts;
3. promoting an interest in different types of reading texts;
4. enlarging the students' vocabulary and providing them with strategies for increasing their vocabulary;
5. developing the students' strategies for reading diverse genres of English for different purposes effectively; and
6. teaching specific skills that increase the students' reading comprehension.

Most importantly, *content* rather than language must be the *point of departure or organizing principle* of ESL reading activities. This will assure that students will acquire English language in the context of meaningful communication. At the beginning levels, ESL learners need to gain the reading skills necessary to understand readings about common, familiar topics in a restricted number of genres. (We use the term *genre* to refer to text types such as narratives, poems, and expository essays.) At the more advanced levels, ESL learners need to concentrate on acquiring the skills necessary to understand more technical, specialized texts as well as more sophisticated pleasure reading. Motivation is central to accomplishing all these objectives.

Motivating Learners

Positive emotions and attitudes can make reading an enjoyable experience for the learner. Teachers can exert a tremendous impact on the emotional atmosphere of the classroom in four different ways: (1) by providing students with reading lessons that are stimulating, informative, and relevant; (2) by changing the social structure of the classroom so that students have more control over their learning; (3) by building the students' confidence; and (4) by teaching students to use affective strategies.

Providing Students with Stimulating, Informative, and Relevant Reading Lessons. Teachers who maintain high levels of motivation conduct well-paced, varied lessons. Tasks are introduced with enthusiasm and with explanations of why doing them helps the students become better readers. Students are encouraged to *read to learn.* The reading material excites the learners and enables them to extend their knowledge. Stories that present problems to be solved also sharpen interest (Wallace 1988). Discussions before reading and discussions and question-and-answer sessions after the reading stimulate high-level thinking, which in turn whets the students' appetite to learn more.

Changing the Social Structure of the Classroom. Allowing students to have more control over their learning increases their motivation to read. There are several ways this can be accomplished: students can choose their own reading material individually, in groups, or as a class; they can express linkages of the reading material and their own life experiences; and they can also be instrumental in choosing classroom reading activities, tasks, and thematic units.

Building the Learners' Confidence. Confidence leads to motivation. Teachers can build their students' confidence by allowing students to prepare for reading exercises, avoiding error correction that embarrasses students, and allowing students to practice reading texts silently before reading these texts in front of others.

Failure is not fun. If students are to *like* reading, they need to experience success in reading.

Teachers can help students attain this success by providing reading activities that are attuned to the students' abilities and by preparing their students well for these activities. Pre-reading activities such as conversations about the reading (which personalize the text by relating it to the students' own experiences) and exercises that include vocabulary overviews prepare the student for the upcoming reading.

Silent reading also builds confidence. As Anderson, Hiebert, Scott, and Wilkinson (1985) suggest, "No one would expect a novice pianist to sight read a new selection every day, but that is exactly what is expected of the beginning reader" *(Becoming a Nation of Readers,* p. 53). Before asking students to read aloud, teachers can ask the students first to read the selections silently.

Another way to build the students' confidence in their reading ability is to ignore most of their mistakes except for those that disrupt the meaning of the text. If students are asked to read aloud, they should not be afraid to make errors.

Teaching Strategies for Creating and Maintaining a High Level of Motivation. Oxford (1990) suggests a number of practical ideas for helping students to create and maintain a high level of motivation. (See also Horwitz and Young 1990 and Cohen 1990.) She describes affective strategies that learners can use to increase their self-esteem and self-confidence as well as lower their anxieties. These strategies help learners to gain control over affective factors (which include emotions, attitudes, motivations, and values) in such a way that their ESL reading development is facilitated.

Choosing Appropriate Reading Materials

Just as ESL students need motivation to read, so too they need rich and continuous reading experiences, "including published literature of acknowledged merit and the work of peers and instructors" (Farr and Daniels 1986, p. 60). Yet to facilitate second language development, readings must be selected carefully. When identifying appropriate reading materials, teachers need to consider whether they are authentic, attuned to their learners' second language proficiency levels, culturally relevant, and sensitive to their students' needs and interests. Too often materials are written by people with a language and literature background who fail to realize that the vast majority of ESL students are not learning English to read Steinbeck, to enjoy a play, or to tell stories; rather, many of these students are learning English to become better managers, engineers, lab technicians, or computer specialists. They need skills to develop the language of business or science, including the ability to read and interpret graphs and tables. This group of students needs to be able to see a graph from the words on a page or, vice versa, put into words the visual depiction of data on a graph (Scovel, personal communication).

Authenticity. A critical consideration in choosing appropriate reading materials for students is *authenticity.* Even beginning students need exposure to *authentic language,* the vehicle of everyday communication that is used in conversations, magazines, books, slogans, traffic signs, menus, schedules, posters, notices, etc. Generally, authentic language is considered unedited, unabridged text that is written for native English speakers. It is always contextualized, that is, part of a larger communicative context.[3] In contrast, unauthentic text rarely can stand on its own as genuine communication. It is often overly-simplified and written explicitly to teach language forms. The following extract from a reader in the *Scope* teaching material is illustrative of unauthentic text.

Example 7.1

This is London airport.
It is Sunday. It is ten o'clock.
This is Ali's father.
This is Ali's uncle.
They are at the airport.
They are wearing coats.
They are wearing coats
because it is cold in England.
They are at the airport.
They are looking at planes.

(*Scope,* Reader 6, *Ali's Coming to England)*

Five reasons we support using authentic texts when possible in ESL reading instruction are:

1. It is difficult to wean beginning readers from a diet of overly-simplified reading texts.
2. The difficulty of a reading text is not so much a function of the language in the text as it is of the conceptual difficulty of the passage, the task, and the activity required of students.
3. Simplifying a text often removes natural redundancy and makes the rhetorical organization somewhat difficult for students to predict. This actually makes a text more difficult to read than if the original were used.
4. Simplified texts lose what we might call the writer's *voice,* his or her identity and purpose.
5. Adults recognize the watered-down nature of simplified texts and often resent it.

This is not to say that authentic text, like unauthentic text, cannot be simplified. Example 7.2 below, suggested by Scovel (personal communication), shows that it can be highly *simplified,* while still retaining authenticity.

Example 7.2
Background: American children frequently ask their parents for money when they are away from home in college. Here is the telegram that a money-hungry son sent his father.

DEAR DAD
NO MON, NO FUN, YOUR SON

Here is the telegram that the father sent back to his son.
DEAR SON
SO SAD, TOO BAD, YOUR DAD

Second Language Proficiency Level A related consideration when choosing reading materials is selecting readings at an appropriate level for the students, neither too easy nor too difficult. (For discussion, see Chapter Three.) When considering the appropriateness of the reading materials for ESL learners of diverse proficiency levels, it is probably best to avoid *readability formulas.* (These mathematical formulas are devised to identify reading difficulty level.) The presidents of the National

Council for Teachers of English and of the International Reading Association issued a joint statement on readability (Cullinan and Fitzgerald 1985) in which they warn against using readability formulas to select texts, especially in the widely used basals (series of books or reading materials that are graded by language proficiency level). Instead of choosing reading materials on the basis of readability formulas, effective teachers select materials for their students on the basis of student interest, needs, and ability level. When they find that a given selection is too easy or too difficult for their students, they choose a different selection. Alternatively, these teachers encourage their students to select their own reading materials, and provide guidelines for selecting the materials: (1) choose interesting materials; (2) select materials that you can understand; and (3) select materials that are neither too difficult (far beyond your capacity to understand) nor too easy (far below your current English proficiency level).

Reading Materials for the Beginning ESL Student. A number of materials provide easy reading for beginning ESL students. Teachers can choose authentic easy readings, engage students in pen-pal activities with native English speakers, use student-produced materials, or use commercial textbooks for ESL students of diverse proficiency levels (that is, semi-authentic reading materials). In addition, teachers can prepare edited, authentic texts for beginning students.

• *Authentic Materials.* Even beginning students can read and understand authentic texts. These texts are written in a relatively simple style and contain predictable structures and content. Once students perceive that a text belongs to a certain familiar genre (be it a fable, a short story, or a narrative), many unfamiliar words and even sentence structures become less difficult. Beginning ESL students enjoy simply written fables and folk stories as well as detective and suspense stories, dialogs, mini-dramas, and science fiction. They also enjoy reading simple narratives, descriptions, and expository passages that have been written by real authors who use simple sentence structures and common vocabulary words.

The authentic reading materials suggested by Paulston and Bruder (1976) work especially well with beginning level ESL learners. These authors suggest using authentic texts with local settings on topics with which students are highly familiar. Such materials include local newspapers, pamphlets, brochures, and booklets about local places of interest or the students' home countries. Because the students are very familiar with the topics of these materials, they are able to comprehend the reading.

• *Pen-Pals.* Letters from peers and the teacher also provide appropriate reading for beginning ESL learners. Heath and Branscombe (1984) found a letter-writing project involving 9th grade basic English students, many of whom spoke English as a second language, and 11th and 12th grade students highly successful in developing English skills of less proficient writers. In this activity, students of diverse proficiency levels are paired with one another and asked to correspond on a regular basis. Another kind of letter writing between students and their teacher called dialog journals has also been successful with ESL students (Kreeft, Shuy, Staton, Reed, and Morrow 1984). In dialog journals, students correspond with their teacher on a regular basis about their personal interests. Instead of correcting their students' grammar, the teacher responds to the content of the letters.

• *Student-Produced Materials.* For beginning ESL learners, the Language Experience Approach (LEA) (Rigg 1981, Dixon and Nessel 1983) provides an excellent means of giving students familiar content and comprehensible English input. This technique uses the students' ideas and the students' own words in the preparation of materials. The students decide what to say and then dictate it to someone else, who acts as a scribe. In dictated stories, the teacher, a more advanced ESL student, or a native English-speaking peer writes down the ESL student's story. The person doing the writing may initiate the sentences for the ESL student, but gradually the ESL student should begin to create his or her own stories. Heald-Taylor (1989) suggests that the writer of the story print exactly what each student desires and after printing the phrase should ask such questions as, *Is this what you wanted to say? Did I get it right?*

Student-produced materials can become a rich source of classroom reading. Students can tell their life histories orally to their teachers or native English-speaking peers, who write these stories down and put them together to form a collection of autobiographies. As an alternative, teachers can put together collections of folk stories or personal narratives. These collections can then serve as student-produced reading materials for the entire class.

• *Commercial Texts.* Teachers can also use semi-authentic texts (professionally written) with their beginning ESL students. While these texts have a limited use and must be balanced with other more authentic texts (refer to the discussion above), their use can be defended. Wallace (1988), for example, states:

> Occasionally, well-known books, including the classics, are abridged and simplified in order to make them more accessible to L2 (second language) readers. Some might object to this "mucking about" with the classics. In defense of simplified readers, however, it might be argued that there are only so many good stories to go around; in simplifying *Great Expectations* or *Wuthering Heights,* writers are easing the path for those who want to read the classics. The mere fact of reduced length, larger print, different format and illustrations makes them less daunting; and, of course, one hopes that at a later stage students may be motivated to read the original books. (p. 35)

• *Edited Authentic Texts.* Many ESL teachers prepare edited authentic texts for their beginning-level students.[4] When creating these texts, they rewrite them to increase their comprehensibility. This often entails simplifying the grammar (for example, breaking up complex sentence structures), repeating main ideas (to give the students additional opportunities to understand the text), and employing familiar vocabulary words. In simplifying texts for their learners, teachers may want to "delete extraneous material (for example, author's asides, unnecessary examples) or add features (for example, sentence connectors, supporting evidence) which render the writing more cohesive" (Brinton, Snow, and Wesche 1989, p. 94). The preparation of supplementary activities, sometimes referred to as learning *crutches* or *aids* (including information grids, graphic organizers, and questions), also makes difficult reading more accessible to beginning level ESL students. Teachers have been successful in editing short stories as well as plays. Short stories are very effective with this level, as novels often overwhelm students who lack sufficient English proficiency to understand them. Similarly, plays are often very useful in beginning level classes, since dialog usually employs simpler sentence structures and conversation is easier for students to understand than other types of text.

Teachers can also make excellent use of narratives that have been abridged or altered to make comprehensible stories for beginning ESL students.[5] In Example 7.3, Stevick (1963) provides an example of the ways in which mini-narratives can be adapted for beginning level ESL students as well as advanced. He suggests writing the story down first in list form, for beginning level students (Version A). (Note the amount of lexical redundancy included in this version. Such redundancy generally increases the second language learner's comprehension of the text.) Next, combine two or three of the items on the list and add introductory phrases for intermediate students (Version B). Finally, introduce more complex clauses for advanced students (Versions C and D). As Stevick's narratives (amplified by Dubin in Version D) demonstrate, even very beginning ESL learners can be given the basics of a good story.

Example 7.3

Ambulance, Version A

1. An ambulance was traveling down a highway.
2. The ambulance was traveling at 80 m.p.h.
3. The siren of the ambulance was wailing.
4. A state policeman was on a motorcycle.
5. A state policeman overtook the ambulance.
6. The state policeman stopped the ambulance.
7. The driver said, "I was speeding."
8. "I know that."
9. "Ambulances carry sick people."
10. "The state allows ambulances to speed."
11. "Why did you stop me?"
12. The policeman replied, "I was trying to tell you something."
13. "There is no patient in your ambulance."
14. "You left your patient's home."
15. "You were in a hurry."
16. "You forgot your patient."

Ambulance, Version B

An ambulance was traveling down a highway at 80 m.p.h. Its siren was wailing. A state policeman on a motorcycle overtook the ambulance and stopped it.

The driver of the ambulance said, "I know that I was speeding, but the state allows ambulances to speed because they carry sick people. Why did you stop me?"

The policeman replied, "I was trying to tell you that there is no patient in your ambulance. You were in a hurry when you left your patient's home and you forgot him."

Ambulance, Version C

An ambulance was traveling down an open highway at 80 m.p.h. with its siren wailing, when a state policeman on a motorcycle overtook it and stopped it.

The driver of the ambulance protested, "I know I was speeding, but ambulances carrying patients are allowed to speed. Why did you stop me?"

The policeman replied, "That's what I was trying to tell you. You were in such a hurry when you left your patient's home that you forgot him!"

Ambulance, Version D — From Dubin (1986, p. 133)

"What's wrong with you? I know I was speeding," the protesting ambulance driver shouted at the policeman. "Are you crazy? You know as well as I do that ambulance drivers are allowed to speed."

"Lay off," the policeman replied. "You're in such a hurry you left your patient's home without him. Just take a look in the back."

Richard-Amato (1988) describes a number of activities that employ simplified reading materials that can be used with beginning ESL students. In one such activity, she suggests giving students simple written directions to follow. "The directions can be on many topics of interest: how to make a model car, how to make paper flowers, how to decoupage" (p. 104).

• *Map Reading.* Map reading is also suitable for beginning students. (See, for instance, Grellet 1981.) In an information gap activity suggested by Krashen and Terrell (1983), students are given maps such as the one contained in Figure 7.2 below. They are asked to work in pairs and trace a route while reading the directions they are given.

Figure 7.2 Maps

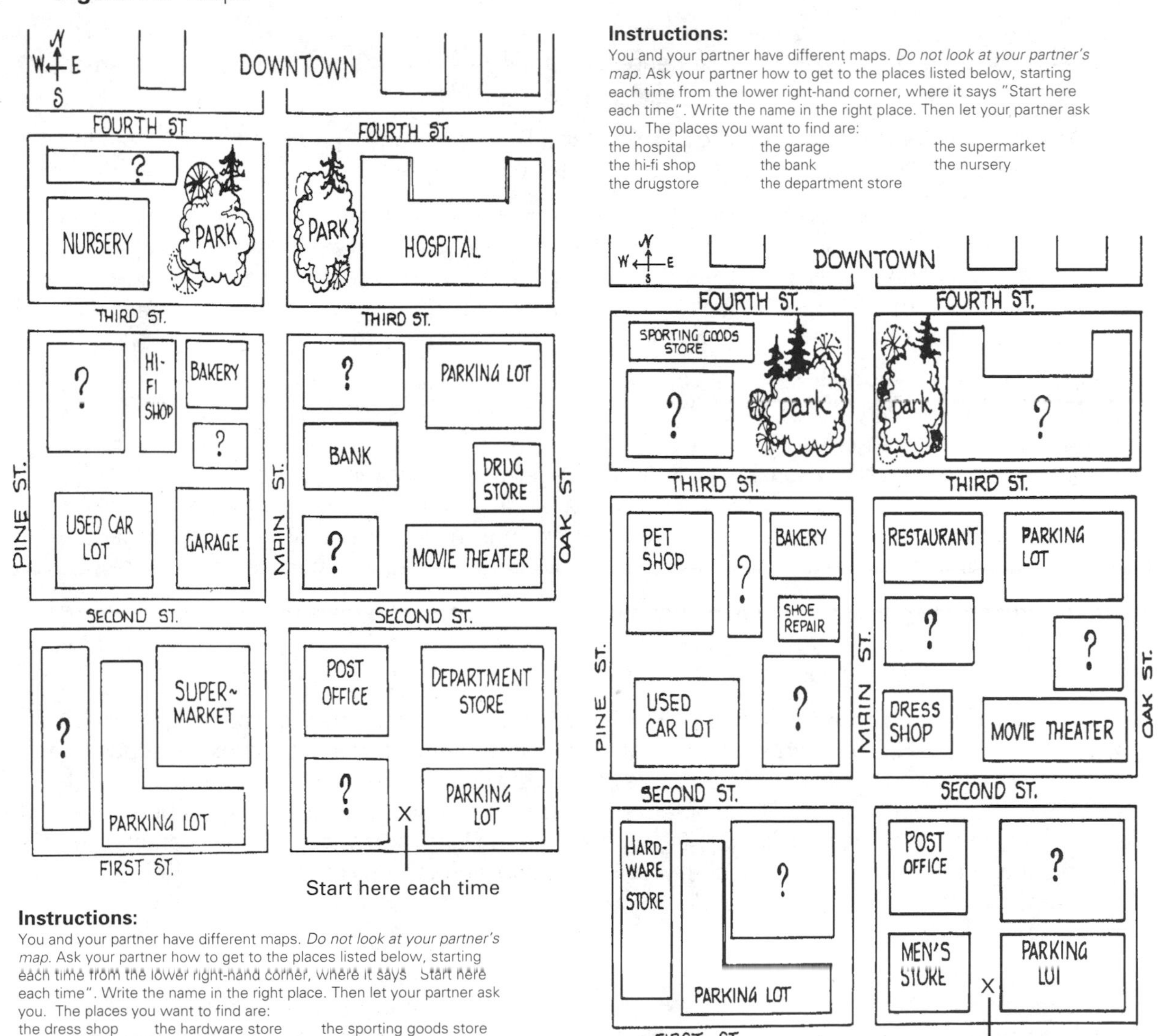

Source: Krashen, S.D., and Terrell, T.D. 1983. *The Natural Approach.* Pergamon Press, pp. 113-114.

A clever alternative combining storytelling and map-reading activities is suggested by Richard-Amato (1988). She suggests that teachers:

> . . . create a story about a fugitive who moves from place to place in different ways: he walks, runs, darts, crawls, skips and drives. The students trace the route on their individual maps as you read. Instead of drawing only straight lines, the students can draw broken lines for "walks" (-------), zigzag lines for "runs" (/\/\/\/\/\ ) sideways carets for "darts" (>>>>>), wavy lines for "crawls" (∿∿∿∿), arches for "skips" (^^^^^) and a series of plus signs for "drives" (+ + + ++). . . Eventually, the students can participate in similar activities using real street maps of cities or highway maps of whole states or countries. (p. 104)

Even beginning ESL learners need a varied reading diet. Teachers need to demonstrate the range of reading functions in English. Different genres and topics expose the learners to the grammar, rhetoric, and vocabulary associated with these genres and topics.

Reading Materials for the Intermediate ESL Student. There are many types of authentic, unedited texts that can be understood by ESL students of intermediate proficiency in English.

• *Newspapers and Popular Magazines.* Intermediate-level ESL students enjoy reading magazine articles that include many illustrations that aid their comprehension. Some enjoy "Dear Abby" selections from the newspaper, easy-to-read selections from *Reader's Digest,* and articles on social issues from popular magazines (Dubin 1986). At this level, it is probably best to avoid technical, academic texts that contain long, embedded sentences and specialized vocabulary.[6]

• *Novels.* Intermediate students can also benefit from reading novels written by authors who tend to use common vocabulary words and simple sentence structures, such as John Steinbeck or Ernest Hemingway. Many students are familiar with World War II and enjoy the *Diary of Anne Frank.* Others enjoy reading books that are based on movies or the classics. Their familiarity with the plot increases their comprehension of the text. Dubin (1986) provides suggestions for making a variety of novels available to students and increasing the likelihood of students finding those that are at an appropriate level and are of interest to them.

• *Other Authentic Texts.* Dubin (1986) points out that there are other excellent sources of material for ESL students who are not yet fluent in English. These include "catalogs, consumer guides, mail-order catalogs, and the campus newspaper, literary, or humor magazine" (p. 139).

Reading Materials for the Advanced ESL Student. A wide range of authentic reading materials is available for advanced ESL readers who often can understand materials without contextual supports. Advanced readers need to read more specialized texts that expose them to the features of English rhetoric, syntax, and vocabulary that characterize diverse registers. For example, those students who are interested in science need to be able to comprehend the language of science — characterized by impersonal forms, such as the impersonal pronoun *one,* and the use of the passive rather than the active voice.

• *Subject Area Reading.* As students gain proficiency in English, they will want to grasp the meaning of the core vocabulary of diverse and specialized subject areas. They will also need to know how this vocabulary is used in particular contexts. That is, they will need to know the co-occurrence restrictions governing the use of specific lexical items. It has been pointed out that introductory college-level textbooks are good sources for reading texts in advanced ESL or English for Academic Purpose courses because students are motivated to read them. Also, the writing tends to be full of redundancy, the syntax is straightforward with few embeddings, and graphic enhancements add meaning.

• *Pleasure Reading.* At the same time advanced ESL learners are gaining proficiency reading advanced specialized texts, they will want to continue reading pleasure material. Many ESL students are interested in reading literature written by speakers of diverse English dialects — including African-American, Chicano English, and Indian English. Some ESL teachers use composition anthologies when teaching advanced ESL students. However, many of these anthologies are inappropriate for international students since they often focus solely on immigrant students or low-achieving native English speaking students.

• *Models.* Valuable sources of reading are models or samples of the specific sorts of writing that teachers may assign (Heath and Branscombe 1984).

> Students are routinely asked to write book reports, dialogues, position papers, lab reports, literary criticism, term papers and other highly conventionalized genres of writing without ever having seen an example of such discourse done well, either by a peer or a professional. Thus students spend much time groping in the dark, trying to imagine or invent the conventions of an assigned genre, when the opportunity to absorb the characteristics of the form have been withheld.
>
> (Farr and Daniels 1966, p. 62)

• *Critical Thinking Exercises.* Critical thinking exercises that involve reading are also particularly suitable for advanced ESL learners. For instance, students could read two newspaper articles on the same issue, but with different viewpoints, and then take a stand on the issue in a debate or in a composition.

• *Student-Produced Reading.* A type of student-produced reading material that is appropriate for high intermediate and advanced ESL students is suggested by Graves (1983). In his approach, the classroom becomes a writing workshop where everyone, including the teacher, is engaged in reading each other's writing. In this approach, the students read each others' writing and their instructor's writing aloud so that both the teacher and the students demonstrate their own writing and writing processes, sharing draft after draft with one another. Bear in mind, however, that students from some cultures are not accustomed to the U.S. concept of writing, in which writers compose several drafts before completing their final product. (Students from Japan, Taiwan, and Korea, for example, may be accustomed to writing a finished product the first time around.) Also keep in mind that the writing your students produce may not resemble native-like writing. If students are sharing their writing with one another, they run the risk of acquiring each others' grammatically incorrect utterances. For this reason, teachers may want to ferret out the students' grammatical errors before the students read one another's essays.

Cultural Relevance. Another concern in choosing appropriate reading material for ESL students is cultural relevance. Cultural relevance is directly related to schema theory. (See discussion above.) ESL students may find a text uninteresting and difficult because it is based on unfamiliar, culturally-determined assumptions. If the reading involves cultural references the students do not understand, cultural gaps will interfere with the students' comprehension. For example, Cantoni-Harvey (1987) tells of a teacher who was reading a story to her class in the United States. In the story, two children brought their sick grandmother some beautiful chrysanthemums. When the teacher interrupted the reading to ask what would happen next, she was amazed that her French students answered that the grandmother was going to die. When the teacher suggested that the chrysanthemums might help the grandmother feel better, the students looked confused. They had been taught in France that chrysanthemums, a symbol of death used to decorate graves, should never be given as presents, especially to the elderly. Had the teacher been acquainted with traditional French culture, she would have explained that in the United States chrysanthemums are not considered an omen of death. As Cantoni-Harvey's story illustrates, students who come from different cultural backgrounds attach somewhat different meanings to words, and these differences can result in misunderstandings. While teachers cannot be expected to understand all the cultural differences that might affect their students' understanding of diverse texts, they can expect different interpretations of text resulting from cross-cultural differences and deal with these differences as they arise.

These misunderstandings arise because second language learners often lack the knowledge of cultural information they need to understand their reading materials. The more ESL readers know about the content of the material, the better they comprehend the material (Rigg 1986). In discussing the selection of culturally relevant materials, Goodman (1967) asserts that the more closely the background knowledge of the reader resembles that of the author, the easier it is for the reader to comprehend the author's ideas. The more familiar the content, the easier to recall. Thus, teachers need to become as informed as possible about the various cultures represented by their students and acknowledge and incorporate their students' cultures whenever possible.

Student Interests. A different consideration when choosing reading materials is student interests. Learners can read far beyond their current proficiency levels when reading materials that they find interesting.[7] Unfortunately, many texts (including discussions of windmills and snails) have absolutely no relevance to a student's life.

Learner needs must also be considered, including, for example, outside-of-school demands such as getting a driver's license and completing rental agreements. In the beginning levels, the reading needs to convey the so-called facts about everyday life. Students should be learning what roles people play in specific situations, what they may say in such roles, and what interpretation is made of what is said. In more advanced levels, learners need exposure "to an ever larger number of registers and genres which they are most likely to use" (Wallace 1988, p. 35).

Providing Enough Reading Materials

Once teachers have selected the appropriate reading material for their learners, they must provide their students with large quantities of it. One way for teachers to provide sufficient amounts of English reading material for students is through pleasure reading. Krashen (1985) claims that silent sustained reading of self-selected material changes students into "good readers, pretty good writers, and better spellers" (p. 176).

Students need an almost endless supply of books and other reading materials. Analyses of university programs that have been successful in promoting independent reading suggest that one of the keys is ready access to books. A book cart or book corner with materials that are written at a variety of levels for learners can be very beneficial. Since students vary widely in their likes and dislikes and there is considerable cross-cultural variation here, teachers will need to survey the students on their interests. If appropriate, depending on the interests and needs of the students, teachers might even require a certain amount of pleasure reading each week. In one university ESL program, for example, students of an advanced English proficiency level are required to read about 50 pages of pleasure reading each week. Students actually receive credit for doing enjoyable reading.

In line with this suggestion, students should be encouraged to take advantage of library materials. Many students do not have pleasure reading materials in their homes. Students who are unaccustomed to library resources may at first be confused by the amount of materials found in our libraries and may be reluctant to use them. Teachers need to show students where materials are located and how to check them out. They also need to assure students that they are welcome to use these materials.

Improving the Students' Reading Comprehension

Just giving students large quantities of reading materials does not guarantee that they will improve their reading skills. To improve their reading abilities, students must develop their comprehension skills. Most beginning ESL learners have difficulty understanding their texts because they pay attention to the literal meaning of the words rather than try to understand the overall meaning. A variety of teaching strategies can be used to improve the ESL learners' reading comprehension. Teachers need to help students guess at meanings first by using context. They can also assure students that they do not have to understand every word to understand the main idea.

Beginning ESL learners also need contextual supports to understand the authentic texts they read. For instance, pictures and diagrams can illustrate key vocabulary effectively. When selecting authentic texts for beginning students, efforts must be made to find topics that are at least partly familiar to the students. If they have already read books on the subject in their first or second language, this will increase their comprehension of the material. It is also helpful to introduce the subjects of these books first in speaking and listening activities.

Sometimes students do not have enough knowledge of the world to understand certain kinds of text and teachers must *fill them in* on what they need to know to comprehend the reading. Teachers need to focus on those concepts that are central to understanding the upcoming reading, concepts that learners either do not possess or may not think of without prompting. To this end, pre-reading activities are beneficial. Stoller (1986) suggests that reading be preceded by pre-reading activities in which the instructor:

> (1) asks students to focus on the title and any illustrations that may accompany the text; (2) asks students to skim the entire passage quickly for the main idea — this is particularly important if the title is not straightforward and/or if there are no illustrations; (3) asks students to scan the passage for specific details considered crucial for overall comprehension; and/or (4) introduces *loaded* cultural presuppositions which would otherwise mislead or confuse students, or perhaps go unnoticed. (pp. 60-61)

ESL students can read *in-depth* on a single topic to increase their comprehension. This is sometimes called *intensive* or *narrow reading*. As Carrell and Eisterhold (1983) suggest, too often reading teachers give beginning ESL students short and varied selections "which never allow students to adjust to an author's style, to become familiar with the specialized vocabulary of the topic, or to develop enough context to facilitate comprehension" (p. 227). When students read a single author or topic, the students have an easier time comprehending their texts. Getting students to read *narrowly* helps students to close the gap between their current knowledge and that assumed by the writer. When students read narrowly (reading, for example, books by the same author or several texts about the same topic), grammatical and discoursal structures repeat themselves so that students get many chances to understand the meanings of the texts they read (Krashen and Terrell 1983).

Mapping, sometimes called word-webbing or clustering, is a different way students can improve their reading comprehension. When students map, individually or in a group, they write down anything and everything they think of when they read a given passage. During this time, they make web diagrams, connecting their ideas in such a way that they display interrelationships within and across subtopics of the reading. If students are given a large poster-sized piece of butcher paper, they can write the core concept in the center, in a rectangle, and then connect details to the main concept.

Important subtopics can be circled. As a group activity, individual differences strengthen the map. As Kagan (1989) suggests, some students see more connections, some go for details, and others are main-idea people. Figure 7.3 below demonstrates this process and gives the reader an idea what a map might look like.

Figure 7.3 Semantic Mapping: Word-Mapping

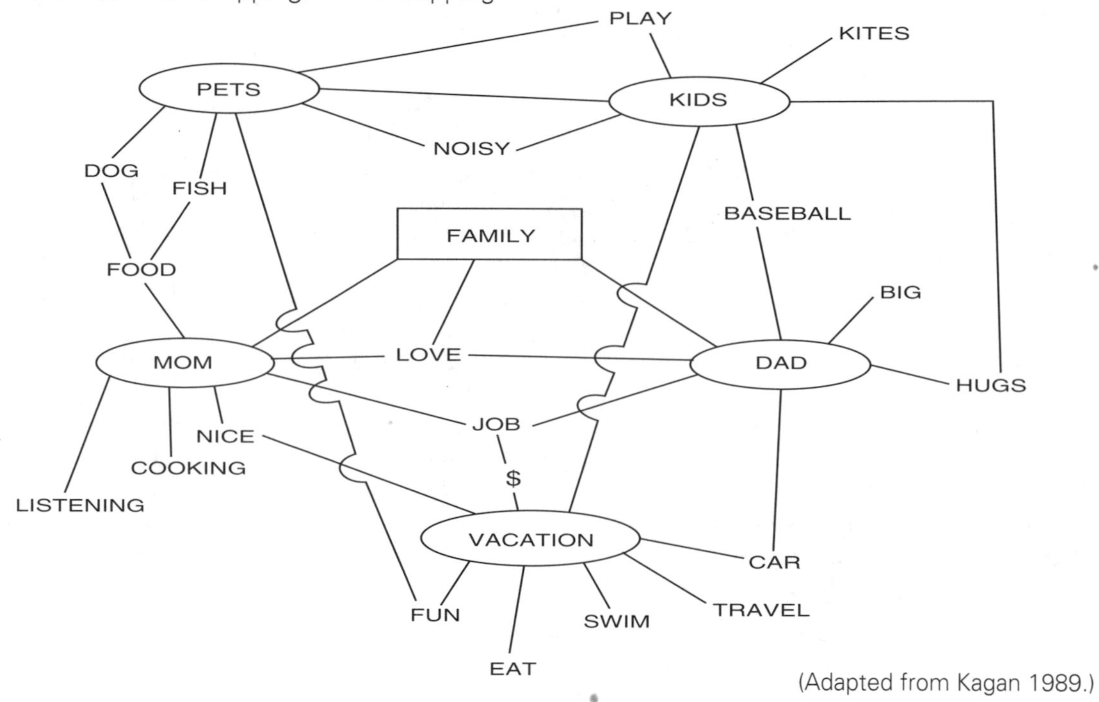

(Adapted from Kagan 1989.)

Dictionaries can also help ESL students understand their reading material.[8] However, students should be discouraged from growing dependent upon them. (If they are looking up more than one or two unknown words per page because they are unable to use contextual clues to understand these words and the words are critical in understanding text they are reading, the reading material is probably too difficult for them.)

Getting Students to Read Purposefully

Just as teachers need to help students improve their reading comprehension, so too they need to help their students to use what they have read. Retelling is one such means. Ashton-Warner, in her autobiographical books *Teacher* (1963) and *I Passed this Way* (1979), describes her experiences in a two-room school for Maori children in rural New Zealand. She used her children's own words as beginning reading texts. Instead of basal readers (which include such sentences as "See Janet, Mother. Janet can run. Janet can jump."), Ashton-Warner wrote down the words her children wanted to know. These included words such as *canoe, knife,* and *kiss.* Students then retold the stories. When the children arrived at school they told their teacher which words they wanted to learn. The words were written on two cards, one to keep at school and the other to carry around all day, take home, and learn. The next morning, the words kept at school were dumped onto the floor and the students scrambled around searching for their own word. The children then paired off to teach each other words. Eventually the words became sentences and the sentences became each other's stories.

One type of group chart can be composed after students have shared a reading. The reading can be written down in the form of a group chart that can be shared with the entire class and used in retelling exercises.

Letter writing also fosters purposeful communication. (See description above.) Students can be encouraged to write to one another, the teacher, or native English-speaking pen-pals.

Richard-Amato (1988) suggests reading activities that are particularly useful for beginning learners. After reading a number of telephone messages, students can write one another memos such as the following:

> You have a job as a receptionist. A salesman has come to sell paper products to your boss. Your boss is not in. The salesman asks you to leave a message. It should say that the salesman will be back later.
>
> You have an appointment with your professor. You must cancel it because your mother is coming to visit that day. Write a message to give to the secretary. Explain the situation. (p. 106)

Figure 7.4 contains other sample student-produced memos.

Figure 7.4 Memos

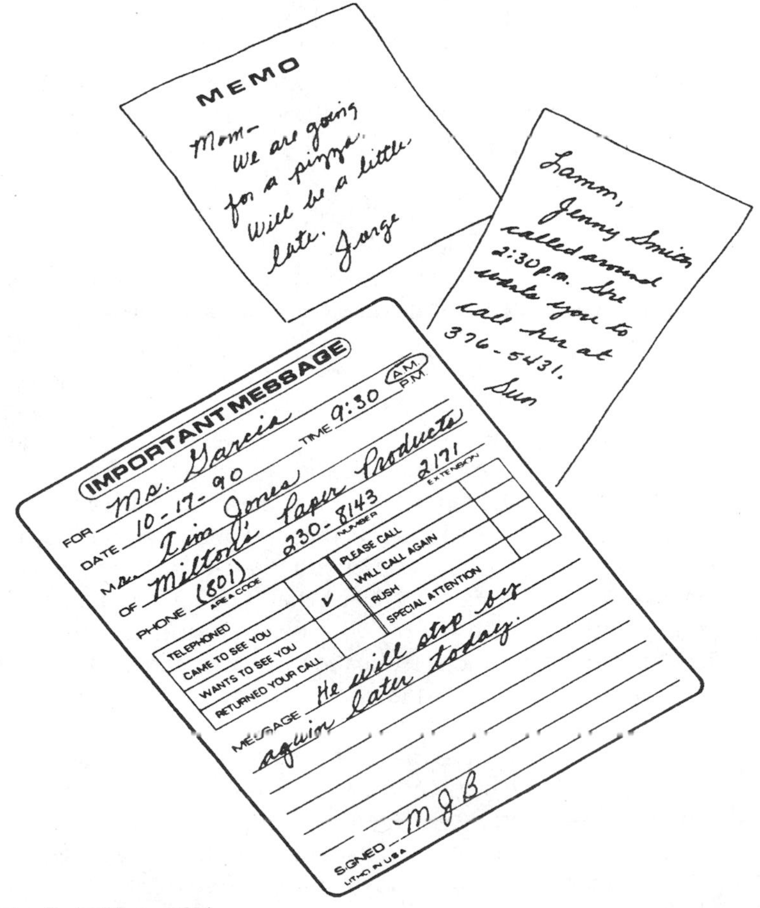

MEMO

Mom-
We are going
for a pizza.
Will be a little
late. Jorge

Lamm,
Jenny Smith
called around
2:30 p.m. She
wants you to
call her at
376-5431.
Sun

IMPORTANT MESSAGE
FOR Ms. Garcia
DATE 10-17-90 TIME 9:30 AM PM
M Tim Jones
OF Milton's Paper Products
PHONE (801) 230-8143 2171
AREA CODE NUMBER EXTENSION
TELEPHONED
CAME TO SEE YOU
WANTS TO SEE YOU
RETURNED YOUR CALL
PLEASE CALL
WILL CALL AGAIN
RUSH
SPECIAL ATTENTION
MESSAGE He will stop by aguin later today.
SIGNED MJB
LITHO IN USA

Source: Richard-Amato, P. 1988, p. 107)

A number of interesting reading activities for using local newspapers are also suggested:

1. Ask the students to find, cut out, and paste on butcher paper a sample of each of the following.
   - the price of a new Volkswagen
   - the price of a 1985 Toyota
   - a picture of a car that costs more than $15,000
   - a picture of a car produced in the United States
   - the cheapest used car
   - the most expensive sports car
   - the least expensive new car
   - a picture of a flashy car
2. Ask the students to use the want ads to look for a car they would like to own. They can discuss the cars that they like and explain why the car they have chosen fits their personal needs.

Jigsaw reading is a well-known means of getting students to guess the meanings of their reading by using contextual and content clues as well as their own background knowledge. In jigsaw reading, learners are asked to put together two or more pieces of a written text that has been divided into shorter segments. This activity can take many forms including matching headlines with stories, advertisements, or articles from which they came, matching cartoons with captions, and matching pictures, captions, and text in the correct sequence. Grellet (1981) suggests that students put an exchange of letters or telegrams in chronological order. More challenging for the students is the matching of various elements (captions, split-up text, pictures) and putting them all in the right order.[9] It is best to have students work in pairs for the more complicated jigsaw reading tasks, but they may work individually for the easier ones.

More advanced students enjoy participating in cooperative learning exercises. In one such activity, described by Kagan (1989), small groups of about four students each are formed. The teacher chooses four different thematically-related articles. Each group is given four copies of one of the short articles that the teacher has chosen. Thus, all the students have the same article. The students read the article and discuss it as a group. They then join a different group, which is composed of four students who have read four *different* articles. The students in the newly-formed groups now have the responsibility to teach the other students in the group the information contained in the articles that they read in their first groups. After this teaching session has ended, all students are quizzed. They receive two grades: one that reflects their own true score, and another that reflects the average score of their last group. When groups develop team spirit, the peer interaction that evolves from the group discussions motivates learners to read more accurately and become more involved in their reading. (See Kagan 1989 for a detailed description of cooperative learning activities.)

There are many other ways to get students to use what they have read. The students can act out a story or, after reading and explaining a story with pictures, the students can participate by pantomiming or performing the actions in the story as the book is reread another time. Students can also write book reviews that are periodically distributed to their peers. Other students can then use their peers' reviews to decide whether to read specific books (Lebauer, personal communication). In addition, students can summarize or analyze their reading in reading logs, discuss it with a partner or group, or use it in a project. They can also participate in simulations and role-play activities that require purposeful reading (Scarcella and Stern 1990).

Most importantly, students should be asked to use the reading purposefully. Lengthy comprehension checks that continue to appear in numerous texts only serve to bore students. Grellet (1981) reminds us that many texts "are meant to be read and enjoyed, that too many exercises might spoil the pleasure of reading."

Teaching Specific Skills and Strategies

Reading teachers have traditionally focused exclusively on the skills needed to develop specific strategies. Drawing on the first language research that identified the strategies used by good readers (skimming, scanning, guessing, and predicting; Munby (1978) discusses the skills associated with two strategies of reading, *intensive* and *extensive* reading. In *intensive reading,* reading functions to obtain detailed information, and students need to understand linguistic as well as semantic detail and pay close attention to the text. Omaggio (1986) describes four types of understanding necessary when teaching students to read intensively:

> (1) understanding the plain sense, or factual, exact surface meanings in the text; (2) understanding implications, which involves making inferences and being sensitive to emotional tone and figurative language; (3) understanding the relationship of ideas in the reading passage, including intersentential relationships and linkages between paragraphs; and (4) being able to relate the reading material to one's own knowledge and experience. (p. 150)

There are many creative exercises that can be developed to aid readers in comprehending text at these various levels. For instance, to help readers understand implications and relationships, the teacher can guide students in matching passages of text and diagrams, labelling parts of the text, or using the information to discover solutions to problems. (See Grellet 1981 for further suggestions.)

In *extensive reading,* students do not need to understand all the details of the text. Instead, speed and skill in getting the overall gist of the text are important. Krashen and Terrell (1983) suggest that one example of extensive reading is *pleasure reading.* Phillips (1983) also suggests that understanding the author's intent, getting the main ideas, and reacting to the material personally are also goals when reading extensively. Grellet (1981) identifies *skimming* (or quickly running one's eyes over the text to get the gist as in extensive reading) and *scanning* (or quickly searching for some particular piece of information in the text). Clearly, the various functions of reading are not mutually exclusive and may be done in succession when approaching a given text. Good readers in both a first and second language use a wide variety of reading strategies to adjust to the material they read (Heath 1982). In Dubin and Olshtain's (1986) words: ". . . good readers quickly and possibly unconsciously fit their attack skills to their personal objectives for reading and to particular styles of writing" (p. 148).

ESL reading teachers need to design activities that develop all of the strategies needed to read a variety of texts effectively. While some adult learners are capable of developing effective reading strategies just by increasing the amount they read, others are not.

Oxford (1990) provides a detailed description of the types of instruction teachers can use to develop strategies that enhance reading skills. Her research suggests that incorporating strategy training sessions into regular communicative classroom activities is more beneficial to students than teaching strategies as a separate entity, disconnected from ongoing classroom activities. (See also Cohen 1990.)

The *Interviewer Guide* developed by Hosenfeld and her colleagues (Hosenfeld et al. 1981) is valuable for assessing reading strategies. (See Appendix 7.1, page 116.) Originally this guide was used for preliminary diagnosis of strategies before training, and then to assess changes in strategy use after training. When using this guide, a student performs a language task and thinks aloud, describing what he or she is doing to accomplish the task. As the learner does this think-aloud task, the teacher notes the learner's general behavior.

Hosenfeld's (1979) earlier research showed that successful second language learners vary the strategies they use according to such variables as the genre (folk story, advertisement, poetry, or report), their familiarity with the topic (or subject matter), and the demands of the reading activity. This suggests that teachers need to help learners develop flexibility in the strategies they choose.

THE TAPESTRY APPROACH TO READING INSTRUCTION AND TRADITIONAL APPROACHES

As seen below, the Tapestry Approach to reading instruction contrasts sharply with traditional approaches. The Tapestry Approach is based on the literature on first and second reading development as well as the experience of ESL reading instructors. Students read extensively and intensively for specific reasons. Considerable emphasis is placed on pleasure reading. Skill development and strategy training are important, though not central, components of the Tapestry reading class. In this approach, meaning is the focus of instruction and reading is integrated with the other language skills.

Comparison of the Tapestry Approach to Reading and Traditional Approaches

The Tapestry Approach	Traditional Approaches
• Meaning is central.	• Form is central. It is important for students to understand the sentence structures and rhetorical devices that occur in the reading.
• Students read both intensively and extensively. However, the primary emphasis is on extensive reading.	• Students read intensively.
• Students are actively guided (by the teacher) to integrate information from the text with their own knowledge. Information from the text and the knowledge possessed by the reader act together to produce meaning.	• Students are not actively guided (by the teacher) to integrate information from the text with their own knowledge.
• Reading flexibility is encouraged. How students read depends on the complexity of the text, their familiarity with the topic, and their purpose for reading. Students are taught a variety of learning strategies that improve their reading.	• Students are encouraged to read in one way regardless of the complexity of the text, their familiarity with the topic, and their purpose for reading. Teachers do not teach learning strategies.
• Teachers treat phonics as helpful, but just one component of reading development.	• Considerable emphasis is placed on phonics.
• Students read in situations where written language serves real functions — such as to entertain (as in novels), to inform (as in manuals), and to direct (as on traffic signals).	• Students do not read material that serves real functions.

TAPESTRY PRINCIPLES CONCERNING READING

The discussion above leads to the following principles for ESL reading instruction.

PRINCIPLES

1. Reading is an enjoyable experience for learners.
2. When selecting materials, experienced teachers are sensitive to the learner's second language reading ability, cultural background, interests, needs, and goals.
3. Through reading extensively, students learn to read communicatively: the more, the better.
4. Skill and strategy instruction enhances reading development and is integrated throughout the lessons.
5. Effective reading instruction is content-oriented and involves authentic materials and situations. Meaning is the focus of effective reading instruction.

CONCLUSION

This chapter has considered ways of developing the ESL learners' reading skills. We have seen that Tapestry teachers vary the reading instruction that they provide students in order to shape their instruction to the particular needs of their students. In Chapter Eight, we will describe ways in which teachers can improve the writing instruction ESL students receive.

ACTIVITIES AND DISCUSSION QUESTIONS

1. What specific exercises can the ESL reading teacher use to help students to build the background knowledge needed to understand their reading material?
2. What are the advantages and disadvantages of using authentic text? In what specific situations would you adapt such text?
3. How can you best determine whether your students understand the reading material you give them?
4. What factors determine the difficulty level of a given text?
5. What specific reading strategies improve the learner's ability to understand the text? Before answering this question, it may be helpful to consider some of these strategies: skimming, scanning, writing key elements in the text, summarizing paragraphs in the margin, using the glossary, relying on schemata to predict forthcoming text, identifying people in the text and their perspectives and actions, relying on summaries given in text, conducting ongoing self-evaluation of reading progress, guessing the meaning of new words from the context, using the illustrations to guess forthcoming text, analyzing the organization of the text.
6. How can teachers encourage students to read outside of class?

NOTES

1. Here, we define reading as the ability to make sense of written or printed symbols and use this information to construct a feasible interpretation).
2. Also, students of some cultures may not be accustomed to reading as much as is often done in the United States. Accessing, using, and critiquing massive amounts of information require a major financial investment and openness to alternative interpretations that are not available in many parts of the world (Kaplan 1983, Grabe and Kaplan 1989). As Grabe (1988) explains, ". . .few countries in the world can offer all those necessary, if not sufficient, criteria for the use of information as is the case in the U.S., Europe and Japan" (p. 31).
3. Authenticity should be defined not only in terms of the actual words but also in terms of the form in which it is presented. Omaggio (1986), for example, states: "A newspaper article, for example, should be presented to students exactly as it appeared in the paper with the same typeface, the same space for headlines, the same accompanying photographs or graphics, etc. Such factors constitute nonlinguistic cues to meaning and should be retained to make the reading task easier" (p. 152).
4. Note, however, that there are many problems associated with simplifying texts. Teachers need to be alerted that their efforts to simplify might in fact make the text more difficult, since it can remove the natural redundancy and make the rhetorical organization difficult for students to predict.
5. Wallace (1988) observes that, in good stories, something must happen, something funny, something exciting or frightening, and there must always be a climax. She provides excellent advice for writing narratives.
6. Coady (1979), for example, states:

   > The subject of reading materials should be of high interest and relate well to the background of the reader, since strong semantic input can help compensate when syntactic control is weak. The interest and background knowledge will enable the student to comprehend at a reasonable rate and keep him [or her] involved in the material in spite of its syntactic difficulty. (p. 12)

7. Note, however, that first year college and high school textbooks, often contain graphic information and familiar concepts that aid the intermediate learner's comprehension of the material.
8. In general, English dictionaries tend to be more helpful than bilingual ones.
9. Note, however, that some texts (such as many ads) do not have a particular order. However, most texts do have an order based on meaning.

SUGGESTED READINGS

• Barnett, M.A. 1989. *More than Meets the Eye: Foreign Language Learner Reading: Theory and Practice.* Englewood Cliffs, NJ: Prentice Hall Regents and Center for Applied Linguistics. This volume reviews first language theory and research and their relevance to second language reading theory. The volume presents various models including bottom-up and top-down ones, as well as interactive ones and various combinations. In addition, it examines schema theory and reading within the ACTFL proficiency movement. The final part discusses techniques for teaching reading and presents a sample reading lesson that is consistent with current research and theory.

• Carrell, P., Devine, J., and Eskey, D. (eds.). 1988. *Interactive Approaches to Second Language Reading.* Cambridge: Cambridge University Press. This edited collection, growing out of the Colloquium on Research in Reading in a Second Language at the TESOL Convention, focuses on an interactive perspective to reading. It provides empirical, theoretical, and pedagogical support for the notion that reading in a second language is an interactive process, involving the reader's own background and knowledge and the text. Several models of reading are presented. In addition, the volume suggests applications to classroom instruction.

• Dubin, F., Eskey, D.E., and Grabe, W. (eds.). 1986. *Teaching Second Language Reading for Academic Purposes.* Reading, MA: Addison-Wesley. This useful collection by eight reading specialists focuses on reading instruction that helps ESL learners advance academically. The first two chapters provide the theoretical framework for the pedagogical chapters that follow. Later chapters provide detailed descriptions of specific reading courses at different levels and for different purposes. The final chapters examine issues of concern to teachers in academic programs. These issues include the selection of appropriate texts, student assessment, and the application of computer technology.

• Grellet, F. 1981. *Developing Reading Skills: A Practical Guide to Reading Comprehension Exercises.* Cambridge: Cambridge University Press. This handbook provides language teachers with many practical suggestions for developing their own reading materials. It classifies and describes various reading activities designed to develop different reading skills. The book helps teachers to introduce variety into their reading classes and to involve the students actively in reading exercises.

• Arens, K.M., Byrnes, H., and Swaffar, J. 1991. *Reading for Meaning: An Integrated Approach to Language Learning.* Englewood Cliffs: NJ: Prentice Hall. Although primarily intended for foreign language instructors, this volume presents a model for the implementation of interactive reading that will be of interest to all language teachers. It provides a useful summary of reading research, suggests ways to integrate reading skills, includes ideas for the diagnostic testing of reading comprehension, and provides many examples of effective reading techniques and strategies.

APPENDIX 7.1

Interviewer Guide for Reading Strategies

Student's Name ____________________

General reading behavior (*Circle one.*)

Rarely translates; guesses contextually	Translates; guesses noncontextually
Translates; guesses contextually	Translates; rarely guesses

Strategies
(Circle the number of the strategies mentioned.)

	Comments
1. Keeps meaning in mind.	____________________
2. Skips unknown words (guesses contextually).	____________________
3. Uses context in preceding and succeeding sentences and paragraphs.	____________________
4. Identifies grammatical category of words.	____________________
5. Evaluates guesses.	____________________
6. Reads title (makes inferences).	____________________
7. Continues if unsuccessful.	____________________
8. Recognizes cognates.	____________________
9. Uses knowledge of the world.	____________________
10. Analyzes unknown words.	____________________
11. Reads as though he or she expects the text to have meaning.	____________________
12. Reads to identify meaning rather than words.	____________________
13. Takes chances in order to identify meaning.	____________________
14. Uses illustrations.	____________________
15. Uses side-gloss.	____________________
16. Uses glossary as last resort.	____________________
17. Looks up words correctly.	____________________
18. Skips unnecessary words.	____________________
19. Follows through with proposed solutions.	____________________
20. Uses a variety of types of context clues.	____________________

(Adapted from Hosenfeld et al. 1981.)

WRITING

8

PREVIEW QUESTIONS

1. Why do some groups of ESL learners seem to enjoy writing more than others?
2. How can teachers make writing enjoyable for all ESL students?
3. What are the components of second language writing proficiency?
4. What facilitates second language writing development?
5. What specific types of writing do ESL students need to use in academic settings?

This chapter focuses on writing, another essential strand in our tapestry design. This strand is tightly interwoven with three other strands, represented in our tapestry motif by reading, listening, and speaking.

Students in ESL programs quickly discover that their survival in academic settings depends on their ability to write well. This is because writing serves a gate-keeping function in universities in the United States. Professors evaluate students on the basis of their written work; those students who acquire strong writing skills usually advance academically, whereas those students who do not acquire these skills advance more slowly.

ORGANIZATION OF THIS CHAPTER

In this chapter, we discuss components of writing proficiency, factors affecting ESL writing development, and traditional approaches to writing instruction. We then describe the Tapestry Approach to writing, an approach consistent with recent research. We end with a summary of Tapestry principles for writing development.

COMPONENTS OF WRITING PROFICIENCY

Effective writers have command of English grammar, spelling conventions, punctuation, and rhetoric. In short, they are proficient in the components of communicative competence outlined by Canale and Swain (1980). (See also Chapter Five.) Figure 8.1 summarizes these components.

Figure 8.1 Abilities underlying writing proficiency

Grammatical Competence
Grammar — morphology and syntax, including rules for subject/verb agreement, reference, etc.
Vocabulary
Mechanics — handwriting, spelling, punctuation

Strategic Competence
The writing process — getting ideas, getting started, writing drafts, revising

WRITING PROFICIENCY

Sociolinguistic Competence
Rules and principles that enable writers to vary their writing according to such factors as the purpose, topic, and audience; includes control of various genres, knowledge of different discourse communities

Discourse Competence
Cohesion
Coherence

Grammatical Competence

As shown in this figure, *grammatical competence* is an important component of writing proficiency. It involves becoming competent in using the grammar, vocabulary, and mechanics of the language. Without grammatical competence, writers generally fail to express their ideas in academic contexts. In such contexts, knowledge of grammar is greatly valued and writers are negatively stereotyped on the basis of the grammatical errors they make. A professor who reads an essay beginning *The Roman Empire collapse for many reason* might judge the student who wrote the essay as an incompetent, illogical thinker.

Sociolinguistic Competence

Added to grammatical competence, skilled writers have developed *sociolinguistic competence*. This type of competence enables them to vary their use of the language with respect to a number of variables, including the topic, the genre, the audience, and the purpose. In this way, the learner is able to write for diverse discourse communities, communities that appreciate widely varying texts. In addition, sociolinguistic competence enables writers to maintain their credibility with these discourse communities. This might mean establishing themselves as authorities in the academic community by using references; or it might mean conveying friendliness to peers by using inclusive *we* (the *we* that includes both the writer and the addressee).

Discourse Competence

In addition to mastering grammatical and sociolinguistic competence, good writers develop *discourse competence,* which enables them to organize their texts cohesively and coherently. (See also Chapter Five.)

Halliday and Hasan (1976) analyzed five linguistic devices that writers use to compose cohesively. These devices indicate "a semantic relation between an element in a text and some other element that is crucial to the interpretation of it" (p. 8). They are: reference, substitution, ellipsis, conjunction, and lexical cohesion. Examples follow.

Example 8.1

- **reference**

  Three blind mice, three blind mice. See how *they* run.
  (The *they* refers not to just any mice, but to three particular blind mice.)

Example 8.2

- **substitution**

  Slowly, James moved the tables away from the door. He moved only the large *ones* that were blocking the doorway.
  (*Ones* is a pronoun substitute for the word *table.)*

Example 8.3

- **ellipsis**

  Huck Finn had eaten most of the *sandwiches*. There were only three *(sandwiches)* left.
  (The word *sandwiches* is deleted in the second sentence.)

Example 8.4

- **conjunction**

  He was a good worker. *Therefore,* he was given a raise.
  (The second sentence is tied to the first by means of the word *therefore.)*

Example 8.5

- **lexical cohesion**

  James gave Michael a present. It was the perfect *present*.
  (The word *present* in the first sentence is repeated in the second.)

The task of the second language learner is to acquire the appropriate uses of these devices. In James' (1980) words, "while every language has at its disposal a set of devices for maintaining textual cohesion, different languages have preference for certain of these devices and neglect others" (p. 104). For instance, lexical cohesion is more prevalent in Korean writing, since Koreans do not normally use pronoun reference in their writing. The example below is illustrative. It comes from a Korean university student who is enrolled in an intermediate level ESL course at the University of California.

Example 8.6

On October 26, 1979, President Park was assassinated. The dictator was killed by one of the cabinet members. The late President Park gained power on May 1961 and continued powerful until President Park was killed.

In this example, the ESL student uses the synonym *dictator* and repeats the noun phrase *President Park* where native English speakers would prefer to use the pronoun *he*. It would appear that the student is using lexical cohesion in English much as he does in Korean.

Appropriate use of these cohesive devices contribute to the overall *coherence* of a text. Following Charrolles (1978), we use the term *coherence* to refer to the unity and organization of ideas within a text. Canale (1982) provides an excellent description of the conditions of coherence:

Development: Presentation of ideas must be orderly and convey a sense of direction.

Continuity: There must be consistency of facts, opinions, and writer perspective, as well as reference to previously mentioned ideas. Newly introduced ideas must be relevant.

Balance: A relative emphasis (main or supportive) must be accorded each idea.

Completeness: The ideas presented must provide a sufficiently thorough discourse.

Strategic Competence

In addition to the three other competence elements, skilled writers also have *strategic competence*, which enables them to use strategies to stretch their competence to write effectively. For example, writers may brainstorm to get their ideas together before composing or rely on their friends for help in ferreting out the mechanical errors that they make. They select those strategies that best fit the particular texts they are composing. For instance, they sometimes follow a writing process that calls for them to brainstorm, draft, compose, revise, and edit (for instance, when they are writing expository essays). At other times they follow a writing process that simply calls for them to write (for example, when making lists). Note that here we are expanding Canale and Swain's (1980) notion of strategic competence. In our view, this type of competence is a means of stretching the students' ability to write well, not just a means of overcoming limitations in language competence.

Interactions among Competencies

All four of these competencies — grammatical, sociolinguistic, discourse, and strategic — interact to produce good writing. Writers sometimes develop one area of competence to a greater extent than others. They might also develop the competence to compose one type of genre (such as laboratory reports) effectively, but not the proficiency to write another (such as expository essays). Similarly, they might develop the competence to write effective texts for some audiences and some topics, but not for other audiences and other topics.

FACTORS AFFECTING ESL WRITING DEVELOPMENT

Having considered the competencies that enable writers to compose effectively in English, we now discuss research pertaining to the development of these competencies in a second language. This research concerns: needs and objectives, motivation, authenticity, cultural and linguistic expectations, background knowledge, skill integration, reading as input for writing, and writing practice.

Needs and Objectives

Scholarly inquiry suggests that ESL writing development is enhanced when instruction is explicitly designed to address student needs and objectives. Some students will need to write *personal genres* — including notes, telegrams, postcards, diaries, and informal letters — while others will need to write *institutional genres* — including advertisements, business letters, instructions, forms, summaries, reports, and essays (White 1981). Not only will students need to write different genres for different instructional and personal learning *objectives*, but they will also need to write different genres for different *functions*. For instance, they will need to write to explain, convince, or describe.

Considerable research has examined the writing demands placed on ESL learners in university settings. This research suggests that writing instruction should emphasize expressive and personal writing. Spack and Sadow (1983), for instance, argue that although personal writing (such as narratives and descriptions) is less cognitively demanding than academic expository writing, personal writing should remain an integral part of the ESL class since it satisfies intellectual and developmental needs, helps students to generate ideas, and provides students with a transition to academic expository writing. (See Hamp-Lyons 1986 for a similar view.) However, there are political, motivational, and academic reasons for introducing all ESL students to some academic writing. Administrators and professors sometimes view classes that solely teach narrative and personal writing as *fluff* — unworthy of funding. Swales (1987) also suggests that students both need and want to know how to write academic research papers. (For similar views, see Johns 1986 and Reid 1989.)

The individual differences discussed in Chapter Four clearly affect writing development. Within ESL programs, distinct learner populations exist, each with different interests and motivations. There are often graduate and undergraduate students, older and younger students, students majoring in diverse fields — including business, computer science, and engineering. The varying writing needs of these groups must be addressed.

Motivation

Closely related to learners' needs and objectives is motivation. Successful ESL writers have positive attitudes about writing. They do not feel overly anxious about it. Gungle and Taylor (1989) remind us that writers' anxiety can directly interfere with the development of ESL writing skills. Students with a high level of writing apprehension "avoid writing when possible and when forced to write do so with great anxiety. . . These students often fail to attend class when writing is required and seldom voluntarily enroll in classes where writing will be required" (p. 236).

Choice is a critical component of writing. When students are allowed to choose the topics they write about, they elaborate their ideas, clarify their thoughts, and revise their texts. In discussing motivation, Hughey, Wormuth, Hartfiel, and Jacobs (1983) urge teachers to satisfy their students' need to feel that their efforts to write are worthwhile. For these ESL writing experts, "the successful teacher looks for something good in each piece of student writing, compliments the student for success, and aids the student in meeting further learning needs" (p. 49).

Authenticity

Using writing purposefully to convey authentic messages to real audiences also facilitates writing development. In Chaudron's (1983) and Mittan's (1989) studies, for instance, university ESL students who wrote to convey authentic messages to real audiences (peers) significantly improved their essays. When the students wrote for real audiences, they became so engrossed in communicating that they focused on the content and organization of their essays as well as the linguistic forms.

Cultural and Linguistic Experiences

Research has also demonstrated that writing practices are often tied to specific sets of beliefs and values of particular cultural groups (Gee 1986, Ochs 1983, Heath 1982, Street 1984). Students from different cultures have a wide variety of preferences in choosing and elaborating on topics and in organizing and developing their writing. Moreover, they hold different expectations of audience (Hinds 1987). As McKay (1989) explains, "the topics students choose to write about, the ways they develop these topics, the kinds of information they include, the ways they organize the information and the kinds of inferences they leave for the reader to make are all related to their own rich cultural experiences" (p. 251).

A number of linguists have provided evidence that specific rhetorical structures may be shaped by one's cultural experience. (For recent collections on contrastive rhetoric, see Connor and Kaplan 1987, Kaplan 1983, Purves 1988; see also Ricento 1987.) Others, however, argue that one's cultural background does not affect one's rhetorical organization in a second language (Mohan and Li 1985).

We suggest here that one's cultural background does affect one's rhetorical organization in a second language, but that cultural background interacts with other variables—such as age, second language proficiency, degree of acculturation, and the ability to write in one's first language. Clearly, the effect of one's cultural background on one's ability to write in a second language diminishes as one acculturates to the United States.

Not only might one's culture affect writing production, one's writing ability in the first language might also affect writing development. Jones and Tetroe (1987) examined the claim that ESL writing is similar to native language writing. These researchers used think-aloud protocols with university students. They found that ESL students (native Spanish speakers) tended to use the same strategies in both their first and second languages—regardless of their proficiency levels in English. Canale, Frennete, and Belanger (1988) found a significant relationship between native writing ability and second language writing ability of French-English bilingual high school students. They conclude that the more capable the writer is in the first language, the more capable the writer is in the second. (See also Cummins 1989.)[1]

Background Knowledge

Just as one's cultural and linguistic background affects one's writing, so too does one's background knowledge. Indeed, the primary reason some ESL students succeed in developing writing skills may lie in their conceptual knowledge. Successful ESL students have, in addition to grammatical competence and other skills, sufficient background information (McKay 1989). In those areas in which ESL students have limited knowledge, they need new experiences to build their knowledge.

Integration of the Four Skills

Along very different lines, researchers have argued that integrating the four language skills — reading, writing, speaking, and listening — leads to improved ESL writing ability. They have pointed out that there are particularly important connections between speaking, and writing, and that these two modes of communication must be integrated in college classrooms (Mangelsdorf 1989).

Researchers have also demonstrated that reading is essential for ESL writing development. In fact, a number of linguists consider reading (written at an appropriate English proficiency level) a key source for the acquisition of writing proficiency. (See, for example, Krashen 1982.) ESL reading specialists are also emphasizing the importance of a reading/writing connection. (See, for instance, Carrell, Devine, and Eskey 1988.) They argue that students need to have an opportunity to acquire grammar, vocabulary, and discourse through reading.

However, while the research indicates that reading can lead to improved writing skills, there is no evidence that this improvement is automatic. (Refer to Eisterhold 1991 for an excellent review of the research.) To improve their writing ability, students must *do* something with the reading. As Hughey, Wormuth, Hartfiel, and Jacobs (1983) suggest: "Being a good reader does not make one a good writer. Reading serves to give the writer ideas, data, model sentence patterns, and structures, but a student will be able to become a good writer only by writing" (p. 49).

Writing Practice

Not surprisingly, the more experience students have writing about specific topics in particular genres and contexts, the more confidence they gain and the more fluent their writing becomes. Students who are unable to write particular types of texts very often simply lack experience writing them.[2]

TRADITIONAL APPROACHES TO WRITING INSTRUCTION

In traditional approaches to writing instruction, language-focused activities rather than learner-focused activities are central. Teachers emphasize grammatical correctness and rhetorical models (such as comparison/contrast). Correct sentence structure is an essential component of the traditional approaches, and grammatical skills receive considerable emphasis. Errors in writing are avoided by providing learners with models to follow or by guiding and controlling what learners write to prevent them from making errors. Examples of traditional writing activities include:

> - providing models to which learners make minor changes and substitutions
> - expanding an outline or summary
> - constructing paragraphs from frames, tables, and other guides
> - producing a text through answering a set of questions
> - sentence combining: developing complex sentences following different rules of combination.
>
> (Richards 1990, p. 107)

THE TAPESTRY APPROACH TO WRITING INSTRUCTION

The characteristics of the Tapestry Approach and traditional approaches are summarized below.

Comparison of the Tapestry Approach to Writing and Traditional Approaches

The Tapestry Approach	Traditional Approaches
• Students discover effective writing techniques and strategies with the guidance of the teacher.	• The teacher imparts knowledge of writing.
• Writing is viewed as a collaborative, social process. Students assist one another in composing texts.	• Students work alone.
• Writing topics are student-controlled.	• Writing topics are teacher-controlled.
• Writing shapes and refines thought. Students create meaning through writing.	• Ideas are formulated before the students write. Writing is the act of transferring ideas to paper. Students do not create meaning.
• Students write for real audiences.	• Students do not write for real audiences.
• Errors are considered natural and are corrected in the final stages of the writing process.	• Students are discouraged from making errors.
• Grammar is taught in the context of writing for communication.	• Grammar is taught in isolation.
• Feedback is given throughout the writing process.	• Feedback is given when the writing is finished.
• Students are evaluated on the basis of the quality of their total writing process.	• Students are evaluated on the basis of their finished texts only.

Much empirical study supports the Tapestry Approach to writing rather than traditional approaches. The Tapestry Approach is designed to motivate learners. As Gungle and Taylor (1989) point out, the messages the students convey receive primary consideration and the students learn to improve their essays gradually over a series of revisions. Gungle and Taylor argue that this offers instructors more opportunities to provide students with positive feedback, which in turn motivates students. Further, the process approach provides students with numerous opportunities to write; students often compose several drafts. In addition, it integrates the four language skills — reading, writing, speaking, and listening — since students are encouraged to read to obtain additional information about their writing topics and interact with peers in group and conference situations. Added to all this, the process approach draws on the students' background knowledge and rich cultural experiences because students have considerable control over their writing.

As shown, the Tapestry Approach is chiefly a process approach, but not totally. In the Tapestry writing classroom, the emphasis is on learner-centered activities in which students assume control over what they write and how they write it (Zamel 1987). Writing is a way of discovering meaning, since it refines thought and empowers students by enabling them to affect their readers. In this approach, meaning is central and form develops from meaning. Writing specialists have long argued that teachers must focus on the writing *process* rather than the writing *product*. They point out that writing is a complex process that leads to the discovery and clarification of meaning. As Flower and Hayes (1977) succinctly put it, "A writer's normal task is a thinking task" (p. 457).

Because the Tapestry Approach is process-oriented, it gives students needed practice in all stages of the writing process, including: pre-writing, writing (or drafting), and revising. Pre-writing involves finding a topic, finding out about the topic, and thinking about it in such a way that ideas are generated, shaped, refined, and organized. In addition, pre-writing includes considering the audience and the purpose of the writing task. Drafting entails writing the words down that express the ideas. In revising, writers rewrite what they have written and delete, substitute, add, and reorganize. What follows are typical Tapestry activities for each of the so-called *stages* of the writing process.

Pre-Writing: Idea-Gathering

In the pre-writing stage, students need multiple opportunities to generate ideas.

Journals. Journals can be an important source of ideas. In these journals, students react to class activities as well as elaborate on their own ideas and perspectives. The writing is functional in that the learners write for their own enjoyment without the pressure of grades. Journals can be content-oriented, oriented toward a particular writing assignment, or personal. Dialog journals in which learners exchange their ideas with their instructor provide a means of making idea-gathering a more interactive process. In these journals, the students write anything they want. The teacher responds with comments — "not in a threatening, red-ink, corrective mode but in a supportive, nonjudgmental, idea-evoking way" (Oxford, 1990, p. 78). Thus, the students receive the teacher's responses to their ideas prior to writing their compositions. (For an excellent description of dialog journal writing, refer to Peyton 1990, and Peyton and Reed 1990.)

Brainstorming. In brainstorming, students spontaneously generate and expand on ideas pertaining to a particular subject. "The rapid exchange allows for exploration, clarification, interpretation, explanation, and insight into different opinions. Since brainstorming is a sharing of ideas, it helps students develop an awareness of other points of view in an uncritical setting, as well as an awareness of their own personal points of view" (Hughey, Wormuth, Hartfiel, and Jacobs 1983, p. 79). Teachers can choose facilitators or moderators to ensure the free flow of ideas and to keep the ideas on-track, devote an entire class period to brainstorming, establish the topic to be discussed, require all students to participate, encourage students to take notes during the session, and make clear the uncritical nature of the session.

Clustering or Word Mapping. Working individually or in small groups, the students write a topic in the middle of a page and organize related words in clusters around the central concept. (See Chapter Seven.) Clustering helps students to pinpoint and organize main ideas and to understand where supporting details are needed.

Cubing. Cubing has been successfully used in ESL classes as a quick means of helping students identify a writing focus. Students write about all six sides of the cube. They spend about five minutes on each side. The sides are:

1. Describe —by using one's senses to examine color, size, shape; to feel; to smell; to touch; to hear.
2. Compare —what it is like or unlike.
3. Associate —it with whatever it brings to mind, similar or dissimilar.
4. Analyze —how it is composed, what it is part of, what is part of it.
5. Apply —it in whatever way it can be used or done.
6. Argue —for it or argue against it, and give reasons for taking that position.

(Adapted from Hughey, Wormuth, Hartfiel, and Jacobs 1983, p. 81.)

Strategic Questioning. Richards (1990) suggests that students examine a set of questions to guide their writing. The questions might be: *What do you really want to write about? What is your primary objective? What do your know about your topic? What do you still need to find out? What interests or surprises you about the topic? What ideas seem to fit together? Who might be interested in reading what you are going to write?*

Quickwriting. In quickwriting, the students get as many of their ideas on paper in a specific time (such as ten minutes) without worrying about the form their writing takes. The advantage of this activity is that learners are forced to write without editing so that they are free to discover their own ideas, thoughts, and feelings.

Pre-Writing: Information-Gathering

Students need possibilities for information-gathering during the pre-writing stage.

Writing Modules. A writing module is a unit that includes many related readings and exercises pertaining to a single, general subject of interest to students. Modules can provide students with valuable background information. Reactions to the modules either in discussions or quickwrites can help the students gather their ideas. Teachers and students can choose which modules to use and, within the module, which readings and exercises to use. This allows for great flexibility in adapting the writing class to the specific interests of the students. (Refer to Lebauer and Scarcella 1992.)

Interviews. Interviews enable students to gain valuable information from others. Usually, they involve talking with and/or questioning someone to discover that person's knowledge of and perspectives about a given subject or problem. Hughey, Wormuth, Hartfiel, and Jacobs (1983) suggest the following procedures: (1) analyze the problem/subject to determine what information is probably needed, (2) decide whom to interview, (3) write questions for the interview, (4) contact the interviewees to set up an appointment, (5) conduct the interview, (6) take notes on the responses to the interview questions, (6) synthesize the information, and (7) decide what information is significant and what is irrelevant to the subject/problem.

Dialogs. In dialogs or unstructured conversations, students share their ideas about a given topic. This activity gives students an opportunity to try out new ideas. During dialogs, teachers encourage students to use such expressions as: *I think. . .; I believe. . .;* and *In my opinion. . .*. These dialogs work well in small groups to help students anticipate audience response. Students can structure the task and establish the subject. Teachers can assure a relaxed atmosphere, set time limits, and encourage all participants to engage freely, sharing their views with other members of the class.

Writing (Drafting)

Once students have gathered their ideas, they need to write them down. They are given practical strategies and guidelines for shaping their ideas, but they are not given *cookie-cutter rhetorical forms. Rather, they are encouraged to focus on what they are trying to say.* Suggested activities for this phase of the writing process include:

Component Writing. The students are asked to write the various components of their texts within a certain time (such as ten minutes, each part). This forces the students to get their ideas onto the page without worrying about accurate use of the language.

One-Sitting Writing. The students are encouraged to write their entire texts (beginning to end) in one sitting. They are told to concentrate on getting their meaning across, not language form.

Leisurely Writing. Students are asked to begin a text in the class and finish it in their leisure at home.

Revision

In the revision stage, writers reconsider the content and organization of their writing and make whatever revisions that they feel appropriate. Sample activities follow.

Peer Reviews. In peer reviews, students read and comment on each others' writing. These reviews offer students reactions from real readers who provide multiple, often mutually reinforcing, perspectives. Such reviews help student writers develop audience awareness. The following procedure is recommended:

1. Students read their peers' writing and respond to it using a peer review sheet, a questionnaire that focuses the reviewer's attention on specific areas of the author's text.
2. Students meet to exchange comments on their writing, further elaborating on their written peer review sheets.
3. The writers respond in writing to the peer review sheets, using a specially prepared response sheet. They express their agreement and/or disagreement with their peers and outline the specific changes they intend to make on the next version of their texts.
4. The teacher reads and responds to each student's writing, peer review sheet, and response sheet. (Refer to Appendix 8.1 for sample peer review and response sheets. See also Mittan 1989, and Lebauer and Scarcella 1992.)

Questions for Revising. In these activities, students are given a set of questions that guide their revision. For example, they may be asked: *In composing your draft, what was the biggest problem that you experienced? What changes do you intend to make? List three important details in your paper. If you had something to add to this paper, what would it be?*

Editing

In the editing phase of the writing process, students are directed to review their writing and find grammatical inaccuracies. Sample activities are described below:

Error Corrections. The teachers read and mark errors with symbols. These symbols draw the students' attention to certain mechanical errors (for instance, VT = verb tense error, WO = wrong order). The teachers limit the number of errors they correct according to their students' proficiency levels and needs. Students then make corrections on their own. As an alternative, teachers mark an X in the margin of those lines containing major errors. Students then find the errors and correct them. This latter type of activity is for those students who have the proficiency needed to identify and correct errors without the benefit of correcting symbols.

Checklists. Students are given checklists of grammatical structures and typical errors. They are asked to analyze their own essays for grammatical difficulties. When students are able to identify their errors, they are more capable of correcting them.

Rewriting Exercises. Students rewrite ungrammatical statements made by their classmates, typed by their teacher, and distributed to the class (Richards 1990).

Non-Linear Process

However, the Tapestry Approach does not focus on these stages indiscriminately. Tapestry teachers emphasize that competent writers do not strictly follow these stages. This is because research into the composing processes of native writers has revealed that many writers do not follow the various stages outlined above (rewriting, writing, revising, and editing). (See, for example, Murray 1978 and Perl 1979.) Writers do not have a linear writing process. Rather, the process of writing is non-linear — a constant interaction among idea generation, rhetorical and lexical shaping, and mechanical revision. It is a messy process for most writers — not the straightforward plan-outline-write process that traditional textbooks describe (Freedman 1987, Hillocks 1986). In Perl's (1979) study of the composing processes of five unskilled college writers, she found that her subjects "began writing without any secure sense of where they were heading, acknowledging only that *they would figure it out as they went along*" (pp. 330–331). Britton (1978) goes so far as to suggest that outlining or advance planning may prevent writers from composing effectively.

Strategies of Competent Writers

The Tapestry Approach helps students to develop effective writing strategies.[3] In this approach, students are taught the effective writing strategies of competent writers during the different stages of the writing process. They vary the use of these strategies as a function of their own learning style. Learners who need closure and those whose style is analytic often do far more organized outlining and advance planning than do learners who do not require closure and those whose style is global. Any generalizations that ignore learning style are likely to be off the mark. (See Chapter Four.)

Similarly, not all second language learners are capable of employing the composing strategies of competent native English writers. Many strategies, such as brainstorming, require English proficiency beyond the capabilities of learners who are still in the process of acquiring English. That is why

Tapestry teachers are sensitive to the English proficiencies of their students. The strategies of competent writers are outlined below.

The Composing Behaviors of Competent Writers

1. Pre-writing behaviors

Competent writers

- Spend time thinking about the task and planning how they will approach it
- Gather and organize information
- Have a variety of different strategies to help them (for example, they take notes, read, and make lists)

Less competent writers

- Spend little time on planning
- Start off confused about the task
- Have few planning and organizing strategies available

2. Drafting and writing behaviors

Competent writers

- Take time to let ideas develop
- Get ideas onto paper quickly and fluently
- Have sufficient language resources available (for instance, grammar and vocabulary) to enable them to concentrate on meaning rather than form
- Spend time reviewing what they write
- Know how to review to solve composing problems
- Use reviewing to trigger planning
- Are primarily concerned with higher levels of meaning

Less competent writers

- Begin the task immediately
- Have limited resources available and quickly become concerned with language matters
- Spend little time reviewing what they have produced
- Review only short segments of text
- Do not use reviewing to solve composing problems
- Are concerned primarily with vocabulary choice and sentence structure formation

3. Revising behaviors

Competent writers

- Make fewer formal changes at the surface level
- Use revisions successfully to clarify meanings
- Make effective revisions that change the direction and focus of the text
- Revise at all levels (lexical, sentence, and discourse)
- Add, delete, substitute, and reorder

- Review and revise throughout the composing process, review what was written to determine where to go next
- Often pause to review and revise while they are rewriting the first draft
- Are not bothered by temporary confusions arising from the composing process
- Use the revision process to generate new content and trigger the need for further revision
- Distance themselves from the text, perhaps leaving it for several days or weeks
- Keep in mind the goals and the audience, make sure that what they write is consistent with their objectives, make their text clear and understandable, adapt their texts for their addressee, considering formality, tone, and so on
- Write multiple drafts

Less competent writers

- Make many formal changes at the surface level
- Make revisions that do not always clarify meanings
- Do not make major revisions in the direction or focus of the text
- Revise primarily at the lexical and sentence level
- Do not make effective use of additions, deletions, substitutions, and reorderings
- Make most revisions only when they write the first draft
- Do not pause to review when copying the first draft
- Revise in such a way that it interferes with the composing process
- Are bothered by the confusion associated with revising, thus reducing the desire to revise
- Use the revision process primarily to correct grammar, spelling, punctuation, and vocabulary

Source: Adapted from Ronald E. Lapp from "The process approach to writing: Toward a curriculum for international students." 1984 Master's Thesis, available as a *Working Paper in ESL,* University of Hawaii.

Beyond a Purely Process Orientation

Clearly, writing is a process and should be taught as one. However, there are some potential drawbacks that exist with process approaches. The Tapestry Approach overcomes these drawbacks by adapting and supplementing purely process-oriented instruction in order to appeal to a wide range of students. This reflects our belief that no single pedagogical orientation is effective in teaching the diverse populations found in ESL classrooms; teachers must vary their orientation to fit the specific students and subject matter they teach.

The Tapestry Approach adapts and supplements the process orientation in several ways. First, unlike exclusively process-oriented approaches, the Tapestry Approach does not teach students to revise *all* types of writing. This is because a number of researchers have suggested that certain types of writing genres do not lend themselves to the multiple revisions of process approaches. For instance, Jenkins and Hinds (1987) discovered that the form and content of business letters written in French, Japanese, and English are highly conventionalized. They argued that such highly formulaic genres can readily be taught to ESL learners through models. (See also Horowitz 1986 for similar arguments.)

Second, unlike some process approaches, which focus on sociolinguistic, discourse, and strategic competence to a greater extent than they focus on grammatical competence, the Tapestry Approach focuses on all aspects of the learner's writing proficiency. Although other approaches may give some students the impression that grammar is unimportant since grammar instruction is left to the last stage of the writing process, the Tapestry Approach does not. In the Tapestry Approach, grammatical competence is just one component of writing proficiency, but a critical one, and Tapestry teachers emphasize its importance. In the Tapestry Approach, grammar instruction stems from students' needs and abilities as demonstrated by their own writing and second language research. The aim of instruction is to treat those specific grammar problems that ESL students actually make and that second language acquisition research suggests can be overcome. (See, for instance, Larsen-Freeman and Long 1991, Long 1982, and Rutherford and Sharwood Smith 1988.) In the Tapestry Approach, grammar exercises never interfere with the composing process. Tapestry teachers instead focus on just a few grammatical features at a time and provide illustrations. They teach their students editing skills. They remind their students of typical errors, such as subject-verb disagreement, to look for and to correct as they edit.

Third, Tapestry teachers are sensitive to the problems of peer revision and, at times, help their students locate their grammar mistakes prior to peer review activities. This is because in peer review activities, students read and comment on each others' essays during the revising stage of the composing process. The students can pick up on each others' inaccurate grammatical structures and incorporate them into their own writing.

Finally, the Tapestry Approach does not focus on the stages of the writing process (rewriting, drafting, revising, editing) as though these stages always existed or were mutually exclusive. Our own view is that writing is in fact a process, but an idiosyncratic one that often, though not always, requires multiple revisions at both a global and local level.

SAMPLE WRITING ACTIVITIES

Some suggested activities follow that allow writing to be taught as an idiosyncratic process. Although the activities are grouped by ESL proficiency levels (high-beginning, intermediate, and advanced), they may be adapted for students of any proficiency level.

Activities for High-Beginning ESL Students

High-beginning ESL learners often need experience writing a wide range of shorter text types — such as letters to pen-pals, journal entries, lists of various kinds, forms, and charts — which rarely call for pre-writing activities and revision. At the same time they are writing these short texts, they need to be writing longer texts that lend themselves to the multiple revisions of process instruction. Suggested activities for high-beginning level ESL learners are listed below.

Ethnographic Histories. In ethnographic histories, students interview one another or someone outside of the class. They write the histories based on their observations and interviews. These observations and interviews can then be turned into feature articles that, after revision and editing, contribute to a class magazine. Students often become so engrossed in their own ethnographic research that they collect data from their own community and produce writing based on their analysis of this information. The students, rather than the teacher, control the writing.

Jigsaw Writing. In jigsaw writing, students are given "unrelated, target story fragments, a sentence or two each, and are required to write a story that weaves all the story lines together into a reasonably coherent whole, transitions and all" (Oxford 1990, p. 78). This activity helps learners to discover new linkages as they interact with one another.

Cooperative Analysis Activity. Cooperative learning can be very valuable in beginning level ESL classrooms (Kagan 1989). Raimes (1983) suggests one type of cooperative learning activity that requires an exchange of information. This activity involves:

> . . . asking a small group of students to read a particular text — short story, poem, essay or graph — and then to produce an analysis of the text. Each student in the group is then assigned an aspect of the analysis. For instance, to describe the purpose of a symbol or to explain an element on the graph. The students share their writing with each other, pool their ideas, and work together to produce a comprehensive analysis. (pp. 140–141)

Narratives. ESL students of all levels need to write about their own immediate experiences. One of the most interesting experiences that even beginning level ESL students can draw upon is stories of their own countries. Students write only what they feel comfortable with sharing and give as accurate an account as possible so that their audience can picture their experiences. Because the students already have a wealth of memories, they can easily tap into these and put their energies into writing.

Activities for Intermediate ESL Students

More advanced learners are capable of writing longer, more complex texts that lend themselves to process approach instruction. (See suggested activities above.) Yet even in intermediate ESL writing classes, process instruction should be supplemented with other types of instruction that do not require repeated revisions. In effective intermediate ESL writing classes, teachers give their students a large number of opportunities to write. Some of the activities include the following.

Cooperative Learning Activities. Cooperative learning activities are just as successful with intermediate and advanced learners as they are with beginning. Jigsaw tasks (Kagan 1989) and report writing, in which students each have information that they teach to others to accomplish a joint goal, can be carried out using a great deal of writing. Students can also write on a cultural topic on which they are the experts.

Other joint writing projects in which students work together, making individual contributions, include: newspapers, newsletters, literary magazines, sports digests, scrapbooks, or scripts for simulated radio and TV programs and news bulletins (Oxford 1990). "Another suggestion for joint writing practice is to have learners interview each other using a semistructured format, and then turn the interviews into feature articles which are, after revisions, published in a class magazine" (Oxford 1990, p. 78). Such magazines can include a variety of genres — news, poetry, stories, pictures, letters to the editor, and even ads.

Letter Writing. Littlejohn and Hicks (1986) suggest numerous letter-writing activities that can be used to create genuine writing tasks for ESL students. For instance, students can react to newspaper articles (in letters to editors), seek advice (in letters to Ann Landers or Abigail Van Buren), ask for information (in letters to travel agencies, embassies, and apartment managers), write persuasive texts (on behalf of Amnesty International), complain (in letters to hospitals, stores, telephone companies), and invite others to parties (in letters to friends and colleagues).

Resumés. Swain (1984) suggests a simulation activity in which students write resumés. In this activity students are asked to choose between two sources of summer employment. A booklet is given to the students that contains information about the two jobs—including the salary, the job qualifications, the benefits, and the precise nature of each job. Once the students decide which job they find most desirable, they write job resumés. They submit their resumés to a panel of students who then selects the best applicants for the jobs. This activity works particularly well for students looking for positions in the United States; however, it is inappropriate for international students who will never work in the United States.

Activities for Advanced ESL Students

The main varieties of advanced writing might be journal writing, short in-class writings, reports, and expository essays. Students need to be able to respond to an author's ideas, write to analyze a character's motivation, write from different points of view, write to clarify their own feelings, and so on. As they develop increased proficiency in English, they will need to write for more specific purposes and in particular domains, such as engineering, business, and medicine. Two other activities, reformulation and literature-based, drama-inspired tasks, are particularly useful with advanced ESL students.

Reformulation. Reformulation, native English speaker refinement of ESL student-produced writing, provides students an opportunity to utilize some of the native English writer's words and phrases in their own texts. (Refer to Levenston 1978.) After spending considerable time on a piece of writing, "advanced ESL students often have the uncomfortable feeling that a native English speaker would not say it the same way" (Cohen 1990, p. 120). The content may be excellent and the vocabulary and grammar free from errors, but students realize that the overall effect of their writing is non-native. Perhaps the ESL learners use vocabulary, grammar, cohesive ties, and discourse devices in manners that deviate in very subtle ways from native English speakers. Cohen (1990) suggests the following stages in using reformulation. The first three are pre-reformulation and the last two are actual reformulation.

Stages

<u>*Pre-reformulation Tasks*</u>

1. Students produce a text, usually a short paper of 200–300 words. They revise it as many times as they like.
2. Students give the paper to a competent native English writer or a teacher — at least once — for feedback.
3. Upon receipt of the reviewer's comments, students revise their paper based on the feedback received. This version is referred to as a *reconstruction* in that it has been corrected so as to reflect what the writer means to say.

<u>*Reformulation Tasks*</u>

4. A native speaker rewrites or reformulates the entire paper or a portion of it. The native speaker tries to preserve as many of the student's ideas as possible, while expressing them in his or her own words so as to make the piece sound as native-like as possible.
5. With the help of a native speaker or on their own, the students compare their original versions with the reformulated ones. They examine the discourse features, the vocabulary, and the choice and ordering of syntactic structures.

Literature-Based, Drama-Inspired Writing Tasks. Proponents of a communicative approach to language teaching emphasize that skills should be taught in a realistic context, one possible context being works of literature. Literary texts "have the potential to provide the basis for intensely interactive, content-based ESL classes because the exploration of literature . . . constitutes real content" (Gadjusek 1988, p. 227; see also Brumfit and Carter 1986 and Povey 1979). Stern (1985, 1990) provides a detailed description of a number of literature-based simulation activities that can be successfully employed in the ESL writing class. In the *dramatic monolog*, for instance, each student selects one of the characters in a literary work and, taking into consideration the character's feelings, ideas, and style of speech, assumes the role of the character and writes about a particular situation or issue. The *dramatic dialog*, which is similar to the dramatic monolog, involves writing conversations between the characters of a story, play, or poem.

TAPESTRY PRINCIPLES CONCERNING WRITING INSTRUCTION

To summarize, the Tapestry Approach to writing embodies the following principles.

PRINCIPLES

1. Writing is viewed as a purposeful process. It is both functional and authentic. Students write for real audiences.
2. Since writing is a social process, in many stages and in many activities, learners collaborate. They assist one another in their writing. Student-teacher and peer interactions are essential.
3. Reading is a critical component. A significant portion of the instructional period is devoted to reading—reading to get information, ideas, content, style, and language for writing, and reading to revise one's own and others' writing.

CONCLUSION

This chapter has provided a detailed description of the Tapestry Approach to writing instruction. In this approach, meaning is central, and all aspects of writing proficiency (grammatical, discourse, sociolinguistic, and strategic) are developed. In the next chapter, we will consider some of the ways in which the oral interaction skills can be taught. Again, we will emphasize the importance of peer collaboration and assistance in communication, and review the necessity of varying instructional orientations for individual learners.

ACTIVITIES AND DISCUSSION QUESTIONS

1. In the Tapestry Approach, writing is considered a social process and students are encouraged to help one another compose. What are some activities that encourage collaboration on writing projects?
2. Some ESL learners experience *writer's block*, anxiety that may prevent them from finishing their writing. How can teachers help students overcome writer's block? (See this chapter and Chapter Four for ideas.)

3. Many writing tasks are so difficult that ESL learners become easily discouraged. Such tasks seem to elicit the students' worst work. What are three types of writing tasks that elicit the students' *best* writing ability?
4. What can teachers do to make writing fun for students?
5. How should grammar be taught in the writing classroom?
6. What factors facilitate ESL writing development? Which of these factors can the ESL teacher control? Why?

NOTES

1. It is also likely that ESL students may lack formal writing instruction or practice writing in their first languages. Many ESL students reveal that they have not had opportunities to write essays of any length during their high school educations.
2. Two studies illustrate the importance of writing practice in ESL writing development. Brière (1966) found that repeated practice in writing freely and rapidly facilitated ESL student writing fluency. In a replication study, Shaw (1982) gave intermediate EFL college students six minutes to write rapidly during class. Shaw compared the writing of these students with the writing of students in a comparison class who wrote only once a week. The students' writing was assessed for length (determined by number of words) and grammaticality. Shaw found that those students who wrote daily composed longer and more grammatically accurate essays than those students who did not.

SUGGESTED READINGS

• Hughey, J.B., Wormuth, D., Hartfiel, V.F., and Jacobs, H. 1983. *Teaching ESL: Composition: Principles and Techniques.* Rowley, MA: Newbury House. This comprehensive and extensively tested textbook offers a number of ideas for teaching writing to ESL university students of intermediate and advanced ESL levels. This volume is part of the English Composition Program series, which includes a student textbook and a volume on testing ESL writing proficiency. The first part of the book provides a philosophy of writing as a creative, discovery-based process. The second part offers practical methods that can be used to develop this process (including methods that strengthen a writer's awareness of invention, purpose, audience, shaping, and evaluating writing). Methods are suggested by the ESL Composition Profile, which the authors suggest as a measuring device that provides students with analysis and feedback valuable in the revising and editing stages of the writing process.

• Johnson, D.M. and Roen, D.H. (eds.). 1989. *Richness in Writing: Empowering Language Minority Students.* New York: Longman. This innovative text combines scholarly research with practical pedagogical suggestions. Emphasis is on nondeficit models of teaching writing. Drawing on the research of Paolo Frière, Part I discusses empowerment approaches to minority education. The contributors discuss the specific contexts in which students learn: the local community, communities across cultures, and organizational structures in schools. Part II discusses specific rhetorical issues (such as audience, purpose, and topic) for ESL writers. The last part examines cultural issues in teaching ESL students writing. Although the volume is primarily intended for teachers of the language minority students living in the United States, teachers of ESL students who are enrolled in intensive English language programs will also find the volume of practical value.

• Krashen, S.D. 1984. *Writing: Research, Theory and Applications.* New York: Alemany. This monograph provides teachers with a short overview of recent research on writing and practical suggestions for teaching writing. The author emphasizes those approaches that are most consistent with his own theory of second language acquisition. The volume mainly focuses on teaching native English writers, but also contains a brief discussion of the research on ESL writing development and instructional practices.

• Kroll, B. (ed.). 1991. *Second Language Writing: Research Insights for the Classroom.* Cambridge: Cambridge University Press. The thirteen original articles in this edited volume describe research findings and practical implications for classroom instruction. Among the topics covered are the composing process of second language writers, variables affecting the second language writing process, the reading/writing connection, and writing assessment. The book provides the most thorough overview of recent trends in ESL writing research.

• McKay, S. (ed.). 1984. *Composing in a Second Language.* Rowley, MA: Newbury House. This anthology examines major issues in helping ESL students acquire ESL writing proficiency. The ten chapters address three issues: theory, teaching, and evaluation. In the first section, Taylor, Flower, Kaplan, and Meyer define the composing process and investigate first and second language similarities and differences. In the second section, Raimes, Reekie, Zamel, Weissberg, and Buker offer numerous practical suggestions for teaching ESL writers and developing ESL writing materials and curriculum. In the final section, Kroll, Schafer, Hendrickson, and Sommers suggest various approaches to error correction that are consistent with the process approach to composition instruction.

• White, R.V. 1980. *Teaching Written English.* London: George Allen and Unwin. This practical guide to teaching writing examines the functional use of writing in real communication and offers suggestions for teaching different types of writing (such as narratives, descriptions, and comparisons) to adult ESL learners of all ESL proficiency levels.

APPENDIX 8.1

REVIEW SHEET: COHESION AND CONTENT

Names of reviewers: ____

Author's name: ____

Please answer the following questions:

1. If you could write a title for this paper, what would it be?
2. Consider the introductory paragraph. Does the author state his or her thesis?
   (Check the appropriate blank.) Yes _____ No _____
   Could the thesis be stated more clearly? Yes _____ No _____
3. How interesting is the introduction of the essay? Rate the interest level of the essay on a scale from 1 to 5. (1 = Boring; 5 = Fascinating) 1 __ 2 __ 3 __ 4 __ 5 __
4. What specific vocabulary words would you change to make the essay more interesting? Please be as specific as possible.

   <u>Example</u>
   In the first paragraph, I would change the words, *learn many things* to *attain much knowledge.* (To advance, he would have to *learn many things*. Better: To advance, he would have to *attain much knowledge.)*
5. Are there places in the essay where the author seems to wander? That is, are there parts of the essay that are not relevant to the thesis statement? Write the words "off-topic" near those sections of the paper that seem "off-topic" to you. You may write directly on the author's paper.
6. How do you rate the organization of this essay? Rate the organization of the essay on a scale from 1 to 5. (1 = Needs much improvement; 5 = Outstanding) 1 __ 2 __ 3 __ 4 __ 5 __
7. How could you improve the organization of the essay? Please be as specific as possible.
8. How do you rate the content of this essay? Rate the content on a scale from 1 to 5.
   (1 = Needs much improvement; 5 = Outstanding) 1 __ 2 __ 3 __ 4 __ 5 __
9. What specific topics in the essay should be expanded upon, clarified, or deleted? Are examples needed?
10. In what specific ways could the conclusion be improved?

(Adapted from Lebauer and Scarcella 1992.)

RESPONSE TO THE REVIEWERS

Name of author: ____

Names of reviewers: ____

Please fill in the blanks below.

1. I agree with the following comments that the reviewers made:
____
2. These are the changes I plan to make in response to the reviewers' comments:
____
3. I disagree with these comments:
____
4. I think I need the most help improving the following (Please check one or more blanks):

_____ the thesis statement; I need a clearer thesis statement.
_____ the introduction; I need to make the introduction more interesting.
_____ the transitions between paragraphs; I need better transitions.
_____ the content; I need to add more detail.
_____ the content; I need to add more examples.
_____ the vocabulary; I need to avoid redundancy.
_____ the vocabulary; I need to use more vivid vocabulary.
_____ the grammar; my grammar is weak.
_____ the conclusion; I need a more interesting conclusion.
_____ the conclusion; I need a conclusion that is more directly related to the thesis.
_____ the coherence; parts of my essay are off-topic.

Other: Please describe. Be as specific as possible.

(Adapted from Lebauer and Scarcella 1992.)

LISTENING

9

PREVIEW QUESTIONS

1. Why is listening a critical skill in the learning of English as a second language?
2. What are the components of listening competence?
3. Why is listening often ignored in ESL classrooms?
4. What main factors influence listening for learners of ESL?
5. What are the primary features of good listening activities in the ESL classroom?

This chapter focuses on the skill of listening, a major area of concern to second language students and those who teach them. In the tapestry of language learning, listening is one of the most significant strands, interwoven with the other language skills of reading, writing, and most especially speaking. The importance of integrating all the language skills is described in Chapter Six.

In this chapter we will point out the linkages with speaking in particular, but we will also try to tease these strands apart, so that we can focus for a moment on the unique characteristics of the listening process.

ORGANIZATION OF THIS CHAPTER

In this chapter we discuss why listening is so important as a contributor to language learning and why listening is nevertheless often ignored or treated only superficially in traditional language instruction. Second, we summarize how the Tapestry Approach to listening contrasts with traditional approaches to listening. Third, we show the relationship between listening and the four aspects of communicative competence. Fourth, we break down the act of listening into various components. Fifth, we cite the main factors influencing the listening process. Sixth, we list and demonstrate characteristics of effective listening exercises and provide examples. Finally, we summarize the main Tapestry principles related to listening.

LISTENING AS A CRUCIAL SKILL

Listening is a significant and essential area of development in the native language and in a second language. Throughout this chapter we use this definition of listening: "*Listening is the process of receiving, attending to, and assigning meaning to aural stimuli*" (Wolvin and Coakley 1985, p. 74).

Why Listening Is Important

The definition above suggests that listening is "a complex, problem-solving skill" (Wipf 1984, p. 345). Listening is more than just perception of sound, although perception is the foundation; listening also requires comprehension of meaning. Effective listening sharpens thinking and creates understanding.

Listening interacts with speaking in the aural-oral communication feedback system. Ordinarily listening is not an isolated skill. In normal, daily communication, listening usually occurs in conjunction with speaking. One person speaks, and the other, through attending by means of the listening process, responds. Only in certain circumstances — for instance, in a lecture situation, at the theater, or when listening to radio or watching television — does listening seem to become an isolated skill, unsupported by and not interacting with other language skills. Yet even in those special circumstances, listening comprehension is not totally isolated because listeners apply what they know from the sociolinguistic "rules" of speaking to predict what they are likely to hear spoken next, and they interpret what they hear based on what they know of the culture, the grammar, and the vocabulary of the language. Therefore, listening operates with the aid of numerous language-related subskills, even in those special cases (lectures, TV, and so on) when listening at first appears to be a process acting on its own.

Listening in almost any setting is the most frequently used language skill. In the United States it is estimated that "close to 90% of class time in high school and college is spent listening to discussion and lectures" (Taylor 1964). This figure might be lower in ESL programs, which tend to be more interactive, but we can be assured that the percentage of time devoted to listening is at least over half. A review of numerous studies showed that "among students who fail [in college], deficient listening skills were a stronger factor than reading skills or academic aptitude" (Conaway 1982, p. 57).

Among ESL students, the difficulties of listening are heightened, and listening may take on an even more critical role than the other skills in overall communication. For many, listening is the basic mechanism through which the rules of the language are internalized (Byrnes 1984). It is also the medium through which much significant cultural information is conveyed.

Listening interacts with a very powerful nonverbal communication system, which sometimes contradicts the messages provided through the verbal listening channel. An ESL student might hear a message of interest and welcome from a native speaker of English; for instance, "Let's get together for lunch sometime," but the nonverbal cues (indifferent facial expression, moving away and onto the next activity, lack of follow-up) give a very different message that must also be interpreted and weighed before action is taken. Mehrabian (1971) claims that as much as 93% of the total meaning of any interaction comes from nonverbal, often visual, clues, although we assert that the specific percentage is arguable. The fact is, though, that what the student observes ("hears" or "sees") through nonverbal messages is every bit as important as what the student hears through careful listening. We must train students to understand how to listen well and how to pick up nonverbal cues at the same time.

Why Listening Is Often Neglected in Language Instruction

Many language instruction experts have traditionally considered listening as the handmaiden, servant, or poor relation of the three other chief language skills: reading, speaking, and writing. Listening is frequently viewed as an enabling skill not worthy of attention on its own. Listening has been relegated to "listening for speaking rather than listening for understanding" (Nord 1981, p. 69). Students have been "trapped in the frenzied 'Hear it, repeat it!', 'Hear it, answer it!', or 'Hear it, translate it!' nightmare," in which listening serves as an instantaneous stepping stone to some other skill (Meyer 1984, p. 343). While it is true that listening is integrally connected with other language skills, particularly speaking, a focus on this connection has often led to a failure to teach students how to listen in the first place. This situation is exemplified by Krashen's (1982) exhortation to provide extensive quantities of comprehensible input without offering any special instruction to learners on how to deal with this input. The concept, shared by other authorities, seems to be that listening comprehension simply takes care of itself without any aid or teaching, and that osmosis is all that is needed. However, listening-comprehension-through-osmosis is not sufficient for most students. (Mendelsohn 1984). Listening instruction should not be ignored, but instead should be included as a very important part of any ESL program.

THE TAPESTRY APPROACH TO LISTENING INSTRUCTION AND TRADITIONAL APPROACHES

Differences between the Tapestry Approach to listening instruction and more traditional treatments of listening is demonstrated below. The Tapestry Approach treats listening as part of the web of communication, not as an isolated skill, and teaches students specific strategies to apply in listening situations. The point of listening in the Tapestry Approach is to receive and share meaning. No "rote" listening exercises are given; meaning is always involved in some way.

Comparison of the Tapestry Approach to Listening and Traditional Approaches

The Tapestry Approach	Traditional Approaches
• Students collaborate on authentic listening tasks (jigsaw, group activities, etc.).	• Students work alone with tapes, if listening is taught at all.
• Listening topics are student-generated to a great extent.	• Listening topics are teacher- or program-controlled.
• Students are encouraged to guess while listening and are given strategies to do so; they also learn other key strategies for listening.	• Students are not given help in guessing while listening; often they do not realize they must guess to understand.
• Tapestry teachers recognize that listening is easier for auditory students than for students with a visual or hands-on style, and they routinely provide help (visuals, realia) for listeners who need it.	• Teachers do not pay attention to differences in listening ability based on learning styles.

HOW LISTENING RELATES TO COMMUNICATIVE COMPETENCE

As noted in earlier chapters, communicative competence is one of the cornerstones of the Tapestry Approach. We have adapted the Canale and Swain model of communicative competence, explained earlier in this book. To review, the four components of communicative competence are grammatical competence, sociolinguistic competence, discourse competence, and strategic competence. We will show how listening relates to each of these. Figure 9.1 graphically shows the relationship between listening proficiency and each of the elements of communicative competence.

Figure 9.1 The Components Underlying Listening Proficiency

Grammatical Competence
Grammar — In listening, understanding, and applying the rules of morphology and syntax to understand what is heard
Vocabulary — recognizing words that are heard
Mechanics — using natural pauses, stress, intonation, etc. to help understand meaning

Strategic Competence
Using any and all clues for guessing the meaning (background knowledge, linguistic clues, etc.)

LISTENING PROFICIENCY

Sociolinguistic Competence
Knowing social and culturalexpectations related to the appropriate use of the new language, and using these expectations as a basis for understanding what is heard

Discourse Competence
Knowing how discourse operates on coherence and cohesion, so as to recognize and understand what is heard in short or extended discourse (above the sentence level)

Grammatical Competence

Figure 9.1 shows that *grammatical competence* is an umbrella concept that includes increasing expertise in grammar (morphology and syntax), lexicon or vocabulary, and mechanics. In regard to listening, the term *mechanics* refers to basic sounds of letters and syllables, pronunciation of words, intonation, and stress.

ESL listeners must understand these elements in order to catch the meaning of what they hear. If an ESL student cannot understand how words are segmented into various sounds, and how sentences are stressed in particular ways to convey meaning, then the student will find it difficult to understand the meaning of the message.

Sociolinguistic Competence

Grammatical competence is enhanced by *sociolinguistic competence* for ESL listeners. Sociolinguistic competence involves knowing what is expected socially and culturally by users of the target language. This information is very important in helping ESL listeners understand what they hear. Particularly important is the listener's grasp of the purpose of any given oral communication. The speaker might want to convey one or more of the following (among other possible purposes): the main idea, specific facts, a feeling or emotion, a persuasive argument, two balanced sides of a question, a sense of authority, or sheer friendliness. The listener who is adept in sociolinguistic aspects of language will automatically look for the purpose of the speaker and adjust his or her own listening focus accordingly; or might decide that the speaker's overt purpose is not the only important one, and that "listening between the lines" for a covert purpose might be crucial as well.

Understanding the sociolinguistic side of language learning helps listeners know when (or if) it is appropriate to comment and to ask questions during a discourse, and how to respond nonverbally as well. Sociolinguistic competence includes recognizing the communication situation for what it is (a formal lecture, an introduction among strangers, an informal greeting among friends, and so on) and then listening for what would be expected in such a situation.

Discourse Competence

In addition to grammatical and sociolinguistic competence, ESL listeners must develop *discourse competence.* Discourse deals with communication above the sentence level. In discourse — whether it is short or extended, formal or informal — the rules of cohesion and coherence apply. These are discussed at length in Chapter Five on communicative competence and are very important in Chapter Eight on writing. Coherence and cohesion aid in holding the communication together in a meaningful way. The various parts are glued to each other rather than being random, unconnected fragments. Even the short, telegraphic communications we sometimes have with our family members or close friends have some internal cohesion and coherence. Because of cohesion and coherence, almost any listening passage possesses a degree of predictability.

If students have discourse competence, they will be able to anticipate what will be said next in any discourse and will be able to understand more easily what they are hearing at any given time. Discourse competence implies that the listener is active, not passive, and is always seeking to know how the parts of any communication relate to each other and what they mean. More specifically, it involves understanding how English, the target language, uses specific conventions for reference, substitution, ellipsis, conjunction, and repetition of words. (For good examples of these conventions, which could occur just as easily in speech as in writing, see Chapter Eight on writing.)

Strategic Competence

We have discussed three aspects of communicative competence that relate to listening proficiency: grammatical, sociolinguistic, and discourse competence. For developing listening skill, *strategic competence* is perhaps the single most important of all the communicative competence elements, and because of this we will discuss this topic in detail. With reference to listening, strategic competence means the ability to tap all possible clues to guess the meaning of unknown expressions heard in the target language. Strategic competence in listening involves using guessing strategies to compensate for missing knowledge while trying to take in what is heard.

Guessing intelligently is one of the most important strategies known to ESL learners, because listening is not just a *bottom-up* skill in which the meaning can be derived from the sum of all the discrete sounds, individual syllables, and separate words or phrases. Listening does indeed involve some bottom-up processing of discrete elements, but at the same time it requires a substantial amount of *top-down* processing in which the meaning is inferred from broad contextual clues and background knowledge. Listening can best be understood as a highly complex, interactive operation in which bottom-up processing is interspersed with top-down processing, the latter involving guessing.

Guessing is thus essential for listening. It helps learners let go of the false belief that they have to recognize and understand every single word before they can comprehend the overall meaning. More importantly, guessing plays a major role in *hypothesis testing* and *comprehension monitoring,* dual processes that occur every time a non-native English user listens to English. (For more on comprehension monitoring, see Henner-Stanchina 1986.)

In all the aspects of listening comprehension, listeners act as detectives who *test out hypotheses* concerning the meaning of what they hear. Listeners must decode the meaning of what is being said, often by means of guessing from context clues. They have to predict what is coming next, so they can keep up with the flow of the communication. Finally, they must make adjustments and resolve discrepancies if the predictions are proved wrong. This implies, of course, that they must be capable of recognizing when comprehension failure has occurred and then of shifting to a new hypothesis. Testing and adjusting hypotheses, in turn, demand a high level of monitoring of one's own comprehension, thus the term *comprehension monitoring.* Students' skill in comprehension monitoring can be checked by repeatedly playing a listening tape and asking students to discuss their changing comprehension of the meaning after each repetition.

The ability to exploit both linguistic and nonlinguistic clues is essential for strategic competence in listening. *Linguistic clues* range from affixes to phrases. Items such as suffixes, prefixes, word order, and cognates all help learners guess unknown expressions. Titles or nicknames also help learners guess the meaning; a term of endearment such as "sweetheart" gives the learner a very different clue to the meaning than if a formal title like "Dr. Smith" is used.

In a formal discourse, the use of discourse markers, such as *first, second, third; the most important concept to remember is . . . ; we will now turn to . . . ;* and *so far we have covered,* signal to the listener the general organization of what is being presented.

In addition, knowing what has already been said provides still further clues, based on rules of discourse competence such as coherence and cohesion (discussed above).

Nonlinguistic clues exist in great abundance. For example, close observation of nonverbal behavior (facial expressions, posture, and proxemics) provides still other clues to what is being said. Background noise offers a context that aids in guessing meanings. For example, even if the listener does not understand exactly what a speaker has just said, the background sound of a crowd cheering indicates that the speaker has expressed something of value or importance. Finally, general background knowledge of any kind — particularly related to the subject at hand — is exceptionally useful in offering hints for inferring meanings of unknown words and expressions. In listening, the individual links what is heard to whatever background information (schemata) is in long-term memory (Byrnes 1984).

ASPECTS OF LISTENING

Now we know how listening proficiency is related to the four aspects of communicative competence. We now turn to aspects of listening as a process.

Listening involves a number of elements. These start with perception and then follow through four areas of comprehension. All these components involve the transformation of *input* to *intake* — a change from the whirling buzz of noise into a meaningful subset that is internalized by the learner (Cohen 1990). The movement from input to intake is discussed at length in Chapter Three of this book.

This distinction between input and intake is very important. Not everything to which a student is exposed becomes intake that contributes to the learner's second language development. At the perception level, the intake is a string of significant sounds. At the various levels of comprehension, the intake is meaning-bearing words, phrases, clauses, sentences, or longer discourse.

Perception

The first component of listening is *perception,* which requires distinguishing the significant stimuli from the stream of sound or noise. The task of the beginning listener is, first of all, to perceive: to break out the important sounds from the ongoing stream, to find "meaningful units in a previously undifferentiated sequence of noises" (Byrnes 1984, p. 325).

This is not as easy as it might at first seem. Learners of ESL in the United States must sometimes struggle to notice the sound differences between *eaten* and *eating* or between *men* and *man,* not to mention the regionally different pronunciations of *pen* and *pin* (which in some regions might sound just alike to Americans). Differences in accent between British and American native speakers of English often cause perceptual confusion for ESL learners in the beginning. Sometimes the differences are so great that learners might not recognize two different pronunciations as representing the very same word. Differences in pronunciation among the various forms of *world English* — rather than the presence of one single, universally accepted standard of English speech — make English language perception rather complicated for some learners, especially those whose ears are not finely attuned.

Perception, the breaking up of sound into potentially meaningful units, is also made difficult because of the different rhythmic patterns of English as compared with the patterns of the native languages of our ESL students (Ur, 1984).

In English, we divide speech into *tone groups*, strings of connected syllables that have one heavily stressed tone (Ur 1984). For example, in English intonation influences the meaning of a statement (by changing the pitch or key to show importance, irony, certainty, humor, and so on). A rising intonation at the end of a sentence implies uncertainty or a question — or in some instances a lack of self-esteem. ESL learners have to learn new patterns like this, which might differ significantly from what they are used to in their own native tongue. The speed with which learners pick up the new rhythmic flow of English influences their success at the perception level of listening as well as their performance at the higher levels of comprehension.

Four Aspects of Comprehension

Four aspects of comprehension exist:

1. isolated word recognition within the sound stream (minimal comprehension of general content);
2. phrase or formula recognition (marginal comprehension);
3. clause or sentence recognition (minimally functional comprehension of content); and
4. extended speech comprehension (general comprehension of unedited speech).

The learner can operate simultaneously in several of these areas, depending on the nature of the communication, the level of proficiency of the listener, the fatigue or energy level of the listener at the particular time, the topic, the interest the listener attaches to the discussion, the importance of understanding the content in a specific situation, the level of discourse complexity, the number of contextual aids available for guessing the meaning, and so on. In other words, a learner is not stuck at a single stage at any given time; he or she may switch back and forth from one comprehension area to another in a nonhierarchical way, depending on the factors noted above. (See also Byrnes 1984 and Joiner 1986.)

Understanding Isolated Words. In this element of listening comprehension, the ESL student catches isolated words such as "worry" or "exam" or "going." By apprehending one or more of these discrete words, the intelligent learner can sometimes guess at the general content. In this instance, the conversation might be about someone worried about going to an exam, and if the learner hears one or two of these words, the general content might be clear enough.

Recognizing Phrases. The learner can recognize whole phrases or routine expressions, such as:

> Example 9.1
> Raining *again!*

Example 9.2:
Our team's gonna win.

Example 9.3
Hi, howya doin'?

Example 9.4
What's goin' on?

Example 9.5
I'm fine, how're you?

Example 9.6
What a hoot!

Example 9.7
It's awesome, pal!

These formulas (some of them based on rather transient slang) grease the wheels and cogs of communication. Because they are so common, listeners can easily learn to recognize and understand them and can learn how to respond appropriately. Tapestry teachers provide learners with as many of these routines as possible. Understanding such commonplace expressions helps learners feel self-confident, aids in fluency, and keeps learners actively involved.

Understanding Clauses or Sentences. Clause or sentence recognition is another element in understanding speech. This involves recognizing clauses or sentences that are not purely routine or formulaic — novel expressions that the learner has probably not heard before.

Example 9.8
My computer's on the fritz, and I need your help!

Example 9.9
Sure looks like it's gonna be a fabulous day, whaddya think?

Example 9.10
I've been looking all over for Frannie, but I can't find her anywhere on campus.

Example 9.11
Victor and Michael have left "L.A. Law," but Gracie is coming back, thank heavens.

In this aspect of listening, the listener's degree of understanding is often based on willingness to guess in order to fill in any gaps in understanding. This willingness to guess in turn depends on risk-taking ability and on general world knowledge (relevant knowledge that helps the learner predict what the speaker will say or guess what the speaker is saying).

Understanding Discourse. This aspect of understanding relates to extended speech, or what we commonly call *discourse* above the sentence level. The accomplished learner doesn't just focus on isolated words to guess the general content, pick out certain formulas, or concentrate on discrete clauses or sentences; instead, the learner is able to move to a greater overall understanding of a lecture, a conversation, or any other oral communication. For instance, if Example 9.12 were read aloud, the listener might be able to understand most of it and would simultaneously try to guess what he or she does not fully understand.

Example 9.12

For some pollutants, the air outside may be safer to breathe than air inside the home! That was the shocking conclusion of a ten-year investigation by the EPA that measured personal exposure to a wide range of environmental pollutants in more than 2,000 people who live in or around 12 U.S. cities. Since most Americans spend up to 90 percent of their lives indoors (half that time is in their own homes), the EPA calls the risks from indoor air pollution "among the top environmental problems" of the 1990's and warns, "For most people, the risks to health may be greater to exposure to air pollution indoors than outdoors."

(Breecher and Linde, Chapter 3, p. 1, 1992)

In all comprehension areas, and particularly in the realm of discourse, the listener must notice the register being used: academic, journalistic, formal-social, informal-social, and so on. Listeners can understand better when they comprehend the purpose behind the communication — especially as that purpose is reflected in the register the speaker uses. In Example 9.12, the register is a combination of both the journalistic and the academic. In earlier examples in this chapter, the register is much more informal-social.

In discourse, memory becomes important to listening comprehension. The longer the discourse, the more the listener must remember what has been said earlier in order to follow the flow of meaning. Memory strategies can assist the learner in improving retention. (See Oxford 1990.)

FACTORS INFLUENCING THE LISTENING PROCESS

Many factors influence the listening process: the nature of speech as related to listening, the nature or purpose of the specific listening task, the degree of attention, the physical mechanism of the ear, the sex of the listener, differences related to learning style, and affective issues in listening.

The Nature of Speech

In real-life, daily communication situations, listening requires understanding meaning on the spot and instantaneously, without having the chance to rewind a tape to listen to the whole communication again. The fleetingness of speech has a terrific impact on the listener, requiring constant attention. The time element separates listening comprehension from reading comprehension; in reading, the material is permanent and the reader controls the pace, but in listening, the message is transitory and the speaker typically controls the pace (Joiner 1986). Comprehending free speech or normal communication is necessary, even though most ESL learners find it difficult to keep up the pace initially.

Ordinary speech contains many ungrammatical, reduced, or incomplete forms; it also has hesitations, false starts, repetitions, fillers, and pauses, all of which make up 30-50% of any informal conversation. In addition, topics often shift. However, redundancy and repetition allow listeners to understand the communication more effectively; if they do not catch the meaning the first time around, repetition often comes to the rescue.

The Nature or Purpose of the Listening Task

The nature of the listening task is critical in understanding the listening process. Different listening tasks require different kinds of listening strategies. For example, listening for specific details (for example, flight information at an airport) calls for the learner to pay selective attention to those details only and to filter out anything that does not relate directly to those particulars. This is a discrimination task that essentially amounts to separating the important from the unimportant.

A very different listening task with contrasting requirements is listening to opposing arguments (as in a political debate) in order to discern their credibility. This task demands a different kind of attention: focusing on the content, structure, and logic of the arguments, using compare-and-contrast techniques, as well as simply dividing facts into significant and insignificant. Critical, analytical judgment is the ultimate goal of this type of listening.

Listening for the main idea (of a lecture or a TV show) involves synthesizing a great deal of material into a general concept, possibly with examples or applications of that concept. Global cognitive behavior is necessary here, rather than analytic.

In therapeutic or empathic listening (Coakley and Wolvin 1986), the listener must focus on the emotional content as well as the facts given by the speaker. The listener provides supportive nonverbal behaviors and verbal responses to enable the speaker to talk through a problem. The attempt is to be as nonjudgmental as possible while providing support, although any listening, no matter how supportive or empathic, involves sifting, sorting, and judging.

In appreciative listening (Coakley and Wolvin 1986), the individual listens in order to enjoy or gain a sensory impression from the material. Appreciative listening can include listening to the speaker's language style, to a movie or stage production, or to environmental sounds, and appreciating them aesthetically and sensually.

The Degree of Attention

If the listener is not paying adequate attention, the information will not be processed (Cohen 1990). It will not be transformed from *input* — the stimuli that are available to the learner — into *intake* — that which the learner actually takes into his or her consciousness.

> Attention is central to the entire process of second language acquisition and, for that matter, to any form of learning. Attention is the learner's window to the world; it is the neuropsychological mechanism that promotes or prohibits acquisition. . . . Attention . . . neurologically and psychologically explains the ways external stimuli enter (or are blocked from) the mind and the way the mind shapes (or does not shape) the individual's perception of the people and the languages that make up the surrounding environment.
>
> (Scovel 1991, pp. 3, 5)

Cohen (1990) emphasizes the importance of attention for listening and provides a self-test of attending that can be used in an ESL classroom, with vocabulary adaptations by the teacher as necessary. Using this questionnaire, Cohen has confirmed what most experienced teachers already know: that students take in less classroom input than teachers might desire, often in the range of 25%–85%. People remember only about 20%-30% of what was said, according to Bostrum (in Breecher 1983).

Thus, attention is important in general; and within this broad phenomenon, the depth of attention is the most significant feature. If students really want to learn the language material, they must analyze and enrich this material by giving it in-depth rather than superficial attention. Superficial attention is acceptable for material that is already well known and automatic, but it is not appropriate for new material that is in the process of being learned.

The Tapestry teacher helps students to use various strategies to focus attention. For example, learners make personal associations (verbal and nonverbal linkages) between new material and what is already known. Students use images, rhymes, physical motion, and color codes to focus attention. While individuals search for cognates and parallel grammatical structures across languages, attention is channeled usefully.

The Physical Mechanism of the Ear

The physical listening mechanism is another important influence on the listening process.

> The auditory reception of the stimulus — the vocal message — is a detailed process involving the intricate hearing mechanism. The sound must enter the middle ear, set into vibration the tympanic membrane, and be conducted through the inner ear to the brain.
>
> (Joiner 1986, p. 15)

Unfortunately, many listeners do not have a perfect hearing mechanism. In fact, in the United States one out of 20 people has a hearing loss or distortion, often caused by loud music or some other kind of noise pollution at home or at work (Breecher and Linde, 1992). It is wrong to believe that hearing problems strike only older people. Probably some students in our ESL classes also have problems that affect their physical hearing capability. Tapestry teachers pay special attention to any listening difficulties and ask, if they are pretty sure that the problem is physical, for students to have their hearing checked.

The Gender of the Listener

Men and women, in general, have distinctly different communication styles, and these styles include different modes of listening. Men often listen for facts and information, while women frequently listen for underlying intentions and feelings (Tannen 1990). This is definitely true for U.S. culture and for most of Western Hemisphere societies, and it might be true for many other cultures as well. Tapestry teachers help their students — female *and* male — to focus on the nature of the particular listening task and to be flexible in what they notice and take into their consciousness. They help students go beyond any culturally-induced gender stereotypes for listening and communicating. Tapestry teachers who aid all students in using appropriate listening strategies can assist students in breaking out of gender-bound limitations.

Differences in Listening Related to Learning Style

During any act of listening, right-brain (global) people tend to prefer focusing on main ideas and on the music and rhythm of the language. In contrast, left-brain (analytic) individuals listen in a more detailed, logical, analytical way.

Auditory students are far more adept at listening than are visual students, who need to be assisted with a variety of visual aids when listening. Auditory students welcome oral instructions and conversational settings, while visual students need handouts and prefer communication in which something visual is involved. See Chapter Four for more details on learning styles and their effects on language learning in general.

Tapestry teachers aid students of all learning styles to learn to listen more effectively through the use of specific strategies. These include paying close attention and understanding and acting on the purpose of a given listening task. (For more details on these and other related strategies for listening, see Oxford 1990.)

Affective Aspects of Listening

Affective refers to self-esteem, emotions, feelings, attitudes, beliefs, and motivation, among other issues. Often students come to the language classroom with a negative "listening self-concept" (Joiner 1986) — that is, low self-esteem in the area of listening. This self-perception is typically based on years of someone's harping at home: *Why don't you ever listen?* or *You aren't listening to me!* or *Why don't you ever pay attention?* Listening itself becomes a strained, painful task when the learner has a poor listening self-concept. Attention spans are often shorter and self-confidence sinks in such instances because the learner comes to believe that he or she simply has no talent for listening or paying attention in *any* language.

Serious anxiety sometimes occurs when students feel they cannot handle a listening task. Highly visual learners are particularly vulnerable to this feeling when faced with complex listening activities. Anxiety is compounded when learners believe they must understand every word they hear — a very unrealistic goal for all but the most advanced. When some language learners fail to understand every word spoken, they might become frightened, thus preventing "their transferring even the most basic first-language coping skills to the second language" (Meyer 1984, p. 343). Anxiety about not understanding everything can lead to discouragement, fatigue, and a general sense of failure.

Native speakers of English, however, do not believe they have to comprehend every word they hear. Native speakers are familiar with *filling in gaps* in meaning if they don't understand a particular word or don't hear it correctly. Tapestry teachers help their students understand that it is not essential to understand everything in order to function well in listening to the language. They provide guessing strategies and hypothesis-checking strategies so learners can feel comfortable in the listening situation.

Tapestry teachers also help students lessen their listening-related anxiety through a series of affective strategies, such as doing deep breathing, using music to relax, giving oneself a reward for good listening, and saying positive statements such as *I am a good listener* or *I can understand a great deal of what I hear in English.* Details on these affective strategies are given in Oxford 1990.

FEATURES OF GOOD LISTENING ACTIVITIES

Sometimes classroom listening activities do not reflect authentic language or meaningful, interesting tasks. Students are correct in perceiving such activities as boring, childish, and irrelevant (Mendelsohn 1984, Ur 1984, Meyer 1984). In contrast, a good listening activity has all or most of the following characteristics:

1. The listening activity has a real, communicative purpose that is clear to the students.
2. It offers content of personal interest to the listeners.
3. The speaker is visible (in person or on a videotape) rather than invisible (as on an audiotape or on the radio) — unless the purpose is to help students understand audiotapes and radio programs.
4. Listeners are required to respond in some meaningful fashion (for example, saying something, following a command or request, asking a question, or taking notes if it's a lecture).
5. The listening activity offers many environmental clues to the meaning.
6. Listeners with typical background knowledge are able to understand the topic of the listening activity; no highly specialized background is required, unless the class focuses on English for special purposes (ESP).
7. The listening activity is "normal" for its own particular speech type; that is, a conversation would have short, redundant, rapid chunks of speech, while a lecture or play might be more formalized and orderly.

Illustrations of good listening activities that fulfill the criteria above are shown here in Examples 9.13 and 9.14 (the first by Oxford from an actual domestic conversation; the second adapted from Ur 1984). Note that these activities can be adapted relatively easily to all levels of listeners, even beginners.

Example 9.13

A wife and husband are shopping at the grocery store. Students must reconstruct the shopping list that is the topic of conversation. This task is useful for intermediate to advanced level students. For lower level students and for highly visual students, be sure to use visual aids to go along with the spoken dialogue. Simplify the language if needed for beginners.

Man (M): Well, honey, let's see, what's in the shopping cart now? Bacon, ham, bread, coffee, chocolate cake mix . . .

Woman (W): Yes, all those were on the shopping list. Did you find the butter, milk, and cheese? They are over in the other section. They are next to the eggs — don't forget the eggs.

M: OK, I'll get them. While I'm over there, I'll get the ice cream, too. Do you want vanilla or chocolate?

W: Chocolate, of course! It says so on the list. I'll go find the lettuce, tomatoes, and apples while you're in the other section.

(a few minutes later)

M: Well, I think we have everything on the list!

W: No. We forgot to pick up the barbecued chicken in the deli section. I'll go get it and meet you at the check-out counter.

M: OK. See you there.

(at the check-out counter)

W: The bill isn't so high this time. I think I'll treat myself to something special that wasn't on the list: a *Newsweek* and a *Cosmo.* You want anything else, sweetheart?

M: Yeah. I think I'll get the *National Informer* while we're here. I haven't read the latest celebrity gossip in a while.

Example 9.14

This is a map activity involving listening comprehension. The students mark a route on a map according to spoken directions given by the teacher. This task can be as simple or as complex as desired, depending on the listening level of the students.

The teacher obtains a clear road map of an interesting area, preferably local. The teacher makes sure the map is visually appealing and contains many pictorial clues, such as a sketch of a bank or a dollar sign on the square that signifies the bank. The map must be photocopied for each student. On the teacher's copy of the map, the route is then sketched.

Then, without the students seeing the marked copy of the road map, the teacher describes in words where to go, adding comments on the scenery and landmarks, discussing the kinds of people who will be met along the way (for example, the minister, the teacher, the baker, the butcher), and mentioning reasons for visiting particular spots. Remember, this can be as simple or as elaborate as the students' listening level warrants. The teacher thus gives a running narrative with many clues. The students mark the route on their individual copies of the map. Then they compare maps with each other and with the teacher's map to determine if they listened accurately.

Alternatively, a student who speaks clearly can serve as the narrator-guide in the road map activity, while the other students mark the route. Another option is to reuse the same map with different routes marked each time, adding humorous details with each iteration.

An optional next step (in a class that is small enough) is for students to draw and photocopy their own maps of special places: nearby places or locations in their own countries. They take turns being the narrator-guide and having the other students chart a route according to oral directions and commentary.

TAPESTRY PRINCIPLES CONCERNING LISTENING DEVELOPMENT

The discussion above leads us to propose the following principles regarding the development of listening skill in our students.

PRINCIPLES

1. Tapestry teachers focus on listening as an important skill in its own right, not just an enabling skill.
2. Tapestry teachers use authentic, realistic listening tasks. Students help determine what they want to listen to based on their interests; teachers facilitate and guide listening activities.
3. Students guess intelligently based on all possible clues to meaning.
4. Tapestry teachers show students how to determine the purpose of a listening task and how to focus their attention appropriately to meet that purpose. They offer students a wide variety of different listening texts and tasks in many different registers, each calling for different types of responses.
5. Tapestry teachers provide special help for students who have trouble with auditory skills. Attempting to strengthen the listening ability and the self-confidence of all students, Tapestry teachers note the existence of listening anxiety and any physical problems related to listening.

CONCLUSION

This chapter has allowed us to follow the listening strand of the tapestry of language learning. Listening is also one of the central strands of all communication. We have summarized the importance of this often neglected skill and have shown how the Tapestry Approach differs from some other approaches in dealing with listening. We have analyzed listening into various elements and have cited a variety of factors influencing the listening process. Finally, we have proposed features of good listening activities, given examples of such activities, and listed Tapestry principles for the development of listening skill.

ACTIVITIES AND DISCUSSION QUESTIONS

1. What kinds of listening activities are most valuable for true beginners in regard to the perceptual level of listening? the comprehension level of listening? Look at Ur's book on listening and gather ideas and examples.

2. How can your students help choose topics and themes for listening activities? How would their personal involvement in such decision-making influence their level of motivation to become better listeners?

3. Why has listening so often been neglected as a skill in the ESL classroom, and why have many listening activities and listening textbooks seemed boring and lifeless to ESL learners? What can be done about such situations?

4. Listening and speaking are often viewed as two sides of the same communicative act. How can you most effectively weave listening and speaking together in activities in the ESL classroom? List as many examples as you can, either by yourself or with one other person. Now compare your list with the list of another person or pair. Consolidate all the good ideas that have been generated.

5. List as many different kinds of oral passages (lectures, telephone conversations, etc.) that you can think of. Now list the purposes for which students might want to listen to any of these oral texts. How can teachers help their students to identify the purposes for listening, as related to the different kinds of oral texts they will encounter in the academic setting and in everyday life?

6. What are some of the emotional stresses that occur while listening in a new language? What can the student do to lower the stress level? What can the teacher do?

SUGGESTED READINGS

• Ur, P. 1984. *Teaching Listening Comprehension.* Cambridge: Cambridge University Press. This book is essential for all teachers of ESL who want to understand the stages of the listening process, from perception through comprehension. Ur explains many factors that affect listening for ESL/EFL students and offers a wide range of hands-on activities for listening. Many are humorous, and all are useful and adaptable. It is the best book available on the topic to date.

• Wing, B.H. (ed.). 1986. *Listening, Reading, and Writing: Analysis and Application.* Middlebury, VT: Northeast Conference on the Teaching of Foreign Languages. This book, though written for foreign language teachers, is one of the best discussions of listening that ESL practitioners can find. The book covers listening in the native language of the learner and listening in the foreign language. Research evidence supports all the statements made in this readable albeit sophisticated volume. (The reading and writing sections are equally valuable, too.)

• Wolvin, A.D., and Coakley, C.G. 1985. *Listening.* (2nd ed.) Dubuque, IA: William C. Brown Company. This is a good general overview of the listening process. For background information on listening, ESL teachers could gain great benefit from this book.

SPEAKING

10

PREVIEW QUESTIONS

1. What competencies must learners acquire to become effective speakers of their second language?
2. What types of activities help learners acquire speaking skills?
3. What activities can ESL teachers use to lower their students' anxieties about speaking in front of their classmates?
4. In ESL discussion activities, some students inevitably take over the discussion while others withdraw. How can teachers promote more balanced participation by students?
5. How can teachers encourage students to interact with native English speakers outside of their ESL classes?

Weavers need multiple opportunities to interact with other more skillful weavers. Through interaction, weavers share ideas and patterns leading to the development of intricate, skillfully designed tapestries. Like weavers, ESL learners need opportunities to speak to more knowledgeable peers. A key factor in second language development is the opportunity given to learners to speak in language-promoting interaction with others who have more linguistic resources than the learners. (See Chapter Three.) The classroom can be especially conducive to providing learners with such speaking opportunities. In the outside world, it is sometimes difficult for ESL students to practice speaking English. Outside of class, the students may have the chance to speak to the clerk in the grocery store or to the bus driver, but sustained speaking practice is often only available with friends from their ESL classes.

ORGANIZATION OF THIS CHAPTER

This chapter focuses on speaking. We first describe the abilities underlying speaking effectiveness. Then we discuss factors affecting the development of speaking skills, including pronunciation. We conclude with a summary of the Tapestry Approach to ESL speaking instruction.

ABILITIES UNDERLYING SPEAKING EFFECTIVENESS

Effective speakers have a variety of abilities. The description of these abilities that follows is based on Canale and Swain (1980) and Canale's (1983) framework. (For a more detailed explanation, see Chapter Five.)

Figure 10.1 Abilities underlying speaking proficiency

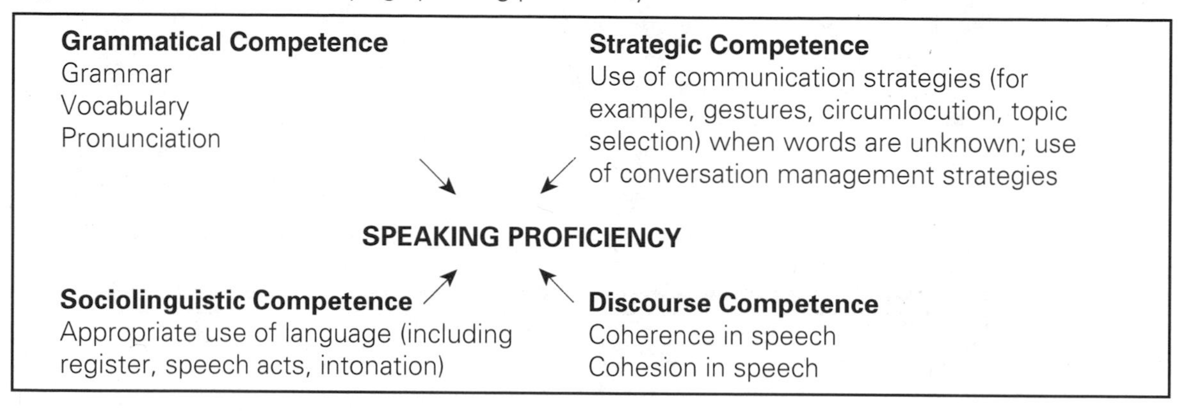

Grammatical Competence
Grammar
Vocabulary
Pronunciation
Strategic Competence
Use of communication strategies (for example, gestures, circumlocution, topic selection) when words are unknown; use of conversation management strategies
SPEAKING PROFICIENCY
Sociolinguistic Competence
Appropriate use of language (including register, speech acts, intonation)
Discourse Competence
Coherence in speech
Cohesion in speech

Grammatical Competence

Grammatical competence enables speakers to use and understand grammatical structures accurately and unhesitatingly, and thus, it contributes to the speakers' fluency.

Sociolinguistic Competence

In addition to grammatical competence, effective speakers have mastered *sociolinguistic competence,* which enables them to use such speech acts as apologies and compliments. Effective speakers also know the routines or phrases associated with these speech acts. (See Table 10.1.)

Table 10.1 Routines used to express disagreement

I can see your point, but...
I think you've missed one important fact which is...
Yes, but on the other hand,...
I really wouldn't put it that way because...
I'm not sure why you believe...

Because effective speakers have sociolinguistic competence, they are also able to vary their speech appropriately according to the purpose of the talk. Thus, they are able to use conversation for *interactional purposes* (to establish social relations) and *transactional purposes* (to convey information or complete tasks). They are also able to use the language that is characteristic of diverse genres — including debates, discussions, and lectures. For instance, they know how to use these routines to highlight information in academic discourse:

to begin with...
as I discussed previously...
in this way...
it's really very interesting that...
as you may recall...

(Adapted from Chaudron and Richards 1986, pp. 113–127.)

They also know when to use formal styles and when to use informal or neutral ones. They know how to talk on the telephone and how to talk at social gatherings. They also can vary their language appropriately. They know just what to say to the service station attendant *(Fill it up.)* and just what to say to the young child *(Nice dolly.)*.

Discourse Competence

Effective speakers also have mastered *discourse competence.* This competence enables them to manage turn-taking in conversation (which entails taking a turn of talk, holding a turn, and relinquishing a turn), to open and close a conversation, to keep a conversation going, and to repair trouble spots in conversation (which may include clearing up communication breakdowns and comprehension problems). Effective speakers and listeners have also acquired a large repertoire of discourse markers, expressions that speakers use to express ideas, show relationships of time, indicate cause, contrast, and emphasis. These discourse markers are summarized in Table 10.2.

Table 10.2 Discourse Markers

• To separate ideas:	well okay now	and right all right
• To show relationships of time:	at that time after this	for the moment
• To indicate cause:	so then	because
• To show contrast:	both but	only on the other hand
• To provide emphasis:	of course you can see you see	obviously as you know in fact
Excerpt from Chaudron and Richards (1986). "The effect of discourse markers on the comprehension of lectures." From *Applied Linguistics*, Vol. 7, No. 2, 113-127, by permission of Oxford University Press.		

Strategic Competence

In addition to the other three competencies, effective speakers have mastered *strategic competence,* which allows them to stretch their ability to communicate effectively in their new language. Thus, although they have not yet mastered all the grammar of the language, they can use turn-taking and conversation management strategies and are able to use small talk to open a conversation and initiate and respond to talk on a broad range of topics. They also use compensatory strategies (for example, gestures, circumlocution, topic selection) to assist when they don't know all the words to say.

FACTORS AFFECTING THE DEVELOPMENT OF SPEAKING ABILITIES

Several factors affect the development of the speaking abilities discussed above. These include the learner's opportunity to interact with more proficient peers and native speakers, fluency and accuracy activities designed to develop the learner's speaking ability, and strategy training.

The Learner's Opportunity to Interact with More Proficient Peers and Native Speakers

As discussed in Chapter Three, students need to participate in the widest possible range of situations with a variety of speakers who can help learners develop their second language proficiency. Teachers may introduce students to a variety of models through films, visitors, team teaching, peer teaching, and teaching by students who have successfully completed the course or who are in the next course. Peers can invite students to movies, sports events, and other activities. Clubs and organizations can involve them in parties and retreats.

Paired and small group activities increase the amount of meaningful and interesting interaction and greatly multiply the number of opportunities available to speak English. (See, for example, Long, Adams, McLean, and Castaños 1976; Enright and Gomez 1985; Long and Porter 1985.) As discussed in Chapter Three, these activities can be structured in specific ways to provide students with assistance in communicating accurately that which they were formerly incapable of communicating alone.

Fluency and Accuracy Activities

Many language educators believe that the conversation class should primarily exist to provide opportunities for learners to practice their speaking skills through communicative tasks and activities. (See, for example, Bygate 1987 and Klippel 1984.) These educators generally believe that it is not necessary to teach conversational features or push students to communicate accurately. In their view, fluency can be developed by simply providing students with lots of conversational practice.[1] However, such practice does not necessarily develop the learner's accuracy. (See Chapter Three.) As Richards (1990) points out, accuracy is important, and tasks should be structured with accuracy as one of the instructional objectives. When students interact with non-native English speakers they are often unable to acquire native-like accuracy (Higgs and Clifford 1982, Wong Fillmore 1986, Schmidt and Frota 1986). While fluency activities (such as unstructured group and pair conversations) provide students with opportunities to practice language that they have already acquired, accuracy activities (such as explicit instruction and carefully structured group and pair work) provide learners with opportunities to perfect their mastery of English (Byrne 1987). We suggest that teachers vary their use of fluency and accuracy activities according to the needs of their learners. For instance, international students who have recently arrived in the United States might need more fluency activities than permanent residents of the United States and are fluent, though inaccurate, in their use of English.

To develop their students' fluency, teachers can provide their students with opportunities to communicate their ideas in unstructured conversational situations. To develop their students' accuracy in conversation, instructors can provide opportunities for students to interact with more knowledgeable peers and native English speakers and teach specific conversation and group skills.

Strategy Training for Speaking

Strategy training can also help students develop speaking skills. Instructors can teach students strategies for taking turns talking and interrupting. They can teach students how to hold back their more vocal classmates and draw out the more timid or self-conscious ones. They can also teach students how to ask for clarification *(What?)*, to ask others to repeat *(Huh? Excuse me)*, to slow down *(Could you please slow down?)*, and to explain *(Could you explain what you mean by that?)*. In addition, they can teach students how to gain time to think (by using hesitation markers such as *Um* and *Let's see)* and how to change the topic *(Hey! That reminds me of my trip to Europe.)*. Teachers can also teach students how to look interested to keep the conversation going (by using such back channel cues as *Right, Uhuh,* and *That's interesting)*. Such tools of conversation enable students to manage their own input and output. Keller and Warner's (1979) pioneering handbooks suggest practical activities for teaching conversational features. Cooperative activities structured to teach specific conversational features also provide rich additional sources of interaction for ESL students.

In addition to these conversational strategies, instructors can also teach effective group management strategies by asking students to evaluate group participation by raising such questions as: *Did everyone have a chance to participate?* and *Did everyone take responsibility for completing the task?* Students can practice group management strategies during cooperative learning activities. In addition, teachers can demonstrate those skills they want students to use in later group work.

THE TAPESTRY APPROACH TO SPEAKING INSTRUCTION AND TRADITIONAL APPROACHES

The Tapestry Approach is designed to help teachers to teach effective speaking skills. A comparison of the Tapestry Approach and traditional approaches is provided below.

Comparison of the Tapestry Approach to Speaking and Traditional Approaches

The Tapestry Approach	Traditional Approaches
• Learners are provided multiple opportunities to interact with more proficient peers and native English speakers.	• Learners interact mainly with other learners.
• Students are encouraged to use English outside of the class and are told how to use it.	• Learners are given little guidance concerning the use of English outside of class.
• Both accuracy and fluency are stressed in speech.	• Accuracy may be stressed, or fluency may be stressed, but rarely are both emphasized.
• Students are taught specific strategies to facilitate their efforts to speak effectively.	• Learners are not taught strategies that help them to speak effectively.
• The goal of pronunciation training is for students to speak with fully acceptable, though not necessarily native-like, pronunciation.	• The goal of pronunciation training is for students to speak in a completely native-like way. (This goal is unrealistic for almost all adults.)
• The primary emphasis in pronunciation is on stress and intonation.	• The primary emphasis in pronunciation is on teaching sounds.

TAPESTRY ACTIVITIES

Below we discuss Tapestry activities designed to develop speaking skills. The effectiveness of these activities directly relates to their relevance to students. Skillful teachers will need to adapt them to the on-going interests, needs, and goals of the ESL students they teach. Although we have divided these activities by proficiency levels, they can be adapted to all levels. The list is neither definitive nor comprehensive. (For additional activities, refer to the suggested readings listed at the end of this chapter.)

Activities for Beginning ESL Students

Cooperative Activities. Cooperative activities require the participation of each group member. All students need to participate since each student's contribution is essential for completion of the activity. In cooperative learning, students help one another to reach goals. They are assessed on their own individual contributions to the group as well as their group's ability to accomplish set objectives. Two specific types of cooperative learning described by Kagan (1989) are outlined below. (See also Johnson, Johnson, and Holubec 1986, and Slavin 1981, 1983, 1989-1990 for additional ideas.)

1. *Peer Tutoring.* Teammates teach each other simple concepts.
2. *Jigsaw.* Each member of a group has responsibility for a specific portion of a lesson. These members work with the members of other groups who have been given the same assignment. They form *expert groups*. Eventually, each member must learn the whole lesson by sharing information with others in his or her group.

Many cooperative learning activities are designed to teach specific group management and conversational skills. The two questionnaires below have been used successfully in cooperative learning tasks to encourage shy students to speak, talkative students to withdraw, and all students to develop effective speaking skills.

Table 10.3 Questionnaire: Conversational Skills

In today's activity	Often	Sometimes	Never
1. I checked to make sure that everyone understood what I said.			
2. I gave explanations whenever I could.			
3. I asked specific questions about what I didn't understand.			
4. I paraphrased what others said to make sure that I understood.			
5. I encouraged others to speak by making such remarks as "I'd like to know what _____ thinks about that" and "I haven't heard from _____ yet" and "What do you think, _____ ?"			

Table 10.4 Group Management Skills Questionnaire

1. What one word would you use to describe how the group was today? ________
2. What one word would describe the way you would like the group to be? ________
3. Is everyone participating?
   Yes, Always_____ Usually_____ Occasionally______ Rarely_____ No, Never_____
   If not, why not?
4. Are you (everyone in the group) trying to make each other feel good?
   Yes, Always_____ Usually_____ Occasionally______ Rarely_____ No, Never_____
5. Are you trying to help each other feel able to talk and say what you think?
   Yes, Always_____ Usually_____ Occasionally______ Rarely_____ No, Never_____
6. Are you listening to each other?
   Yes, Always_____ Usually_____ Occasionally______ Rarely_____ No, Never_____
7. Are you showing you are listening by nodding at each other?
   Yes, Always_____ Usually_____ Occasionally______ Rarely_____ No, Never_____
8. Are you saying "That's good" to each other when you like something?
   Yes, Always_____ Usually_____ Occasionally______ Rarely_____ No, Never_____
9. Are you asking each other questions?
   Yes, Always_____ Usually_____ Occasionally______ Rarely_____ No, Never_____
10. Are you listening and really trying to answer these questions?
    Yes, Always_____ Usually_____ Occasionally______ Rarely_____ No, Never_____
11. Are you paying attention to each other?
    Yes, Always_____ Usually_____ Occasionally______ Rarely_____ No, Never_____
12. Is any one person talking most of the time?
    Yes____ No____

Adapted from: Aronson, Blaney, Stephan, Sikes, and Snapp, 1978.
The Jigsaw Classroom. Beverly Hills, CA: Sage.

Pair Activities. Pair activities allow students to work one-on-one with others in the class. Because such activities involve students simultaneously working in dyads, often those students who are self-conscious speaking in front of a group feel free to interact. Krashen and Terrell (1983) give this example:

> Each pair of students must have a game board of squares; a grid of four by six squares is probably a good size. Each student is then given a set of small cards to fit the squares, each with a sketch or a picture on it. The two sets are identical. The first student arranges the cards on the grid in any fashion. Then this student must give directions to the other student for placing the second set of cards in identical fashion. After the directions are complete, the students match grids to see how accurate the directions were. If the students do not know the name of an object on the cards, they may explain or describe the object, but they should not use native language equivalents.

This activity is particularly useful when the objects pertain to a thematic lesson and the student will soon need to use the vocabulary presented to accomplish a task of real-life relevance. (For excellent suggestions, refer to Gaies 1985.)

Movement. Movement activities require students to get up from their chairs and to interact physically as a group. Two different types of movement exercises are suggested by Bassano and Christison (1987) in Examples 10.1 and 10.2.

Example 10.1

How Well Do You Know Me?

Directions: Read the descriptions below. Look around you to see which students in your class match the descriptions. Ask those students to sign their names next to the descriptions. If you can't see a match, ask several students for information until you find one who can sign his or her name next to the description. The person with the most signatures is the winner.

1. has brown eyes ______
2. likes chocolate ice cream ______
3. is married ______
4. wears glasses ______
5. has dimples ______
6. has a birthday in the same month as yours ______
7. is wearing a watch ______
8. is wearing white socks ______
9. has more than four brothers and sisters ______
10. has been in the United States less time than you have ______
11. has a moustache ______
12. drinks apple juice ______
13. does not like hamburgers ______
14. is wearing stripes ______

(Bassano and Christison 1987, p. 7)

[Allow 10 minutes for the activity itself and extra time to check signatures. Move furniture from the center of the room so that students are free to move about.]

Example 10.2

Everybody Votes

Focus: personal
Time: 20 minutes

Materials: sheets of newsprint (23" x 27")
tape; colored pens

Hang several sheets of newsprint around the room, each sheet headed with a general conversation topic, such as Politics, Religion, Family, Fun and Recreation, Love and Romance, Work, Friendship. Ask students to consider their most favorite conversation topic and to go stand by the sheet that best represents their choice. After noting the balance of interests, ask students to go stand by the sheet that represents their least favorite conversation topic.

Once students are aware of one another's interests, distribute colored pens. Ask students to write a personal comment on each of the newsprint sheets about the indicated conversation topic. Continue the activity until everyone has had a chance to write something on every sheet and to read the other comments.

As a wrap up, reconvene the class and ask students how they felt doing the activity, what things they noticed, what comments they heard. Or have students work in small groups to comment on what they didn't agree with, what they felt compelled to write, and so on.

This activity may be organized around any number of topics, such as Plans for a Saturday Night, Vacation Spots, Things We Can't Live Without, Household Chores, Classroom Activities, and so on.

(Bassano and Christison 1987, p. 3)

One-Centered. One-centered activities always concentrate on one student for a short time. Volunteers are interviewed by the rest of the class. Depending on the student's self-confidence, he or she may participate in front of the class or from his or her seat. Shy students may be asked to respond nonverbally. Krashen and Terrell (1983) provide this example: "A single student thinks of something which happened to him or her yesterday. The other students have to ask questions until they can guess what the event was." (p. 125). Suggestions include a visit, a trip, something the student ate or someone who called the student.

Story Telling. There are a variety of story telling activities that enable students to practice speaking skills. For example, after hearing half a story, students can finish the story orally, or after hearing an entire story, students can retell the story in their own words. (For other suggestions, see Morgan and Rinvolucri 1983 and Richard-Amato 1988.)

Activities for Intermediate ESL Students

Problem-Solving. Long and Crookes (1986) have been experimenting with problem-solving activities for promoting second language acquisition in the classroom. They have found that two-way tasks, in which two participants must share information in order to solve a problem (such as how to get to the train station on time), are effective in promoting the development of interactional features. These tasks encourage learners to push their linguistic knowledge to the limit, negotiate meaning, and develop accuracy as well as fluency.

Discussions. Ur (1981) provides useful strategies for carefully orchestrating discussions. Many effective discussions involve the use of authentic materials. Melvin and Stout (1987) list these: city street maps, public transportation guides, relief maps, lists of hotels, menus from local restaurants, tourist brochures, cultural publications announcing opening times of museums, theaters, or art galleries, catalogues, entertainment sections of local papers, guides to sports and recreational activities, movie listings, shopping guides, and sales advertising. ESL students can use authentic materials in designing and discussing imaginary (or real) travel itineraries. This activity is highly useful to international students who intend to spend some time travelling; however, it is less useful to those who are not planning to travel.

Socio-Dramas. In socio-drama, students act out solutions to social problems, generally determining their own courses of action. The student enactments are open-ended, but center around a clearly stated conflict of relevance to the students. The steps include introducing a topic, stimulating student interest, reading a story that clearly identifies a problem and stopping the story at the climax, discussing the dilemma, selecting students to play the roles, preparing the audience to listen and later offer advice, acting out the rest of the story, discussing alternative ways to solve the problem, and replaying the drama using new solutions when necessary. (For a more detailed description, refer to Scarcella 1983c.)

One socio-drama involves asking students to take on the roles of an administrator, a student named Marie, and a professor. Marie has cheated on a major exam, and the students must decide how she should get herself out of this difficult situation. The socio-drama is given in Example 10.3.

Example 10.3

Marie was a lazy student who attended San Francisco State University. She never paid attention in her classes and completely forgot the date when a term paper was due in her history class. Fortunately, she ran into Jose, a student in her history class, the day before the term paper was due. "I spent the last two weeks working on my term paper. It's due tomorrow, ya know. Did you finish it?" Joe asked.

Marie lied. "Uh, er um yeah. Thanks for reminding me to bring it tomorrow," she said.

That afternoon, Marie went to the library. She found a dissertation on the Civil War. It was written by someone named Jerry Bently. Without hesitating, Marie quickly copied a portion of it. After she handed the paper in, her professor told the class, "I have a surprise for you. I'd like to submit these papers for a consideration to an academic journal of history that publishes student papers once a year. The best paper wins $500. Are there any objections?" Marie thought a brief moment and put her head down. She was not about to draw attention to herself.

A few weeks later, Marie's professor made an announcement to the class. "Class, I have an announcement to make. I'm very proud that one of my students has won the history contest. Marie Hucklebee, you've just won $500 for that great term paper. Please come to the front of the class and receive the money and the congratulatory letter."

"Thank you, Professor Brown," Marie replied. She was thrilled. She grabbed the money, and that afternoon she spent it all on clothes.

The next day, while Professor Brown was home reading, he received a call from his old friend, Jerry Bently. Jerry and he had studied together at Columbia University. Jerry's call brought back old memories — of their graduate days in the dorm, of summer vacations at Jerry's ranch, and of Jerry's dissertation on the Civil War. Thinking about Jerry's dissertation brought the sudden realization that Marie Hucklebee's thinking was oddly similar to Jerry's. Professor Brown went to his bookcase and picked up his friend's dissertation. He thumbed through it until he came to the familiar part, the part Marie had copied. Immediately, Professor Brown called Marie.

"Marie," Professor Brown said. "I need to see you as soon as possible in my office. Is two o'clock today okay?"

"Sure. That's fine," Marie said.

That afternoon, Marie knocked on her professor's door.

"Come in," he said. "Do you have something to tell me?" Marie said,"...

Role-Plays. Role-plays involve less extensive enactments than socio-dramas. Students can role-play people in a variety of situations, including going shopping, eating out, attending movies, visiting the doctor, or looking for an apartment. The procedure described by Richards (1985) for utilizing role-play with intermediate learners is as follows:

> 1. Learners participate in a preliminary activity in which the topic and situation are introduced.
> 2. They then work through a model dialogue on a related topic which provides examples of the type of language which will be required.
> 3. Assisted by role cards, learners perform the role-play.
> 4. Learners listen to recordings of native speakers performing the role-play with the role cards.
> 5. Follow-up activities exploit the native speaker performance.
> 6. The entire sequence is then repeated with a second transaction on the same topic.
>
> (Richards 1985, pp. 85–88)

By selecting topics and settings from the information obtained from learners through needs analysis, the classroom role-plays can be made relevant to the perceived needs of the learners. (See Di Pietro 1987 for excellent suggestions for modifying role-plays so that they have real-world relevance.)

Plays. Smith (1984) suggests a variety of strategies that help learners develop speaking skills through drama. (See, for example, Holden 1981, Maley and Duff 1982, Via 1987, 1976.) Similarly, others have suggested that learners can make literature come alive by acting out the roles of characters from literature. For instance, after students have just read John Steinbeck's (1947) *The Pearl,* they can be asked to play the roles of Juana and Kino. Again, before using such activities it is important for teachers to determine whether the activities have real-world relevance for learners and whether they help the learners acquire the language they need to know.

Activities for Advanced ESL Learners

Reporting Information, Summarizing, Synthesizing, and Debating. Advanced ESL students also need opportunities to speak in a variety of academic situations — reporting information, summarizing, synthesizing, and debating. Cummins (1981) points out that ESL students frequently acquire conversational skills in their first few years in the United States, but lack the ability to communicate in academic, decontextualized situations (in which they cannot guess the meaning of the language they read or hear from the context). He maintains that communicative demands of academia and the acquisition of literacy and academic skills require more than daily face-to-face, one-to-one interaction.

Simulations. Simulations simulate real-life situations. They have been successfully used to teach ESL students of diverse backgrounds. (See Jones 1982 and Crookall and Oxford 1990.) One simulation involves having students take the roles of the college administration, community, and college students. These groups meet to determine whether new off-campus housing should be built, and, if it should, what facilities it should contain. Case studies also make excellent simulations.

The case study method has been used to teach advanced ESL students at Harvard University for over ten years. In this method, students are asked to participate in a simulation concerning an actual decision-making situation. Based on the students' analysis of the data, as well as their experience, readings, and interviews with others, students recommend a solution to the problem. Details of a business case study method are given in Dow and Ryan (1987). They give the following sample (adapted in Example 10.4):

Example 10.4

Bob Smith

The first National Bank of Littleton, Massachusetts, has received a loan application from Bob Smith. He wants to borrow $20,000 to start a shoe store in his hometown. From the application itself and from conversations with people in Bob's hometown, the loan officer has the following information to consider.

1. Born on a farm in western Massachusetts.
2. Mother died when he was six years old.
3. Delivered newspapers after school as a boy.
4. Worked while in high school as a grocery clerk every Saturday.
5. Bought his first car at age 18 for $300.
6. Used his car to deliver groceries for the local store.
7. Served in the army as a private for two years; no promotions.
8. Fined once at age 19 for speeding; no other traffic violations.
9. Applied at age 22 to a bank for loan of $10,000 to start a shoe store in his hometown; bank refused him the loan.
10. Worked as clerk in shoe store for six years; promoted to assistant manager after three years.
11. Has just applied at age 28 to bank for loan of $20,000 to start a shoe store in his hometown.

The problem in this case study is that the loan officer needs to decide whether to loan money to open the shoe store. Students must make a recommendation in written and oral analyses of the case. The case discussion class examines all the issues involved in cases and teaches specific speaking skills such as getting to the point and expressing the point succinctly. Dow and Ryan (1987) present a methodology for using case studies in ESL classes.

Activities for All ESL Learners

Community-Based Learning Activities. An important goal of the Tapestry Approach is to assist learners to use English outside of the ESL classroom. Tapestry teachers encourage learner involvement in the community. Teachers do this by activities such as taking students on field trips and bringing in guest speakers from the outside community. There is a need to convince the learners of the importance of these activities and to structure them in such a way as to validate them. Montgomery and Eisenstein (1985) report that when appropriately managed, community-based learning experiences can lead to significant language gains.

Field Trips. Field trips are important to the success of ESL programs designed for international students. They can reinforce a particular unit of study, expose students to United States culture, motivate students, stimulate intellectual growth, and provide students with opportunities to receive meaningful input and to interact in real world situations. There are many interesting field trip possibilities available to students. Ideas for inexpensive field trips suggested by Maculaitis and Scheraga (1990) include:

- industrial plants and agricultural centers;
- artistic and historic sites;
- communication centers;
- aquariums, zoos, archeology digs, planetariums, and wildlife preserves; and
- recreation areas.

Guest speakers. Guest speakers can enhance a theme-based lesson and provide students with exposure to diverse dialects and registers of English. In preparation for guest presentations, students can write interview questions. Consider speakers such as hospital emergency room workers, politicians, police officers, store workers, postal workers, counselors, nutritionists, family practice physicians, psychiatrists, psychologists, teachers, industry leaders, and Chamber of Commerce heads.

Community Contact. Conversation clubs and buddies enable ESL students to meet informally with native English speaking peers and instructors. Students can also be sent into the community on community contact assignments in which they are asked to collect questionnaire data. Strevens (1988) suggests that teachers create projects for their students that involve data collecting in unobtrusive, culturally acceptable ways. In addition, students can be assisted in developing telephone friendships, working in the local business community, and participating in a number of religious, sports, and recreational organizations.

All of the above activities can be easily adapted to theme- and task-based instruction typical of the Tapestry Approach. Teachers vary the use of such activities on the basis of student needs. (See Appendix 10.1.) During these activities, teachers can monitor students' progress in acquiring speaking skills. (See Appendix 10.2.)

A WORD ON PRONUNCIATION

The goal of teaching pronunciation in the Tapestry Approach is not to make learners sound like native speakers. Only a small segment of the adult population can learn to pronounce a second language in a native-like way. After childhood years, the ability to pronounce a new language natively diminishes (Krashen, Scarcella, and Long 1982; Larsen-Freeman and Long 1991; Scovel 1988). Many traditional approaches imply that they try to teach people to speak in a native-like way, but these approaches cannot achieve such a lofty goal. A more realistic goal, the one adopted by the Tapestry Approach, is to help learners past the age of childhood to develop clear, understandable pronunciation with appropriate intonation and stress. This does not mean native-like speech, which is almost impossible to attain for adults, but it does mean the kind of pronunciation that native speakers of the language will fully accept and comprehend. Problems with intonation and stress cause some of the worst misunderstandings among learners and native speakers, and these problems are avoidable through proper pronunciation training. The teaching of mere sounds is not sufficient, but the teaching of intonation and stress along with sounds provides a much stronger instructional program for pronunciation.

In the Tapestry Approach, pronunciation training is integrated into regular language activities. Students learn self monitoring skills. They go on field assignments outside of class in which they talk with native speakers and note the circumstances under which they themselves are not understood because of pronunciation difficulties (Wong 1987). In this way they discover when they are unintelligible and learn to respond to feedback cues. They make taped speech samples for their teacher to diagnose according to sounds, stress, and intonation. They receive individual help on their specific pronunciation problems, and they practice the needed remediation in communicative activities of many different kinds (for examples, see Celce-Murcia 1987). Students also learn relaxation strategies to help them improve their pronunciation.

TAPESTRY PRINCIPLES CONCERNING SPEAKING

The discussion above brings us to propose the following Tapestry principles pertaining to ESL speaking instruction.

PRINCIPLES

1. Students are encouraged to speak in a wide variety of situations.
2. Learners interact both inside and outside of the class.
3. Both accuracy and fluency are stressed.
4. Teachers help students acquire useful speaking strategies.
5. Teachers aid students in learning appropriate stress and intonation.

CONCLUSION

In conclusion, effective Tapestry speaking instruction includes a careful consideration of the types of speaking tasks that provide learners with multiple opportunities to practice speaking skills with native and non-native English speakers, accuracy and fluency activities, and the learners' use of English inside and outside the ESL classroom. Speaking activities need to be integrated into other activities involving other skill areas such as listening. Tapestry teachers need to be sensitive to the communicative needs of their students and vary the activities they use accordingly.

ACTIVITIES AND DISCUSSION QUESTIONS

1. Make a list of guest speakers you might invite to an ESL class. Include names, addresses, and phone numbers as well as a description of what each might contribute to specific thematic units you are teaching.
2. Sometimes students fail to see the value of ESL speaking activities because they think that the activities are too entertaining. What are three strategies teachers can use to help students see the usefulness of the speaking activities they use?
3. What are the major differences between memorizing a dialog and participating in a role-play?
4. What advantages and disadvantages can you see in the use of simulations and games? What kinds of simulations and games would interest your students?
5. What particular conversational features should teachers model for their students?
6. What activities described in this chapter would you consider most appropriate for the purpose of lowering the students' anxieties about speaking in front of others? For lowering anxieties about pronunciation?

NOTES

1. Fluency has been defined in numerous ways (Van Ek 1976, Van Ek and Alexander 1980, and Fillmore 1979). We use the term to refer to the ability to fill time with talk easily without unnecessary hesitations. It includes the ability to speak appropriately in a wide range of contexts, but does not include the ability to use grammatically correct sentences. In contrast, we use the term accuracy to refer to the speaker's control of grammar, vocabulary, and pronunciation.

SUGGESTED READINGS

- Cristison, M.A., and Bassano, S. 1981. *Look Who's Talking.* San Francisco: Alemany. This interesting volume guides teachers in the development of successful conversation groups in intermediate and advanced ESL classrooms. It provides junior high school, high school, and adult education teachers with a practical set of classroom activities and strategies for fostering interaction in the ESL classroom.

- Richards, J.C., and Schmidt, R.W. (eds.). 1983. *Language and Communication.* London: Longman. This collection of papers offers a comprehensive account of research on the components of communication and of the application of this research to ESL teaching methodology.

- Rivers, W. (ed.). 1987. *Interactive Language Teaching.* Cambridge: Cambridge University Press. This edited volume contains a description of approaches and techniques that facilitate interaction in small and large groups. Activities are suggested for using speaking, reading, writing, testing, poetry, song, drama, grammar, the community, and computer software in interactive contexts.

- Savignon, S.J. 1983. *Communicative Competence: Theory and Classroom Practice.* Reading, MA: Addison-Wesley. Intended for classroom teachers and teachers-in-training, this book contains worthwhile suggestions for ways in which programs can be made more responsive to the communicative goals of both learners and teachers.

- Morley, J. 1987. *Current Perspectives on Pronunciation: Practices Anchored in Theory.* Washington, D.C.: Teachers of English to Speakers of Other Languages. This volume contains practical articles focused on pronunciation teaching. It examines such issues as the role of pronunciation in communication, the effect of learner variables on the development of pronunciation skills, the role of applied phonetics in speech awareness, and communicative approaches to pronunciation.

- Wong, R. 1987. *Teaching Pronunciation: Focus on English Rhythm and Intonation.* Englewood Cliffs, NJ: Prentice Hall Regents and Center for Applied Linguistics. This monograph emphasizes the role of the learner in acquiring pronunciation skills and the teaching of English rhythm and intonation. It provides teachers with a wealth of practical suggestions for personalizing their pronunciation instruction.

APPENDIX 10.1

SELF-EVALUATION OF SPEAKING ACTIVITIES

Activity	I like	It's okay	I don't like
Participating in discussions			
Participating in role-plays			
Singing songs			
Playing games			
Doing pronunciation exercises			
Working on specific projects in small groups			
Going on field trips			
Interviewing guest speakers			

(Adapted from Nunan 1988, p. 132.)

APPENDIX 10.2

SAMPLE RATING SCALE

Indicate the degree to which learners contribute to small-group discussions or conversation classes by circling the appropriate number.

(Key: 5–outstanding, 4–above average, 3–average, 2–below average, 1–unsatisfactory)

1.	The learner participates in discussions.	1	2	3	4	5
2.	The learner uses appropriate nonverbal signals.	1	2	3	4	5
3.	The learner's contributions are relevant.	1	2	3	4	5
4.	The learner is able to negotiate meaning.	1	2	3	4	5
5.	The learner is able to convey factual information.	1	2	3	4	5
6.	The learner can give personal opinions.	1	2	3	4	5
7.	The learner can invite contributions from others.	1	2	3	4	5
8.	The learner can agree/disagree appropriately.	1	2	3	4	5
9.	The learner can change the topic appropriately.	1	2	3	4	5

(Nunan 1988, pp. 142–143)

GRAMMAR

11

PREVIEW QUESTIONS

1. Which groups of students most benefit from grammar instruction? Why? (In answering this question, you may want to consider students from various cultural backgrounds, with different second language proficiency levels, and with diverse learning styles.)
2. Should ESL teachers present grammar rules deductively (through the presentation of rules) or inductively (through examples that lead learners to discover rules by themselves)? Why?
3. What specific grammar rules should be taught?
4. Is the goal of grammar instruction always native-like mastery? Why or why not?
5. How can teachers best determine their students' grammar needs?
6. What learner characteristics affect the grammar instruction teachers provide their students? (Consider such characteristics as age and length of residence in the United States as well as personality variables such as extroversion and introversion.)

Just as the ability to weave involves many aspects, so too does the ability to produce a second language. One important aspect of second language learning is grammar.

ORGANIZATION OF THIS CHAPTER

This chapter concerns the role of grammar in the Tapestry Approach. The purpose is to lay out some important theoretical principles based on the research and then to indicate practical implications for teaching. First, we explain what it means to know English grammar. Then, we provide a rationale for teaching grammar and consider important questions related to grammar instruction. Finally, we outline the treatment of grammar in the Tapestry Approach.

WHAT IT MEANS TO KNOW ENGLISH GRAMMAR

Grammar includes many aspects of linguistic knowledge, including morphology and syntax.

Morphology

Morphology is sometimes referred to as word structure. It concerns the rules and principles underlying the use of *morphemes,* the smallest units of meaningful sound. An example of a morpheme is the *-ing* ending on the word *running. Inflectional suffixes* (that is, meaningful word endings such as *-ing)* are particularly important in English. These particular morphemes function to mark the base form of the word for case, number, person, or tense. To give the reader an idea of the complexity of inflectional morphemes, consider the agentive ending *-er/-or.* While most inflectional endings can attach to only one part of speech (such as a noun, verb, or adjective), the agentive ending *-er/-or,* which usually attaches to verb bases (as in the words *singer, teacher,* and *catcher),* also attaches to nouns (such as *prisoner)* and adjectives (such as the comparative adjective, *stranger).*

In contrast to inflectional suffixes, derivational suffixes (such as *-ment* in the word *government)* change the part of speech of their base. For instance, the derivational suffix *-ly* changes the noun form *friend* to the adverb form *friendly.*

However, knowledge of morphemes includes more than just learning the correct forms. Morphemes not only have specific forms, but also semantic, syntactic, relational, phonological, and distributional properties.

Semantic Properties. Morphemes always have some meaning. For instance, the progressive verb ending *-ing* carries the meaning of duration.

Syntactic Properties. Morphemes also have syntactic properties. The morpheme *-ing* can occur only at the end of verbs in specific sentence structures. For instance, one cannot write, *Last night I went to the movies, saw my friend, and was playing the guitar.*

Relational Properties. In addition to syntactic properties, morphemes have relational properties. These properties refer to the fact that morphemes are related semantically to their base forms such that competent English speakers know that the word *run* is related to *running* and the word *govern* is related to *government.*

Phonological Properties. Morphemes also have distinct phonological properties. In the case of inflectional morphemes, the base of a word affects the pronunciation of the morpheme. (This is the opposite in the case of derivational suffixes.) For instance, the plural morpheme *-s* assimilates or borrows the phonetic feature of voicing of the final sound in the base. As a result, students pronounce the *-s* in the word *bees* as a [z] and the *-s* in the word *tops* as a [s]. This is because the vowel *e* that precedes the *-s* in *bees* is voiced and the consonant sound *p* that precedes the *-s* in *tops* is voiceless.

Distributional Properties. In addition, there are distributional properties of morphemes. The *-ing* ending can attach to any new verb entering English. This is not the case with other inflectional endings. For instance, the verb suffix *-en* can attach only to adjectives of Germanic origin, such as *strengthen, whiten,* and *darken.* As the reader notices, distributional constraints are often idiosyncratic.

Knowledge of morphemes is further complicated by the fact that many morphemes are structurally ambiguous with other morphemes and with meaningless sequences of letters. For instance, compare the *-er* on the agentive morpheme in *butcher,* the comparative morpheme in *smaller* and the non-morpheme in *butter.* (Note that the *-er* in the word *butter* is not a morpheme, since it carries no meaning.)

The reader will note that knowing the morphology of English overlaps knowing English pronunciation, semantics, lexicon, and syntax. Learners acquire all these aspects of the language with varying degrees of accuracy when listening, speaking, reading, and writing. Recognizing the overlap and similarity in acquisition, Canale and Swain (1980) included pronunciation, semantics, lexicon, and syntax in their description of grammatical competence.

Syntax

Knowing English grammar also entails knowing its syntax. *Syntax* refers to the order of words in a sentence. As Hatch explains, "In language production, sentence syntax allows us to choose just how we wish to present our ideas in linear sequence" (p. 75). We can combine words to change the meaning of our sentences. For instance, we can say, *I saw a man commit murder last night in the dark.* Or we can say, *Someone I saw was murdered last night in the dark.* Or *It was dark when the person committed murder.* Syntax allows us to combine ideas in different ways. We can use juxtaposition; that is, simply string sentences together *(I saw a man. He committed murder. It was last night. It was dark.)*, or we can use conjunction *(I saw a man commit murder and it was last night.)*, relativization *(I saw the man who committed murder last night)*, or complementation *(I was surprised that the man committed murder last night.)*. In addition to learning how to combine parts of speech to form sentences and the meanings of these parts, we must know how the elements of language can be put together in specific ways, what functions these elements have, where they can occur, and what grammatical co-occurrence restrictions govern their use. Such restrictions prevent speakers from using imperatives (such as *Sit down)* with pause fillers (such as *ya know)* as in the sentences *Ya know sit down* or *Go to hell ya know.* On top of all this, we must know how frequently to use specific language elements in specific situational contexts. (See Chapter Five.)

In this section, we have presented only a partial description of what it means to know English grammar. Our purpose has been to display the richness and complexity of grammar. Some would argue that because grammar is complex, it cannot be taught. In the section below, we present a different view. We argue that not only is it advisable to teach grammar, it is also necessary.

RATIONALE FOR TEACHING GRAMMAR

As noted in the earlier chapter on communicative competence, grammar is a cornerstone of communicative language teaching. To many people this is a novel idea. For a while, as the crest of the communicative wave swept the language instruction community worldwide, grammar was sometimes lost in the tide. (See, for instance, Dulay, Burt, and Krashen 1982; Krashen and Terrell 1983).

Many teachers in the last decade had the mistaken idea that grammar instruction had little or no place in a communicative classroom. For these teachers, grammar instruction was equated with boring language drills. Such individuals believed that students could simply absorb all the grammar they needed from communicative activities, and that if students wanted to acquire more grammar, they could learn it on their own through homework and reference books.

Support for the idea that students are capable of acquiring grammar through natural exposure to input rather than instruction primarily comes from Krashen (1981, 1982; Krashen and Terrell 1983). In attempting to explain the role of grammar in language development, Krashen proposed a model that de-emphasizes the role of instruction in grammatical development. Central to his model is the distinction that he makes between acquisition and learning. He uses the term *acquisition* to refer to picking up the language subconsciously — much as children acquire their first language. *Learning* is the term he uses to refer to the conscious study of the formal properties of language. Krashen argues that learned knowledge is only available for use by the Monitor — in editing or ferreting out errors in language performance. In Krashen's view acquisition and learning constitute two separate processes. Learning does not lead to acquisition.[1]

Because Krashen believes that the memorization of rules has little effect on language development, he encouraged others to downplay grammar in language classrooms.[2] This severe downplaying of grammar was perhaps a necessary antidote to the grammatical overexposure language learners experienced in the heyday of the cognitive approaches to language teaching. However, the pendulum is now swinging back to a more reasonable point, a state at which grammar is again considered an essential element of language learning. Below we present several practical arguments for the teaching of grammar.

The Role of Grammar in Communicative Competence

The communicative competence model of Canale and Swain (1980; see also Canale 1983) clearly illustrates the significance of grammar. In this model, grammar is an essential component. Without grammar, learners can communicate effectively only in a limited number of situations. They may be able to say *Fill it up* at the gas station, but if they find that their car is low on oil, and they lack the grammatical competence to say *Would you mind checking my oil?,* they might find themselves in serious difficulty. They might be able to get away with ungrammatical sentences such as *Excuse my vocabularies. I no speak English good.* at the corner market, but they will be penalized for using such sentences when they are making oral presentations during graduate seminars.

The Role of Instruction in Acquisition

Many researchers have suggested that instruction helps learners to increase the rate at which they acquire grammatical features and to attain higher levels of grammatical accuracy. These investigators are identifying the specific situations in which adult ESL learners benefit from grammar instruction. Pienemann (1984), for example, found that while acquisition orders are impervious to instruction, classroom instruction can speed the acquisition of specific grammatical structures when learners are psychologically ready to receive this instruction. He uses the term *psychologically ready* to refer to well-timed instruction. Such instruction is given at a time when the learners have already acquired the prerequisite knowledge they need to process the instruction, are paying attention to the instruction, and are sufficiently motivated to attend to and use the instruction. According to Pienemann's *teachability hypothesis,* the learnability of a given linguistic structure constrains the effectiveness of instruction. Long 1983a summarizes the results of 11 studies and shows that while it is impossible to alter developmental sequences, instruction is beneficial. Six of the studies Long analyzed showed faster development in children and adults receiving formal instruction, two arguably had similar results, and three showed that instruction had a minor or nonsignificant effect on learner production. Long concludes that grammar instruction can help ESL learners of all proficiency levels. Others who have reported similar findings include Pica 1983, Weslander and Stephany 1983, Gass 1982, and Pavesi 1986. (For a useful review of the literature, see Long 1988 and Larsen-Freeman and Long 1991.)[3]

Input

Grammar instruction can provide learners with valuable input for language development. Like McLaughlin (1978) and others (see, for instance, Stevick 1980 and Bialystok 1982), we believe that there is a considerable amount of seepage between what Krashen considers learned and what is acquired. This is because, for us, learners memorize rules to produce language (output) and then that language often serves as the learners' own input and leads to further language acquisition. (See Figure 11.1.)

Figure 11.1 The role of learning and acquisition

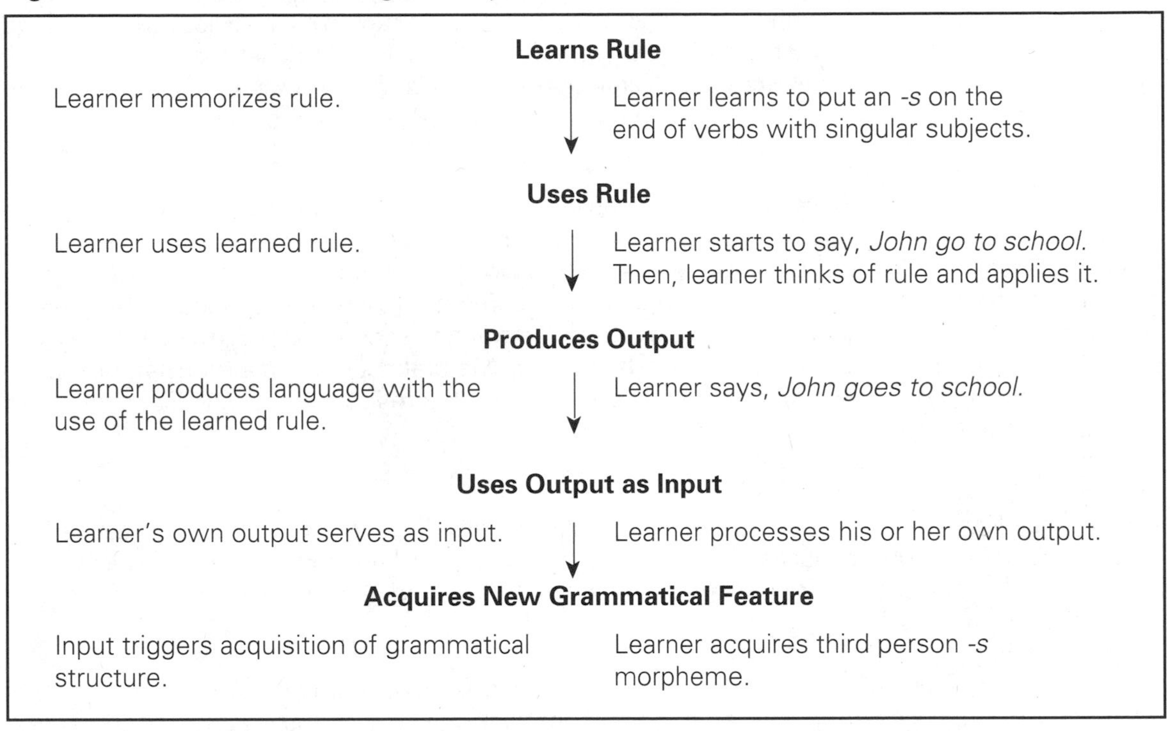

Learns Rule
Learner memorizes rule.
Learner learns to put an -s on the end of verbs with singular subjects.
Uses Rule
Learner uses learned rule.
Learner starts to say, John go to school. Then, learner thinks of rule and applies it.
Produces Output
Learner produces language with the use of the learned rule.
Learner says, John goes to school.
Uses Output as Input
Learner's own output serves as input.
Learner processes his or her own output.
Acquires New Grammatical Feature
Input triggers acquisition of grammatical structure.
Learner acquires third person -s morpheme.

Although it has sometimes been argued that learners are exposed in conversation to all the grammatical structures they need (Krashen 1981, 1982), considerable research demonstrates that this is not the case. (See, for example, Schmidt 1983, Swain 1985, and Schmidt and Frota, 1986.) For instance, it may be important for some learners to learn to use passive structures, such as *The novel was written by James,* to understand their academic textbooks; however, passives occur infrequently in informal casual conversations. Teachers need to consider the grammar their students need and to expose their students to this grammar in a principled way. The grammar of engineering is different from the grammar of history. The grammar of writing is different from the grammar of speaking.

Motivation and Individual Differences

Many students demand grammar instruction because it fulfills cultural expectations. Some cultures place great value on grammatical correctness. For instance, in examining classroom practices by French teachers, Dannequin (1977) observes that students do not have the right to make grammar mistakes, but must instead conform to teachers' standards. One important aspect of Japanese life is learning the proper grammatical form. Great value is placed on doing things *right*. Thompson (1987a) states that "the traditional Japanese regard for authority and formality is in tune with teacher-dominated lessons where much heed is paid to the *correct* answer, learning of grammar rules and item-by-item (rather than contextualized) vocabulary" (p. 223). A salient feature of Chinese education is also obsessive concern with grammatical correctness (Maley 1987). Lewis (1974) observes the stress in Soviet pedagogy on the value of formal grammar presentation. It is not surprising then that learners from these cultures experience frustration when participating in classes in which there is no grammar instruction.

Also, many learners have an analytic learning style preference and often feel completely adrift unless they have analytic grammar activities. They find systematic, analytic/logical exercises and teacher explanations of grammar appealing. While such exercises and explanations may not always in themselves be instructional, they put learning in a format that lowers student anxieties and motivates certain learners. This in itself is an important justification for direct grammar instruction.

Maturational Constraints

Grammar instruction also takes on increased importance given the adult's diminishing capacity to acquire grammar in natural situations. The classroom can help to compensate for the adults' inability to acquire language on their own. A number of studies have shown that maturational constraints affect the natural acquisition of grammatical competence in a second language. In general, adults are capable of acquiring high levels of proficiency in their second language, but for the most part, lack the capability of acquiring native-like proficiency. Maturational constraints on natural second language development are particularly well documented in the area of morphology. (For a review of the studies, see Chapter Two; see also Long 1990.)

Testing

As Celce-Murcia and Hilles (1988) point out, many students have to pass exams, such as the Test of English as a Foreign Language (TOEFL), that rely largely on knowledge of grammatical rules. Students can significantly improve the scores they receive on these exams by studying grammar.

Understanding

Grammar instruction is often helpful to make language input more comprehensible. In comprehending sentences, listeners often begin to construct meaning by focusing on those content words that they understand, their own background knowledge, and word order (Clark and Clark 1977). However, listeners are able to understand sentences more accurately when they complement this knowledge with their knowledge of the relevant grammar. Without any grammar instruction, it is sometimes difficult for students to comprehend what they are hearing.

Enjoyment

Grammar instruction can be enjoyable (Swain 1985). Many students look forward to discovering the way English grammar works.

ISSUES PERTAINING TO GRAMMAR INSTRUCTION

The above rationale for grammar instruction necessitates support for grammar instruction in ESL classes. The issues below must be carefully examined.

The Selection of Grammatical Structures to be Presented in Class

In the Tapestry Approach, teachers do not attempt to teach all the grammatical properties of the English language. Rather, they focus on those grammatical features which are: (1) useful to students, and (2) teachable and learnable. Teachers determine student needs and goals carefully and constantly evaluate the teachability and learnability of the grammatical features that they present to students in class.

For high-beginning ESL learners, teachers select the most basic rules of English grammar and the most common exceptions to these general rules. Whenever possible, they teach common patterns or systems that work for nearly all students all the time. (For instance, when teaching students how to use noncount nouns, they provide such generalizations as "Use noncount nouns to refer to particles too small to count — such as *hair, sugar, rice,* and *sand;* also use noncount nouns to refer to liquids — such as *gas, lemonade, coffee,* and *tea.*" The grammatical structures teachers present have immediate use to students in daily interactions. The patterns include: basic sentence structures (such as declarative, wh-questions, and tag questions such as *That's your friend, isn't it?),* filler subjects (*it* and *there),* adverbs, (*very, too,* and *enough),* prepositions (such as *in, on, at),* articles *(the, a, an),* quantifiers (such as *some, many),* proper and common nouns *(Mr. Brown, chair),* noncount nouns *(love, hate),* count nouns *(table, chair),* pronouns *(he, she, it),* verb tense (present/past) and aspect (present perfect/present progressive), coordination (with *or* and *and),* subordination (with *because),* modal auxiliaries (such as *can, may, must, will,* and *would),* and two- and three-word verbs (such as *I* ***walked out*** *on him.)*

For intermediate ESL learners, teachers select those specific aspects of the grammar that the students need to learn to fill gaps in their knowledge. They do not attempt to teach every nuance of the English language. (For instance, they couldn't care less whether students recognize the common roots of *gyp*sy and *Egyp*tian and *ptero*dactyl and helico*pter!)* Teachers explain that familiar grammatical structures take on different functions in a variety of contexts. They provide students with increased exposure to input that displays the use of the grammatical features in diverse settings. They also provide students with multiple opportunities to use the features. At the same time they provide learners with meaningful input and interaction that contains the target grammatical features, they also provide learners with direct grammar instruction. In this way, students' knowledge of the functions, distribution, and grammatical constraints of the features increases. The grammatical features that are presented are similar to those presented to high-beginning ESL students and include: articles and quantifiers, mass and count nouns, plural forms, verb tense and aspect, passives, relative clauses, modal auxiliaries, causatives, conditional clauses, subordination, complementizers, pronoun reference, two- and three-word verbs, and subject/verb agreement. Note, however, that it is assumed that intermediate students have acquired basic word order.

Also, intermediate ESL courses are more academically oriented than beginning ones, and intermediate ESL students often complete lengthier writing tasks than beginning ESL students. For this reason, some of the grammatical features characterizing academic English (such as passive structures) are presented along with punctuation lessons that complement the presentation and practice of grammatical features.

For advanced ESL learners, teachers review those specific features that students lack. Instruction becomes more individualized and more academically content-oriented. The grammar characterizing the specialized registers students need to learn is also presented. While no effort is made to cover all the subtleties of English, more specific grammatical detail is given to help students increase their communicative effectiveness. Although the same grammatical features that were presented to intermediate students are presented to advanced students (including articles and quantifiers, mass and count nouns, plural forms, verb tense and aspect, passives, relative clauses, modal auxiliaries, conditional clauses, subordination, causatives, complementizers, two- and three-word verbs), more information is provided about these features, and they are presented in ways that require more sophisticated use of English. Also, other additional grammatical features are presented such as parallel structures, cohesive markers, troublesome verb forms, and adjectives formed from *-ing* or the *-ed/-en* participle. In addition to these grammatical features, increased emphasis is placed on helping learners gain effective editing skills that will improve their written work.

The Means by which Teachers Make Grammatical Features Salient

In the Tapestry Approach, teachers make the grammatical structures salient through a variety of means. They recycle grammatical features periodically according to student needs and present features through a variety of activity types. The grammar explanations are presented clearly in simple, nontechnical language. Tapestry teachers use words such as *subject, noun,* and *verb,* and they explain these words carefully. They avoid using confusing linguistic labels such as *preposition stranding.* Boxes, examples, illustrations, charts, and tables are used whenever possible. Also, students are given overviews of those sets of related grammatical features that can be presented as whole systems, such as verb tense and aspect, determiners, modal auxiliaries, and active/passive structures.

The Frequency in which Grammatical Features are Presented

The grammatical features presented in the Tapestry Approach are constantly recycled. In other instructional approaches, students are sometimes given one or two exercises on a given grammatical feature and expected to use the feature effectively, or grammatical features are taught one at a time, in a feature-each-week approach. The *feature-a-week syllabus* is disastrous for learners who are sick for a week or who already know the structure being taught. For this reason, the Tapestry Approach provides students with multiple exposure to grammatical features in a variety of situations designed to increase the students' knowledge of the use of the features. The explanations, examples, and activities are diverse to prevent boredom and to appeal to different learning styles and interests. Multiple explanations are presented in various styles and formats. An ample number of illustrations and examples always follows these explanations. Numerous activities allow students to increase their awareness of a given grammatical feature by focusing on it in written and oral exercises and in authentic reading and listening texts. Other activities challenge students to use their knowledge in cooperative learning exercises, games, and editing exercises.

The Persons Who Provide Instruction

In the Tapestry Approach, both students and teacher are involved in grammar instruction. The Tapestry Approach emphasizes the importance of gradually releasing responsibility from teacher to students. The teacher defines the instructional objectives and normally presents the grammar lesson to the students through explanations, examples, and communicative exercises, and/or practice with the text. However, the teacher gradually releases the responsibility of teaching grammar to students in pair and group work in the context of language-promoting conversation. (See Chapter Three.) Native English-speaking peers also play an important role in teaching grammar.

The Roles of Accuracy and Fluency

For a few students, the goal of instruction is native-like mastery. However, for most students, the goal is only the grammatical proficiency they need to communicate effectively. To gain fluency, students are asked to complete a variety of tasks in which accuracy is unimportant. Such tasks include conversing informally with friends and participating in informal role-play situations. To gain accuracy, students are asked to complete a variety of tasks in which the accurate use of the language is important. Such tasks include writing formal reports, making academic presentations, and participating in debates. Formal instruction and practice also facilitate the development of accuracy.

The Role of Corrective Feedback

In the Tapestry Approach, not all errors are corrected. Error correction in this approach takes a variety of forms. While most students who are just beginning to acquire English benefit more from encouragement than error correction, many students demand error correction. Tapestry teachers know their students' preferences and needs. They tailor the feedback that they provide their students.[4] They consider the ways in which native English speakers react to different types of errors and the educational and affective impact of error correction on specific ESL learners in the course of particular activities. Thus, they do not correct every error their students make. They recognize that errors often indicate developmental trends in language development rather than language deficiencies that can be overcome through constructive, supportive criticism.

Error correction in fluency activities is different than that in accuracy exercises. During fluency activities, teachers never interrupt students to give corrections. This disturbs the flow of communication and negatively affects the students' self-confidence. During accuracy activities, teachers select a few basic features of the language that students are using incorrectly, but are capable of learning. They offer students feedback on these specific features in constructive ways.

It should be noted that in the Tapestry Approach, editing exercises are corrected according to the proficiency level of the learners. When the students are unable to identify their own errors, the teacher assists them — by marking the major errors with correcting symbols that help the learners identify their errors and fix them. Later, when the students have gained more competence as editors, the teachers indicate where the major errors have occurred by placing X's in the margins of the students' written papers. This helps the learners develop strong editing skills that enable them to become independent of their instructors. (See Raimes 1991 for an excellent discussion.)

Means of Presenting Grammatical Features

In the Tapestry Approach, a variety of activities are used to foster the learners' grammatical development. These include presentations, demonstrations, and analytical activities. However, the majority of Tapestry Activities are communicative. This is because, like Nunan (1989), we believe that activities must "... require conclusions, and construct their own [grammatical] rules from instances and examples of language use" (p. 36). These activities differ from the drill-and-kill exercises characteristic of some traditional approaches and include:

Contextualized Communicative Activities. Larsen-Freeman (1991) suggests several innovative communicative activities for teaching specific grammatical features. These activities provide learners with exposure to grammatical structures in the context of meaningful communication. This is what is meant by *contextualized*. (See also Richards, 1985.) In one activity, suggested by Fowler, Pidcock, and Rycroft (1979), learners read and write postcards that contextualize the progressive. As Richards (1985) explains, this activity is ideal for teaching the progressive since the present progressive is used to denote actions that are seen as temporary. In an activity on sports, the students hear a commentary on a sports event that also contextualizes the present progressive:

> The rain is falling heavily here at Monza. Don Braken is lapping at 237 kilometers an hour. He's leading Piero Angelo by eight seconds. Angelo is trying to close the gap but Braken's driving the race of his life today. Now they're in the straight and smoke is pouring from Bracken's engine. His manager is signaling to him desperately. He's coming in to the pit. The mechanics are working on the car and the smoke is dying down, but Bracken is losing precious time. Angelo's opening up a big gap . . . every second is vital.
>
> (Reported in Richards 1985, pp. 168–169.)

Celce-Murcia and Hilles (1988) also offer a variety of useful techniques and resources for grammar instruction: listening and responding, telling stories, participating in dramatic activities and role-plays, describing pictures, realia, and graphics, singing songs and reciting verse, playing games, and participating in problem-solving activities and text-based exercises and activities. In addition, Frank and Rinvolucri (1983) suggest a wide array of useful communicative, contextualized grammar activities. (See also Celce-Murcia 1991.)

Explicit, Deductive Instruction. Both research and teaching experience tell us that many ESL learners benefit from *explicit, deductive instruction*. In such instruction, grammatical rules are made salient through teacher-directed instruction.[5] This is not to say that a return to the exclusive teaching of discrete grammatical points with lengthy grammatical explanations and decontextualized grammar exercises is warranted. Rather, we suggest that most adult learners benefit from teacher-direct grammar instruction that is tailored to specific needs and preferences.

Implicit, Inductive Instruction. Although many learners prefer deductive learning, many others prefer inductive. In inductive learning, learners are asked to discover grammatical rules by themselves. They are given input and asked to make sense of it by discovering the rules. While there is little research that suggests that deductive or inductive learning is inherently better, researchers who support implicit, inductive instruction over explicit, deductive learning argue that students remember grammatical rules better when they discover them on their own. We argue here that the research is inconclusive and until there are more definitive findings, it is best to provide learners with both inductive and deductive types of grammatical activities.

Editing Exercises. Many learners can benefit from exercises in which their grammatical errors are made salient, and they are required to edit their errors. (See also Chapter Eight.)

THE TAPESTRY APPROACH TO GRAMMAR INSTRUCTION AND TRADITIONAL APPROACHES

As seen in the discussion above, the Tapestry Approach differs from traditional approaches to grammar instruction in many ways. A comparison of these two approaches is given below. We have magnified the differences to make the characteristics of the Tapestry Approach salient. We are not suggesting that all traditional classrooms are taught exactly the same, or that traditional grammar instruction is bad for all learners.

Comparison of the Tapestry Approach to Grammar and Traditional Approaches

The Tapestry Approach	Traditional Approaches
• Teachers vary the goals that they have for students based on student needs and preferences.	• Teachers have the same goal for all students: native-like grammatical accuracy.
• Teachers focus on those grammatical features that are: (1) useful to students and (2) teachable and learnable.	• Teachers attempt to teach all grammatical features.
• Themes drive tasks and tasks determine the grammatical features that are taught and the order in which they are presented.	• The focus of the class is grammar. Teachers follow a grammatical syllabus.
• Teachers tailor the feedback they provide their students to the needs and preferences of their students.	• Teachers correct all student grammar errors.
• Teachers gradually release the responsibility of teaching grammar to students in pair and group work — in the context of language-promoting conversation. (See Chapter Three.)	• All grammar instruction is teacher-centered and controlled.

In the Tapestry Approach, intensive grammar instruction that focuses exclusively on grammatical features is the wrong way to go.[6] Tapestry teachers first and foremost follow functional, purposeful principles to second language learning.

TAPESTRY PRINCIPLES CONCERNING GRAMMAR INSTRUCTION

The discussion above brings us to propose the following principles pertaining to grammar instruction.

PRINCIPLES

1. Grammatical forms are presented in authentic language contexts. The teacher and other native speakers demonstrate the use of grammatical structures within the context of authentic, communicative activities (such as writing notes, making lists, or requesting information). These demonstrations consist of exposing students to native speaker use of grammatical structures in a host of activities including role-plays, simulations, and problem-solving and cooperative activities. The teacher invites learners to use the grammatical structures they study in purposeful communication. The communication arouses and maintains the students' interest and attention.
2. Teachers organize and present specific grammatical structures as needs for instruction transpire. In addition, they teach students grammatical structures that are roughly sequenced based on such factors as developmental trends, communicative value, frequency and salience of input, importance of errors to native speakers, and the need for varied activities.
3. Learning about grammatical forms occurs in tandem with learning about other concepts pertaining to the functions of the structures and their purpose in communication. Grammatical forms are never taught in isolation.
4. Grammatical structures are learned from multiple sources of assistance — students teach one another during cooperative learning activities, the teacher provides direct teaching of grammatical points, learners acquire grammar through their listening and reading experiences, and students learn grammar from a variety of analytical and communicative exercises specifically designed with the individual differences of learners in mind. (See Chapters Three and Four.)

CONCLUSION

In the Tapestry Approach, there is no place for purely rote drills. However, unstructured lessons without any grammar instruction equates disaster for many language learners. Grammar instruction cannot be incidental. It must be taught in a principled manner. Not to do so is to do a disservice to ESL students. Moreover, eclecticism is not the answer. Teachers cannot simply mix communicative activities with a few grammar explanations. They must integrate grammar instruction throughout ESL lessons in principled ways. Grammar must be selected and presented in a sensible manner, keeping in mind factors such as developmental factors that affect second language acquisition (see Chapter Two), communicative value, frequency and salience of input, importance of errors to native speakers, and the need for varied activities.

The topic of grammar is once again at the forefront of discussions in language teaching, due in large part to the recent research of Long (1988), Larsen-Freeman and Long (1991), Rutherford and Sharwood Smith (1988), and others. Virtually everyone believes that there is a need for both explicit, formal instruction of grammar and implicit, unstructured task-based instruction — in which learners are exposed to grammatical structures through listening and reading input and required to use these structures in a variety of classroom activities. The Tapestry Approach is designed to meet this need. In so doing, it provides a grammar emphasis where the teacher is the decision-maker and grammatical objectives are defined in advance. In addition, it includes a communicative task emphasis, where the learner and teacher act as joint decision-makers and the grammar instruction emerges from authentic tasks requiring meaningful communication.

ACTIVITIES AND DISCUSSION QUESTIONS

1. What factors affect grammatical development in a second language?
2. How do you determine when a learner is *psychologically ready* to benefit from the instruction you provide?
3. Describe a specific task and explain the grammatical structures that you would present to your learners when teaching the task.
4. Imagine you teach a group of 14 learners. Seven of the learners prefer explicit, deductive explanations of grammar that are followed by numerous examples and analytical exercises. Seven prefer implicit, inductive explanations of grammar that are followed by communicative activities. What activities would you use to appeal to both types of learners?
5. Discuss the differences between the grammar of informal conversation and the grammar of academic, expository prose.
6. What makes an effective ESL grammar teacher? List the reasons that account for the teaching effectiveness.

NOTES

1. As illustrated in the figure below, the Monitor utilizes learned knowledge by acting upon and modifying utterances that are generated from acquired knowledge.

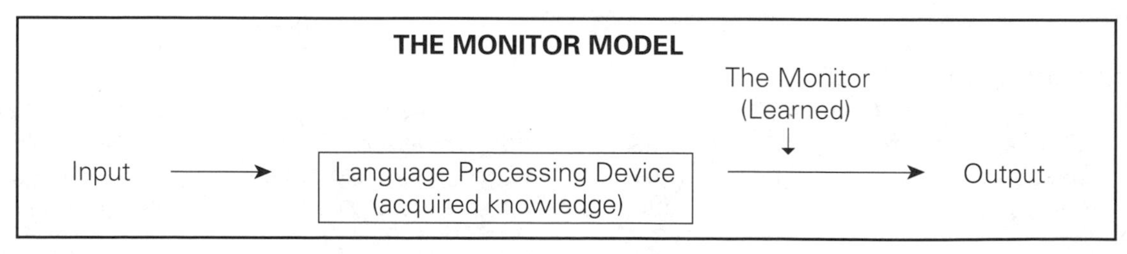

According to this model, the learners' input is processed and becomes acquired competence. At this point, learners may or may not be able to produce grammatically correct sentences. For instance, learners may hear the word *runs*, but process it as *run*, as in the sentence *John run to school.* However, learners may then use a learned rule *(third person verbs end in -s)* to correct their output prior to producing *John runs to school.*

2. Krashen argues that Monitoring has an extremely limited function in language performance. He gives three conditions for its use: (1) there must be sufficient time to think of the appropriate grammar rule and use it; (2) the focus must be on form; and (3) the user must know the rule.
3. Our own view of grammar is very different than Krashen's. We use the two terms *acquisition* and *learning* interchangeably, regardless of whether subconscious or conscious processes are involved.
4. These preferences and needs change in the course of the interaction. They vary as a function of such variables as the learner's feelings and beliefs, topic of conversation, interlocutors, goals, and materials. (See Chapter Three.)
5. The first language literature also suggests that learning is facilitated when learners are told that patterns exist, when they are instructed to look for these patterns, and when the patterns are made salient through explicit presentation followed by sufficient examples (see, for instance, Reber, Kassin, Lewis, and Cantor 1980).
6. The future direction of the grammar controversy rests on further research. We need information from varying perspectives that examine the teachability and learnability of grammatical structures. Research that considers the influence of context, as well as the learner's responses to instruction will help to clarify issues related to the grammar debate. Firsthand classroom accounts from teachers are also needed. Finally, studies investigating the function, form, and use of grammatical structures and their acquisition in a wide variety of contexts will provide information on learner's orchestration of knowledge about grammar and other skills.

SUGGESTED READINGS

• Celce-Murcia, M., and Hilles, S., 1988. *Techniques and Resources in Teaching Grammar.* Oxford: Oxford University Press. This practical volume provides a description of many excellent communicative activities. Grammar structures are contextualized in meaningful discourse.

• Frank, D., and Rinvolucri, M., 1983. *Grammar in Action: Awareness Activities for Language Learning.* Oxford: Pergamon. This book suggests innovative activities that are designed to improve the student's grammatical accuracy in the context of purposeful communication.

CULTURE

12

PREVIEW QUESTIONS

1. Why is culture learning important to language learning?
2. How can we define culture?
3. What should be our goals in teaching culture?
4. How can the new culture and the learner's native culture be simultaneously honored in the ESL classroom?
5. What are the best ways to teach culture and language together?

This chapter focuses on a greatly varied and exciting aspect of the tapestry of language learning: culture. Culture learning and language learning are in many ways inextricable. Most of the communicative approaches to language learning pay heed to the strong relationship between language and culture. The Tapestry Approach, however, particularly highlights this association.

ORGANIZATION OF THIS CHAPTER

In this chapter we define culture and discuss the relationship between culture and language. We cite the importance of culture in language learning and contrast the ways culture is taught in the Tapestry Approach with the ways it is handled in many traditional approaches. We describe and illustrate four levels of cultural awareness that can exist among our ESL students, examine possible goals for teaching culture, mention ways of handling culture shock, and provide illustrative activities for teaching culture. We end with a summary of Tapestry principles for the teaching of culture to ESL students.

DEFINITIONS OF CULTURE

Many definitions of culture exist, all of them valid to one degree or another. Definitions range from terse one-liners to much more detailed expositions.

The Tapestry Approach	Traditional Approaches
• Culture is a central feature.	• Culture is a diversion from *real* language work.
• The definition of culture includes behaviors, attitudes, implicit rules, and the individual's perceptions and interpretations of these.	• The definition of culture is often far more restricted and does not allow for the individual's perceptions and interpretations.
• Students help set their own goals for cultural awareness.	• The teacher sets the same cultural awareness goals for all students.
• The focus concerns U.S. culture, the native culture of the student, and the many cultures of the classmates. Multiculturalism is encouraged.	• The focus is on helping students fit into U.S. culture (often at a superficial level).
• Emotional and social aspects of culture are highlighted, along with cognitive understanding or knowledge of cultural differences.	• Cognitive understanding or knowledge of cultural differences is much more important than emotional or social aspects of culture.

Comparison of the Tapestry Approach to Culture and Traditional Approaches

DEVELOPING CULTURAL AWARENESS

Various degrees of cultural awareness exist, ranging from the level of stereotyping to the level of true empathy. Many degrees of awareness lie between these two poles. Hanvey (1976, 1987) simplifies all the possible levels of cultural awareness. His typology shows four levels into which most of our ESL students can be distributed. We will describe these levels in our own words and provide ESL-related illustrations.

Level 1

Facts, Stereotypes, and Deficiencies. At the first level, information about the culture consists of facts, stereotypes, and what the learner might consider "deficiencies." Some ESL students arrive at our doorstep with preconceptions such as these: all U.S. citizens drive big cars and talk loudly, all U.S. men drink beer and wear cowboy boots, all U.S. women are sexually "free," and all or most U.S. Southerners are prejudiced against minorities and foreigners (as said the other day by an intelligent, newly arrived Japanese student who had seen the movie "To Kill a Mockingbird").

Level 2

Shallow Comprehension. At the second level, the learner notices more subtle traits and processes and may sometimes find them frustrating. In this phase the learner shows only shallow understanding rather than in-depth comprehension of that which is observed. For instance, the ESL student discovers that some U.S. citizens are truly friendly, that is, interested in a real friendship or collegial relationship, while others are only superficially friendly. ESL students learn that invitations such as "Let's get together sometime" might be serious or instead might be just a conventional and rather meaningless form of politeness. These discoveries tend to be confusing and annoying at times, and the learner does not understand the reasons behind them.

Level 3

In-Depth Comprehension. At the third level, the learner begins to understand cultural phenomena from the culture bearers' own frame of reference. This level involves in-depth comprehension and a degree of acceptance of the culture. The ESL student at this level starts to comprehend the internal, "distancing" defense mechanisms that commingle with U.S. courtesy conventions to produce all the mixed messages that U.S. citizens sometimes give to international students. The ESL student begins to relate to the U.S. viewpoint, which is conditioned by the presence of so many different ethnic and cultural groups, and he or she starts to accept, if not condone fully, how some U.S. citizens feel and act.

Level 4

Empathy. This level is true empathy, achievable only through immersion in the culture. Schumann might call this true acculturation. Schumann proposed an important model (Schumann 1978, 1986) that involves the distance between the individual learner and the target culture. When the distance between the two is small, the person has become acculturated to the new culture and feels an identification with that culture. The few ESL students who have reached this level identify with the United States as "their country" and often decide to stay and make their careers here. They use U.S. slang and colloquialisms profusely, sometimes take American names, convert to U.S.-based religions, and even try to out-do U.S. citizens in following cultural norms such as celebrating holidays. They constantly try, consciously or not, to "be inside the heads" of U.S. citizens and to understand, empathize, and act on what they feel these citizens might expect.

Some ESL students avidly desire to acculturate into U.S. society as soon as possible. However, many ESL students have not come here to identify themselves with our culture or to acculturate completely. Indeed, sometimes our students want to preserve their own cultural understandings and behaviors without becoming too much changed or acculturated during their stay in the United States. Sometimes their ultimate goal is to return home, armed with English skills and a U.S. higher education but preserving their own cultural identity. Accompanying families are often even more eager to maintain their cultural roots; sometimes the wives of male Middle Easterners maintain an Arabic-speaking enclave, not venturing into the community or trying to learn English even if they live here for four or five years.

Nevertheless, most ESL students cannot help but expand their cultural horizons simply by being here, by observing the cultural mores around them, and by managing to survive and negotiate in our culture on a daily basis. By virtue of living in the United States and attending ESL programs to prepare themselves for further education and careers, many ESL students are getting a first-hand look at U.S. culture. They see this culture through their own cultural lenses, but at the same time they begin to see themselves and their native culture in new ways.

The ESL classroom is typically a cultural microcosm of the world. Not only are ESL students exposed to U.S. culture, but they are also often exposed to the cultures of many lands throughout the world. Therefore, most ESL students who return to their home countries after studying here find that their experiences in this culture have significantly broadened their cultural vantage point. Sometimes these students have gained the perspective that there is no one "fixed" or "correct" way to do things, but that instead many possible ways exist, depending on the cultural milieu. These students might still find their own country's ways to be the most comfortable and the best for them. However, they can no longer deny that other people's beliefs and behaviors — though opposed to their own ways — might be valid in the cultures from which the people come.

OUR GOALS IN TEACHING CULTURE

Given all the possible levels of cultural awareness, what then should be the goals of ESL teachers in terms of teaching culture? Should we let students happily stay at the level of stereotypes or let them drift along, strictly on their own, to the level of shallow comprehension? Should we press for students to develop in-depth comprehension of the culture in which they are now learning English? Should we push even harder for them to develop the level of empathy or acculturation into their new culture?

Should ESL teachers focus strictly on U.S. cultural awareness? On awareness of the student's own native culture compared with U.S. culture? On a more comprehensive, global awareness of many cultures: U.S. culture, the individual student's native culture, and the cultures of other students in the ESL classroom?

The goals of the ESL teacher regarding culture instruction depend in large part on the needs and goals of the ESL students themselves. However, the Tapestry Approach suggests the following goals:

1. For *every* student, to move beyond Hanvey's level 1, the level of generalized and sometimes inaccurate stereotypes.

2. For *every* student, to acquire at least a shallow understanding (Hanvey's level 2) and preferably a more in-depth understanding and appreciation (Hanvey's level 3) of the following:
   a. the target culture of the United States, where the student is currently learning ESL;
   b. the U.S. culture compared with the learner's own native culture.

3. For *every* learner, to develop at least a shallow understanding (Hanvey's level 2) and, we hope, some degree of in-depth appreciation (Hanvey's level 3) of the other cultures represented in the ESL classroom — not just U.S. culture but the multiple cultures of the student's classmates from around the world. Hanvey's level 2 must be the *minimum* acceptable level in this regard. This goal is, essentially, the development of global awareness, with specific instances related to understanding the cultures of the ESL student's own classmates.

4. For those *self-selected few* ESL students who plan to stay in the United States for the greatest part of their lives and who need to adjust as quickly as possible, to develop true empathy with U.S. people and cultural norms (Hanvey's level 4). Many ESL students will not need or desire this goal. The ESL teacher can assist in this objective by providing introductions and helping to set the scene for close friendships with U.S. citizens, but most of the motivation and action must come from those ESL students who want to acculturate as completely as possible. This process, however, takes years even at its most rapid pace.

We assert that cultural understanding is best viewed as a long-lasting, ever deepening process (Galloway 1985, Seelye 1987, Crawford-Lange and Lange 1987) that can reach different levels, rather than as the collection of tidbits of cultural trivia. Of the many metaphors that Kramsch (1990) offers for culture learning, she distinctly rejects the image of a *container* for the transfer of facts. Culture learning is a personal, individual matter, and the ultimate choice of what level of cultural awareness is to be reached is up to the learner. Culture learning can touch the soul of the learner if he or she allows it. The ESL teacher needs to identify — usually through personal or class discussions or through private interactions — the cultural-awareness goals of the learners and help facilitate the goals to the extent possible, keeping in mind that the level of stereotypes (Hanvey's level 1) should not be the permanent station-stop of any ESL learner but should only be a way-station.

HANDLING CULTURE SHOCK

Somewhere along the line almost every ESL student who is far from home will experience a degree of culture shock — the situation in which the person's identity is challenged and various emotional and sometimes even physical symptoms begin to occur. Chapter Four describes culture shock briefly, noting that it can involve fear, anxiety, anger, depression, withdrawal, stress, alienation, and illness, among other related phenomena.

To reinterpret Scovel (1991), we might say that culture shock occurs in several stages, which fall in the middle of the learner's experience. Culture-shock stages are sandwiched between the stage of initial delight felt by many travelers or visitors and the stage of deeper, more comfortable resolution.

In this chapter on culture learning, we need to reemphasize the possibility of culture shock occurring among our ESL students. What can be done about culture shock? Can it be prevented?

Culture shock cannot be prevented, least of all by the ESL teacher. However, ESL teachers can cushion the blow somewhat. Sensitive teachers who follow the Tapestry Approach allow their students the opportunity to discuss their feelings freely and to express any culture shock they may experience. Some of the best ways to open up the flow of communication about culture shock include literary opportunities, such as writing a poem or an essay for the class magazine, or role-play activities in which free expression of feelings is accepted.

Occasionally, ESL students wish to express their personal feelings about what they perceive as slights or incomprehensible behavior on the part of native speakers of English. One safe way to allow this expression without disrupting the class is to use student journals or diaries on a regular basis. In these journals students are free to state their positive and negative feelings without any fear of embarrassment. Dialog journals allow teachers to respond to the students personally and supportively in writing. If journals indicate that many students are experiencing culture shock, the teacher can lead a discussion about the situation, emphasizing that culture shock is an expectable stage that they will sooner or later leave.

The Tapestry teacher should, when possible, emphasize the commonalities between U.S. culture and the native cultures represented in the classroom, so that students feel more at home and less in a state of culture shock. Across all societies there are common elements, and these should be stressed along with the important differences.

TYPES OF CULTURAL INSTRUCTION ACTIVITIES

Many types of cultural instruction activities exist — an almost bewilderingly large array. We have organized these into eight specific categories to make them simpler and more accessible. The ideas come from many sources, such as Omaggio (1986), Oxford, Ehrman, and Lavine (1991), Oxford (forthcoming), Kramsch (1990), Gaston (1984), Jorstad (1981), and Crawford-Lange and Lange (1987). Nevertheless, the general categorizations are ours.

1. *Native Informants.* This can involve a variety of activities, such as lectures by experts on specific cultural subjects, question and answer sessions, conversation-partner arrangements, and social events. Many of these techniques are often used in ESL classes, but more need to be employed. Any events that mix ESL learners with native informants are to be encouraged. We recommend the use of native informants who are close to the age of the ESL learners and who share many of the same interests.

2. *Teacher Presentations.* Lectures and demonstrations can be successful, but culture instruction should by no means be limited to teacher-centered and teacher-presented activities. Students learn more culture from each other and from a variety of native informants than they can possibly learn from the ESL teacher alone. The ESL teacher should not be the constant presenter, but should instead be the facilitator of a range of different cultural activities involving many people.

3. *Music.* Music is an international language all its own, and it can lead students into a better understanding of ESL. Musical activities include singing, writing songs, watching musical plays, listening to different kinds of music (rock'n'roll, jazz, blues, classical music) from the culture, and even learning to play instruments from the culture.

4. *Pictures and Real Objects.* ESL students are fortunately surrounded by real objects, photos, and pictures from their new culture. Every time they look around the classroom or look out the window, they see signs and symbols of the culture. These can be used to stimulate multicultural, compare-and-contrast demonstrations in which students share items from their own culture and compare those with any parallel (or different) items in U.S. culture. Culture clusters, culture capsules, guessing uses of objects, and ordering items from mail-order catalogues are all related to this theme. Omaggio (1986) provides many ideas about this approach.

5. *Simulations.* Cultural simulations of any kind help ESL learners know and understand the culture of the U.S. They can also assist students in analyzing miscommunications (through the debriefing afterwards). Simulations, including role-plays, provide a relatively safe, protected situation in which students can make cultural and language mistakes without feeling too threatened. See Crookall and Oxford (1990) for many ideas about cultural simulations in the ESL classroom.

6. *Project-Based Culture Learning Activities.* These are student-chosen, student-developed, individual or cooperative demonstrations that concern any aspect of the target culture. See Oxford (forthcoming) on Heritage Projects, which have been used very successfully in intensive ESL programs at the university level. Projects that ESL students have created include: U.S. cooking demonstrations with recipes shared among class members in the new language; formal or informal opinion surveys of people passing by at the local shopping mall; tapes and written reports on the development of American music in the 1960s and 1970s; current-events projects with background information on the First Amendment to the U.S. Constitution; video specials on U.S. football, accompanied by posters on the legal moves and plays of different football team members; a "travelogue" (complete with maps and information about cover charges) of the local nightclubs and dancing spots; a student-guided tour of the town, complete with prearranged interviews with dignitaries; a report, based on discussions with university students and administrators, on how best to get along and make friends in the university; an illustrated dictionary of U.S. slang, idioms, sayings, proverbs, and colloquialisms useful to ESL students for understanding both the language and the culture; and a student-made TV program containing skits, singing, dancing, and typical U.S.-style commercials. Almost any project is fair game, as long as the students choose and develop it themselves (perhaps from a list of initial ideas given by the teacher and expanded by the students).

7. *Style Inventories.* One of the most informative and interesting aspects of culture is the learning and working styles exhibited by students from different cultures. Chapter Four explains style as an important aspect of language learning. It is also a manifestation of cultural beliefs and attitudes (Oxford, Ehrman, and Lavine 1991). Students enjoy taking learning style inventories of many kinds. Dozens of these inventories already exist, some specifically for ESL students (Reid 1987, Oxford 1991). Comparing style results across cultural groups is a fascinating activity, one that

often explains significant differences in how people perceive learning and the strategies or behaviors they choose to help them learn. Of course, not all students from a given cultural background will have identical style profiles, but there will be some cultural similarities that almost invariably appear. For instance, some Hispanic students show themselves to be more global and extroverted in style, while most Asian students (due to their educational system) appear more analytic and introverted.

8. *Discussions.* These can be informal, unstructured cultural discussions or structured, hypothesis-testing discussions concerning a specific cultural aspect. Discussions can be very helpful but should not be the only mode of culture instruction and should not typically be used without some kind of stimuli or input. Cultural readings, cultural videotapes, ordinary movies (a very rich source of cultural material!) rented from the local video store, style surveys, and culture-related simulations of all types can serve as input for discussions.

All of the activities above can be altered to meet the needs of ESL students of different proficiency levels in English. For instance, sophisticated role-plays can be made much simpler by the provision of vocabulary lists and streamlined rules, along with the addition of visual aids and objects. No matter what cultural activities are chosen, students will need pre-activity preparation in the form of brainstorming relevant concepts, listing or mapping relevant vocabulary on the board, bringing in pertinent objects or photos — anything that will help increase students' understanding and stimulate the appropriate background knowledge.

Tapestry teachers are aware of their students' levels of language development and always attempt to allow cultural instruction to mesh well with those language levels. *Tapestry teachers provide the language scaffolding or assistance that learners need when they are learning the culture, and these teachers reduce the aid when it is no longer essential.*

TAPESTRY PRINCIPLES CONCERNING DEVELOPMENT OF CULTURAL AWARENESS

Based on the discussion above, we offer the following Tapestry principles relevant to helping ESL students develop cultural awareness.

PRINCIPLES

1. Culture is not a frill but instead an integral part of the Tapestry Approach.
2. Goals of culture learning will vary by student, but at the very least all ESL students need to move beyond the level of cultural stereotyping and go to the level of comprehension of cultural norms and situations.
3. The concern is not just about understanding the U.S. culture, but also about understanding other cultures represented in the ESL classroom.
4. Culture can be used as content, not just as an explainer of content or as a playful diversion from "real" language work.
5. ESL students can learn a great deal about U.S. culture by understanding the sociolinguistic nuances of English itself.

CONCLUSION

This chapter has centered on culture instruction, a key element in the Tapestry Approach. We have demonstrated that language is a major aspect of culture and that culture therefore deserves significant attention in ESL classes. We have illustrated the four levels of cultural awareness with ESL examples and have examined possible goals for culture instruction in ESL classes in relation to these four levels. We have mentioned culture shock and how to deal with it. We have provided a variety of activities to teach culture in the ESL classroom and have offered a set of Tapestry principles that summarize some of our basic beliefs about culture instruction. We have tried to emphasize the most colorful aspects of culture in the ESL classroom as reflected in the tapestry of language learning.

ACTIVITIES AND DISCUSSION QUESTIONS

1. Which of the definitions of culture do you espouse? Do you have a definition of your own that is better or more comprehensive than any of those given in this chapter? If so, what is it?
2. Summarize the most important reasons, in your opinion, for teaching culture in ESL classes.
3. Given the kinds of students you have dealt with most in your career, or that you expect to deal with, which of the goals for culture instruction in this chapter do you find to be the most reasonable? Which of the levels of Hanvey's taxonomy of cultural awareness would you prefer to aim toward? How will this vary according to the individual needs of your students? What will you do if, in a single class, you have students who show very different cultural-awareness goals and requirements?
4. Look up any of the kinds of culture instruction activities mentioned in this chapter with which you are not very familiar. Do some research to find out what they are, who has used them, and how successful they have been. Try out some of these new ideas and see what you think of them. Observe your students to see their responses. Are there any of these activities that you need to adapt to meet the specific needs of your students?
5. With which of the cultural activities in this chapter are you most familiar? Which have you used yourself, and which have you seen other people use? To what degree were they successful, and why? At what level of Hanvey's taxonomy did the students operate when doing these activities?
6. How can cultural discussions be made most valuable and stimulating? What kinds of input can be used to "charge" discussions effectively? If a discussion lags, how do you handle this? Have you ever broken a discussion into two sides to create a spontaneous debate on a cultural issue? If not, try it and see how it works for you.

SUGGESTED READINGS

• Luce, L.F., and Smith, E.C. (eds.). 1987. *Towards Internationalism: Readings in Cross-Cultural Communication.* (2nd ed.) New York: Newbury House / Harper & Row. This book contains numerous articles on all aspects of cross-culturalism. One very important article concerns culture shock, and another discusses Hanvey's taxonomy of cultural awareness. This book is a "must" for those who want to understand in greater depth the many aspects of cross-cultural communication.

- Omaggio, A.C. 1986. *Teaching Language in Context: Proficiency-Oriented Instruction.* Boston: Heinle & Heinle. This book has a strong chapter on different ways to approach culture teaching. For teachers who would like to see a wide array of ideas with examples, this is a good book with which to begin.

- Stewart, E.C. 1972. *American Cultural Patterns: A Cross-Cultural Perspective.* Yarmouth, ME: Intercultural Press. This is an excellent book for understanding various aspects of our own culture that we take for granted. Often we forget to analyze our own culturally-inculcated behaviors and attitudes. Included in the volume are great reminders about how and why to look at our culture as others might are offered here.

- Seelye, H.N. 1987. *Teaching Culture: Strategies for Intercultural Communication.* Lincolnwood, IL: National Textbook Co. This book is a classic in its genre. It provides a theoretical foundation as well as good ideas for language teachers. No ESL teacher should fail to take a close look at what Seelye has to say about the importance of culture in communication.

EPILOGUE

Together we have explored the world of second language development through the metaphor of the *tapestry of language learning.* In a sense, we have woven our own tapestry in this book. Every chapter fitted into an ever-expanding tapestry, explaining bit by bit the amazing and intricate pattern of second language growth. At this point, the fundamental fabric of the Tapestry Approach is almost complete, but more can be added as greater amounts of information become available.

Let's consider some of the key elements in the Tapestry Approach. Especially important is the concept that the teacher provides learner-tailored assistance in a way that pushes students to seek their greatest communicative potential. To offer this kind of help, the teacher takes on — among other roles — the roles of facilitator, diagnostician of learning styles and proficiency levels, encourager, counselor, provider of interactional opportunities using multiple language skills, and instructor of language learning strategies. In this approach, the learner accepts increasing responsibility for learning and has the strategies to do so comfortably. Students take pride in their own native cultures and in the culture they are now learning. The language classroom is a place of excitement and positive growth instead of a place of boredom or anxiety.

The Tapestry Approach, as many readers have surmised by now, is an amalgam of all that we consider to be the best theory and practice in many related fields: second language acquisition and learning; cognitive, educational, humanistic, and clinical psychology; sociology and sociolinguistics; cross-cultural understanding; and native language reading and composition. The approach draws from many areas, because no single field offers all that language teachers need to know and use. Language learning is a process involving the mind, heart, and bodily senses of students, and any approach that seeks to address the *whole person* must integrate a variety of disciplines.

Some readers might not have found every single strand they were seeking. For instance, pronunciation is covered only lightly in the chapter on speaking. Vocabulary is touched briefly in many chapters but does not have a chapter of its own. We know that pronunciation and vocabulary are exceptionally important, and our large original manuscript contained separate chapters on each. These had to be cut to prevent the text from becoming unwieldy for readers.

We offer a tapestry that we hope is beautiful and useful, but we are sure readers will add their own embellishments and colors. The rich resources shown in the reference list and in the Suggested Readings will help readers expand the tapestry and use it for their own teaching/learning needs.

REFERENCES

NOTE: As of 1991, Newbury House materials are available from Heinle & Heinle Publishers, Boston.

Adler, R. S. (1987). Culture shock and the cross-cultural learning experience. In L. F. Luce & E. C. Smith (Eds.), *Toward internationalism: Readings in cross-cultural communication* (2nd ed.) (pp. 24-35). New York: Newbury House/Harper & Row.

Allwright, R. (1980). Turns, topics, and tasks: Patterns of participation in language learning and teaching. In D. Larsen-Freeman (Ed.), *Discourse analysis in second language research* (pp. 165-187). Rowley, MA: Newbury House.

Andersen, E. (1977). *Learning to speak with style.* Unpublished doctoral dissertation, Stanford University, Stanford, CA.

Andersen, E. (1990). Acquiring communicative competence: Knowledge of register variation. In R. Scarcella, E. S. Andersen, & S. D. Krashen (Eds.), *Developing communicative competence in a second language* (pp. 5-26). New York: Newbury House/Harper & Row.

Andersen, R. (1989). The theoretical status of variation in interlanguage development. In S. M. Gass, C. G. Madden, D. Preston, & L. Selinker (Eds.), *Variation in second language acquisition: psycholinguistic issues* (pp. 46-64). Clevedon, Avon: Multilingual Matters.

Anderson, R. C., Hiebert, E. H., Scott, J. A., & Wilkinson, I. A. G. (1985). *Becoming a nation of readers.* Washington, DC: National Institute of Education.

Arens, K. M., Byrnes, H., & Swaffar, J. (1991). *Reading for meaning: An integrated approach to language learning.* Englewood Cliffs, NJ: Prentice Hall.

Aronson, E., Blaney, N., Stephan, C., Sikes, J., & Snapper, M. (1978). *The jigsaw classroom.* Beverly Hills, CA: Sage.

Ashton-Warner, S. (1963). *Teacher.* New York: Bantam.

Ashton-Warner, S. (1979). *I passed this way.* New York: Knopf.

Au, S. Y. (1988). A critical appraisal of Gardner's socio-psychological theory of second language (L2) learning. *Language Learning, 38*(1), 75-100.

Austin, J. L. (1962). *How to do things with words.* Cambridge, MA: Harvard University Press.

Bailey, K. N. (1983). Competitiveness and anxiety in adult second language learning: Looking at and through the diary studies. In H. W. Seliger & M. H. Long (Eds.), *Classroom-oriented research in second language acquisition* (pp. 67-103). Rowley, MA: Newbury House.

Bailey, K. N., Madden, C., & Krashen, S. D. (1974). Is there a *natural sequence* in adult second language learning? *Language Learning, 24*, 235-244.

Barnett, M. A. (1989). *More than meets the eye: Foreign language learner reading: Theory and practice.* Englewood Cliffs, NJ: Prentice Hall Regents and Center for Applied Linguistics.

Barth, R. (1990). *Improving schools from within: Teachers, parents, and principals can make the difference.* San Francisco: Jossey-Bass.

Bassano, S., & Christison, M. A. (1987). Developing successful conversation groups. In M. H. Long & J. C. Richards (Eds.), *Methodology in TESOL: A book of readings.* New York: Newbury House/Harper & Row.

Bassano, S., & Christison M. A. (1988). Cooperative learning in the ESL classroom. *TESOL Newletter, 22*(2), 1, 8-9.

Beebe, L. M. (1983). Risk-taking and the language learner. In H. W. Seliger & M. H. Long (Eds.), *Classroom-oriented research in second language acquisition* (pp. 39-66). Rowley, MA: Newbury House.

Beebe, L. M. (1988). *Issues in second language acquisition: Multiple perspectives.* New York: Newbury House/Harper & Row.

Bejarano, Y. (1987). A cooperative small-group methodology in the language classroom. *TESOL Quarterly, 21*(3), 483-504.

Bialystok, E. (1982). On the relationship between knowing and using linguistic forms. *Applied Linguistics, 2*(3), 181-206.

Bley-Vroman, B. (1986). Hypothesis testing in second-language acquisition theory. *Language Learning* 36:353-376.

Breecher, M. M. (1983). How to be a better listener and get more out of life. Article syndicated by *Los Angeles Times Syndicate*, published in newspapers throughout the U.S.

Breecher, M. M., & Linde, S. (1992). *Healthy homes in a toxic world.* New York: John Wiley.

Brière, E. J. (1966). Quantity before quality in second language composition. *Language Learning, 16*, 141-151.

Brinton, D. M., Snow, M. A., & Wesche, M. (1989). *Content-based second language instruction.* New York: Newbury House/Harper & Row.

Britton, J. (1978). The composing processes and the functions of writing. In C. Cooper & L. Odell (Eds.), *Research on composing: Points of departure.* Urbana-Champaign, IL: National Council of Teachers of English.

Brooks, N. (1968). Teaching culture in the foreign language classroom. *Foreign Language Annals*, 204-217.

Brown, H. D. (1987). *Principles of language learning and teaching.* (2nd ed.) Englewood Cliffs, NJ: Prentice Hall.

Brumfit, C. J. (1984). *Communicative methodology in language teaching: The roles of fluency and accuracy.* Cambridge: Cambridge University Press.

Brumfit, C. J., & Carter, R. A. (1986). *Literature and language teaching.* Oxford: Oxford University Press.

Bruner, J. (1983). *Child's talk: Learning to use language.* New York: Norton.

Burt, M. K., & Kiparsky, C. (1972). *The Gooficon: A repair manual for English.* Rowley, MA: Newbury House.

Bygate, M. (1987). *Speaking.* Oxford: Oxford University Press.

Byrne, D. (1987). *Techniques for classroom interaction.* London: Longman.

Byrnes, H. (1984). The role of listening comprehension: A theoretical base. *Foreign Language Annals, 17*, 317-329.

Canale, M. (1982). Evaluating the coherence of student writing in L1 and L2. Paper presented at the annual TESOL convention, Honolulu, HI.

Canale, M. (1983). Communicative competence to communicative language pedagogy. In J. Richards & R. Schmidt (Eds.), *Language and communication.* London: Longman.

Canale, M., & Swain, M. (1980). Theoretical bases of communicative approaches to second language teaching and testing. *Applied Linguistics, 1*(1), 1-47.

Cantoni-Harvey, G. (1987). *Content-area language instruction: Approaches and strategies.* Reading, MA; Addison-Wesley.

Carrell, P. (1984). Evidence of a formal schema in second language comprehension. *Language Learning* 34(2): 87-112.

Carrell, P., & Eisterhold, J. (1983). Schema theory and ESL reading pedagogy. *TESOL Quarterly* 17(4): 553-573.

Carrell, P., Devine, J., & Eskey, D. (Eds.). (1988). *Interactive approaches to second language reading.* Cambridge: Cambridge University Press.

Cathcart-Strong, R. (1986). Input generation by young second language learners. *TESOL Quarterly, 20*(3) 515-530.

Cazden, C. (1988). *Classroom discourse: The language of teaching and learning.* Portsmouth, NH: Heinemann.

Celce-Murcia, M. (1987). Teaching pronunciation as communication. In J. Morley (Ed.), *Current perspectives on pronunciation* (pp. 1-12). Washington, DC: TESOL.

Celce-Murcia, M., & Hilles, S. (1988). *Techniques and resources in teaching grammar.* Oxford: Oxford University Press.

Chamot, A. U., & Küpper, L. (1989). Learning strategies in foreign language instruction. *Foreign Language Annals, 22*(1), 13-24.

Chapelle, C. A. (1983). *The relationship between ambiguity tolerance and success in acquiring English as a second language in adult learners.* Unpublished doctoral dissertation, University of Illinois, Urbana-Champaign, IL.

Charrolles, M. (1978). Introduction aux problemes de la coherence des textes. *Langue française, 38,* 7-41.

Chaudron, C. (1977). A descriptive model of discourse in the corrective treatment of learners' errors. *Language Learning, 27,* 29-46.

Chaudron, C. (1982a). *Simplicity and salience in instruction in English as a second language classes: Variations in topic reinstatement and their effect on comprehension.* Unpublished doctoral dissertation, University of Toronto.

Chaudron, C. (1982b). Vocabulary elaboration in teachers' speech to L2 learners. *Studies in Second Language Acquisition, 4*(2), 170-180.

Chaudron, C. (1983). Evaluating writing: Effects of feedback on writing. Paper presented at the annual TESOL convention, Toronto. [ERIC Document No. ED 227 706].

Chaudron, C. (1985). Comprehension, comprehensibility, and learning in the second language classroom. *Studies in Second Language Acquisition, 7,* 216-232.

Chaudron, C. (1988). *Second language classrooms: Research on teaching and learning.* Cambridge: Cambridge University Press.

Chaudron, C., & Richards, J. (1986). The effect of discourse markers on the comprehension of lectures. *Applied Linguistics, 7*(2), 113-127.

Cheng, L. R. (1987). *Assessing Asian language performance: Guidelines for evaluating limited English-proficient students.* Canada: Aspen.

Chomsky, N. (1965). *Aspects of the theory of syntax.* The Hague: Mouton.

Chomsky, N. (1981a). Principles and parameters in syntactic theory. In N. Hornstein & D. Lightfoot (Eds.), *Explanations in linguistics: The logical problem of language acquisition.* London: Longman.

Chomsky, N. (1981b). Markedness and core grammar. In A. Belleti & L. Rizzi (Eds.), *Theory of markedness in generative grammar.* Pisa: Scuola Normale Superiore di Pisa.

Christison, M. A., & Bassano, S. (1981). *Look who's talking.* San Francisco: Alemany.

Clark, E. (1976). What's in a word: On the child's acquisition of semantics in his first language. In T. Moore (Ed.), *Cognitive development and the acquisition of language.* (pp. 65-110). New York: Academic Press.

Clark, E., & Clark, H. (1977). *Psychology and language: An introduction to psycholinguistics.* New York: Harcourt Brace Jovanovich.

Clément, R., Major, L., Gardner, R. C., & Smythe, P. C. (1977). Attitudes and motivation in second language acquisition: An investigation of Ontario francophones. *Working Papers on Bilingualism, 12,* 1-20.

Clyne, M. (Ed.). (1981). *Foreigner talk.* Special issue of *International Journal of the Sociology of Language, 28.*

Coady, J. (1979). A psycholinguistic model of the ESL reader. In R. Mackay, B. Barkman, & R. R. Jordan (Eds.), *Reading a second language* (pp. 5-12). Rowley, MA: Newbury House.

Cohen, A. D. (1990). *Language learning: Insights for learners, teachers, and researchers.* New York: Newbury House/Harper & Row.

Cohen, A. D., & Olshtain, E. (1981). Developing a measure of sociolinguistic competence: The case of apology. *Language Learning, 31*(1), 113-134.

Collier, V. (1989). How long? A synthesis of research on academic achievement in second language. *TESOL Quarterly* 238(3): 509-531.

Conaway, M. (1982). Listening: learning tool and retention agent. In A. S. Algier & K. W. Algier (Eds.), *Improving reading and study skills.* San Francisco: Jossey-Bass.

Connor, U., & Kaplan, R. (Eds.). (1987). *Writing across languages: Analysis of L2 text.* Reading, MA: Addison-Wesley.

Cook, V. (1985). Chomsky's universal grammar and second language learning. *Applied Linguistics, 6*(1), 2-18.

Corder, S. P. (1967). The significance of learner errors. *IRAL, 5,* 161-169.

Corsaro, W. (1979). Sociolinguistic patterns in adult-child interaction. In E. Ochs & B. Schieffelin (Eds.), *Developmental pragmatics* (pp. 373-389). New York: Academic Press.

Coulthard, M. (1985). *An introduction to discourse analysis.* London: Longman.

Crawford-Lange, L. M., & Lange, D. L. (1987). Doing the unthinkable in the second-language classroom: A process for integration of language and culture. In T. V. Higgs (Ed.), *Teaching for proficiency, the organizing principle* (pp. 139-178). Lincolnwood, IL: National Textbook Company.

Crookall, D., & Oxford, R. L. (1990). *Simulation, gaming, and language learning.* New York: Newbury House/Harper & Row.

Crookes, G., & Schmidt, R. (1989). Motivation: Reopening the research agenda. *University of Hawaii Working Papers in ESL, 8,* 217-256.

Cross, T. (1977). Mothers' speech adjustments: The contribution of selected child listener variables. In C. Snow & C. Ferguson (Eds.), *Talking to children: Language input and acquisition* (pp. 151-188). Cambridge: Cambridge University Press.

Cullinan, B., & Fitzgerald, S. (1985). *Background information bulletin on the use of readability formulae: Joint statement of the President, International Reading Association, and the President, National Council of Teachers of English.* Urbana-Champaign, IL: National Council of Teachers of English.

Cummins, J. (1979). Linguistic interdependence and the educational development of bilingual children. *Review of Educational Research, 49* 92): 222-251.

Cummins, J. (1981). Age of arrival and immigrant second language learning in Canada: A reassessment. *Applied Linguistics. 2,* 132-149.

Dannequin, C. (1977). *Les enfants bâillonnés.* Paris: CEDIC, Diffusion Nathan.

Day, R. R. (1986). *Talking to learn: Conversation in second language acquisition.* Rowley, MA: Newbury House.

DiPietro, R. (1987). *Strategic interaction.* Cambridge: Cambridge University Press.

Dixon, C., & Nessel, D. (1983). *Language experience approach to reading and writing: LEA for ESL*. Hayward, CA: Alemany.

Dore, J. (1975). Holophrases, speech acts and language universals. *Journal of Child Language, 2,* 21-40.

Doughty, C., & Pica, T. (1985). Information gap tasks: Do they facilitate second language acquisition? *TESOL Quarterly, 20*(2), 305-325.

Dow, A. R., & Ryan, J. T. (1987). Preparing the language student for professional interaction. In W. M. Rivers (Ed.), *Interactive language teaching.* Cambridge: Cambridge University Press.

Dubin, F. (1986). Dealing with texts. In F. Dubin, D. E. Eskey, & W. Grabe (Eds.), *Teaching second language reading for academic purposes* (pp. 127-160). Reading, MA: Addison-Wesley.

Dubin, F., Eskey, D. E., & Grabe, W. (Eds.). (1986). *Teaching second language reading for academic purposes.* Reading, MA: Addison-Wesley.

Dubin, F., & Olshtain, E. (1986). *Course design: Developing programs and materials for language learners.* Cambridge: Cambridge University Press.

Duffy, G. G. (1981). Teacher effectiveness research: Implications for the reading professions. In M. Kamil (Ed.), *Directions in reading: Research and instruction: 30th yearbook of the National Reading Conference.* Washington, DC: National Reading Conference.

Dulay, H. C., & Burt, M. K. (1974). Natural sequences in child second language acquisition. *Language Learning, 24,* 327-353.

Dulay, H., Burt, M., & Krashen, S. D. (1982). *Language two.* New York: Oxford University Press.

Durkin, D. (1978-1979). What classroom observations reveal about reading comprehension instruction. *Reading Research Quarterly, 14,* 481-533.

Eckman, F. R., Bell, L. H., & Nelson, D. (1984). *Universals in second language acquisition.* Rowley, MA: Newbury House.

Edelsky, C. (Ed.). (1986). *Writing in a bilingual program: Habia una vez.* Norwood, NJ: Ablex.

Edwards, H., Wesche, M., Krashen, S., Clément, R., & Kruidenier, B. (1984). Second language acquisition through subject-matter learning: A study of sheltered psychology classes at the University of Ottawa. *Canadian Modern Language Review, 41*(2):268-282.

Ehrman, M. E., & Oxford, R. L. (1989). Effects of sex differences, career choice, and psychological type on adults' language learning strategies. *Modern Language Journal, 73*(1), 1-13.

Eisenstein, M. (1989). *The dynamic interlanguage: Empirical studies in second language variation.* New York: Plenum.

Eisterhold, J. (1991). Reading-writing connections: Toward a description for second language learners. In B. Kroll (Ed.), *Second language writing: Research insights for the classroom* (pp. 81-101). Cambridge: Cambridge University Press.

Ellis, J., & Ure, J. (1969). Language varieties: Register. In R. Meacham (Ed.), *Encyclopedia of linguistics: Information and control* (pp. 251-259). Oxford: Pergamon.

Ellis, R. (1986). *Understanding second language acquisition.* Oxford: Oxford University Press.

Ellis, R. (1987). *Second language acquisition in context.* London: Prentice Hall.

Ellis, R. (1988). The effects of linguistic environment on the second language acquisition of grammatical rules. *Applied Linguistics, 9*(3), 257-274.

Enright, S. D., & Gomez, B. (1985). PRO-ACT: Six strategies for organizing peer interaction in elementary classrooms. *NABE Journal, 9*(3), 431-453.

Enright, D. S., & McCloskey, M. (1988). *Integrating English: Developing English language and literacy in the multilingual classroom.* Reading, MA: Addison-Wesley.

Ervin-Tripp, S., & Mitchell-Kernan, C. (1977). *Child discourse.* New York: Academic Press.

Faerch, C., & Kasper, G. (Eds.). (1983). *Strategies in interlanguage communication.* London: Longman.

Fanselow, J. (1977). Beyond Rashomon: Conceptualizing and describing the teaching act. *TESOL Quarterly, 11*, 17-40.

Farr, M., & Daniels, H. (1986). *Diversity and writing instruction.* New York: ERIC Clearinghouse on Reading and Communication Skills, National Council of Teachers of English.

Felix, S. (1984). Two problems of language acquisition: The relevance of grammatical studies to the theory of interlanguage. In A. Davies, C. Criper, & A. Howatt (Eds.), *Interlanguage* (pp. 133-161). Edinburgh: Edinburgh University Press.

Ferguson, C. (1971). Absence of copula and the notion of simplicity: A study of normal speech, baby talk, foreigner talk, and pidgins. In D. Hymes (Ed.), *Pidginization and creolization in language* (pp. 141-150). Cambridge: Cambridge University Press.

Ferguson, C. (1975). Toward a characterization of English foreigner talk. *Anthropological Linguistics, 17*, 1-14.

Fillmore, C. (1979). On fluency. In C. Fillmore (Ed.), *Individual differences in language ability and language behavior* (pp. 85-101). New York: Academic Press.

Fine, J. (1988). *Discourse analysis in second language research.* Norwood, NJ: Ablex.

Flanders, N. (1970). *Analyzing teaching behavior.* Reading, MA: Addison-Wesley.

Flower, L. S., & Hayes, J. R. (1977). Problem-solving strategies and the writing process. *College English, 39*(4), 449-461.

Fowler, W. S., Pidock, J., & Rycroft, R. (1979). *Incentive English* (Book 1). Middlesex: Nelson.

Frank, C., & Rinvolucri, M. (1983). *Grammar in action: Awareness activities for language learning.* Oxford: Pergamon.

Freedman, S. (1987). *Response to student writing.* Urbana-Champaign, IL: National Council of Teachers of English.

Gadjusek, L. (1988). Toward wider use of literature in English as a second language: Why and how. *TESOL Quarterly, 22*(2), 227-257.

Gaies, S. J. (1977). The nature of linguistic input in formal second language learning: linguistic and communicative strategies. In H. Brown, C. Yorio, & R. Crymes (Eds.), *On TESOL '77.* Washington, DC: TESOL.

Gaies, S. J. (1981). T-Unit analysis in second language research: Applications, problems and limitations. *TESOL Quarterly, 14.*

Gaies, S. J. (1985). *Peer involvement in language learning.* New York: Harcourt Brace Jovanovich.

Galloway, V. B. (1985). A design for the improvement of the teaching of culture in foreign language classrooms. ACTFL project proposal. Hastings-on-Hudson, NY: ACTFL.

Gardner, R. C. (1985). *Social psychology and second language learning: The role of attitudes and motivation.* London, Ontario: Edward Arnold.

Gardner, R. C., Lalonde, R. H., Moorcroft, R., & Evers, F. T. (1985). *Second language attrition: The role of motivation and use.* London, Ontario: University of Western Ontario.

Gardner, R. C., & Lambert, W. E. (1959). Motivational variables in second language acquisition. *Canadian Journal of Psychology, 13,* 266-272.

Gardner, R. C., & Lambert, W. E. (1972). *Attitudes and motivation in second language learning.* Rowley, MA: Newbury House.

Garnica, O. (1977). Some prosodic and para-linguistic features of speech to young children. In C. Snow & C. Ferguson (Eds.), *Talking to children: Language input and acquisition* (pp. 63-88). Cambridge: Cambridge University Press.

Gass, S. (1982). From theory to practice. In M. Hines & W. Rutherford (Eds.), *On TESOL '81* (pp.129-139). Washington DC: TESOL.

Gass, S., & Madden, C. (Eds.). (1985). *Input in second language acquisition.* Rowley, MA: Newbury House.

Gass, S. M., & Schachter, J. (1989). *Linguistic perspectives on second language acquisition.* Cambridge: Cambridge University Press.

Gass, S. M., & Varonis, E. (1984). The effect of familiarity on the comprehensibility of non-native speech. *Language Learning, 24*, 65-89.

Gass, S. M., & Varonis, E. (1985). Task variation and nonnative/nonnative negotiation of meaning. In S. M. Gass & C. G. Madden (Eds.), *Input in second language acquisition* (pp. 149-161). Rowley, MA: Newbury House.

Gass, S. M., & Varonis, E. (1989). Incorporated repairs in non-native discourse. In M. Eisenstein (Ed.), *The dynamic interlanguage: Empirical studies in second language variation.* New York: Plenum.

Gaston, J. (1984). *Cultural awareness teaching techniques.* Brattleboro, VT: Prolingua.

Gee, J. (1986). Orality and literacy: From the *Savage Mind* to *Ways with Words. TESOL Quarterly, 20*(4), 719-746.

Genesee, F. (1978). Is there an optimal age for starting second language instruction? Unpublished manuscript, McGill University, Montreal.

George, H. (1972). *Common errors in language learning: Insights from English.* Rowley, MA: Newbury House.

Giles, H., & Byrne, J. L. (1982). An intergroup approach to second language acquisition. *Journal of Multicultural and Multilingual Development, 3*, 17-40.

Giles, H., & Smith (1979). Accomodation theory: Optimal levels of convergence. In H. Giles & R. N. St. Clair (Eds.), *Language and social psychology* (pp. 45-65). Oxford: Basil Blackwell.

Gilligan, C. (1982). *In a different voice: Psychological theory and women's development.* Cambridge, MA: Harvard University Press.

Gleason, J. B., & Weintraub, S. (1978). Input language and the acquisition of communicative competence. In K. Nelson (Ed.), *Children's language* (Vol. 1). (pp. 163-210). New York: Gardner Press.

Goldenberg, C. (1991). *Instructional conversations.* Unpublished manuscript, Center for Cultural Diversity, University of California at Santa Cruz.

Goodlad, J. (1984). *A place called school.* New York: McGraw Hill.

Goodman, F. (1967). Reading: A psycholinguistic guessing game. *Journal of the Reading Specialist, 4*, 126-135.

Grabe, W. (1986). The transition from theory to practice in teaching reading. In F. Dubin, D. E. Eskey, & W. Grabe (Eds.), *Teaching second language reading for academic purposes* (pp. 25-48). Cambridge: Cambridge University Press.

Grabe, W. (1988). Reassessing the term "interactive." In P. Carrell, J. Devine, & D. Eskey (Eds.), *Interactive approaches to second language reading.* Cambridge: Cambridge University Press.

Grabe, W., & Kaplan, R. (1989). Writing in a second language: Contrastive rhetoric. In D. M. Johnson & D. H. Roen (Eds.), *Richness in writing: Empowering language minority students* (pp. 263-283). New York: Longman.

Graves, D. (1983). *Writing: Teachers and children at work.* Exeter, NH: Heinemann.

Gregg, K. (1984). Krashen's monitor and Occam's razor. *Applied Linguistics, 5*(2), 79-100.

Grellet, F. (1981). *Developing reading skills: A practical guide to reading comprehension exercises.* Cambridge: Cambridge University Press.

Griffin, P., & Cole, M. (1984). Current activity for the future: The Zo-ped. In B. Rogoff & J. V. Wertsch (Eds.), *Children's learning in the "zone of proximal development". New Directions for Child Language Development* (Vol. 23). (pp. 45-64). San Francisco: Jossey-Bass.

Grimshaw, A. D., & Holden, L. (1976). Postchild modifications of linguistic and social competence. *Items, 30*, 33-42.

Gumperz, J. (1977). The conversational analysis of interethnic communication. In E. L. Ross (Ed.), *Interethnic communication: Proceedings of the Southern Anthropological Society.* Athens: University of Georgia Press.

Gunderson, B., & Johnson, D. (1980). Building positive attitudes by using cooperative learning groups. *Foreign Language Annals, 13*(1), 39-43.

Gungle, B. W., & Taylor, V. (1989). Writing apprehension and second language writers. In D. M. Johnson & D. H. Roen (Eds.), *Richness in writing: Empowering language minority students* (pp. 235-248). New York: Longman.

Hakansson, G. (1986). Quantitative aspects of teacher talk. In G. Kasper (Ed.), *Learning, teaching and communication in the foreign language classroom* (pp. 83-98). Denmark: Aarhus University Press.

Halliday, M. A. K. (1970). Language structure and language functions. In J. Lyons (Ed.), *New horizons in linguistics* (pp. 140-165). Harmondsworth, England: Penguin.

Halliday, M. A. K., & Hasan, R. (1976). *Cohesion in English.* London: Longman.

Halliday, M. A. K., McIntosh, A., & Strevens, P. (1970). The users and use of language. In J. Fishman (Ed.), *Readings in the sociology of language.* The Hague: Mouton.

Hamp-Lyons, L. (1986). No new lamps for old yet, please. *TESOL Quarterly, 20*(4), 790-795.

Hanvey, R. G. (1976). Cross-cultural awareness. In R. G. Hanvey (Ed.), *An attainable global perspective.* New York: Center for Global Perspectives.

Hanvey, R. G. (1987). Cross-cultural awareness. In L. F. Luce & E. C. Smith, (Eds.), *Towards internationalism: Readings in cross-cultural communication* (2nd ed.). New York: Newbury House/Harper & Row.

Hatch, E. (1983). *Psycholinguistics: A second language perspective.* Rowley, MA: Newbury House.

Hatch, E., Flashner, V., & Hunt, L. (1986). In R. Day (Ed.), *Talking to learn: Conversation in second language acquisition* (pp. 5-22). Rowley, MA: Newbury House.

Heald-Taylor, G. (1989). *Whole language strategies for ESL students.* San Diego: DORMAC.

Heath, S. B. (1982). *Ways with words.* Cambridge: Cambridge University Press.

Heath, S. B. (1986). Sociocultural contexts of language development. In *Beyond language: Social and cultural factors in schooling language minority students* (pp. 143-186). Sacramento: Bilingual Education Office, California State Department of Education.

Heath, S. B., & Hanscombe, J. (1984). "Intelligent writing" in an audience community: Teacher, students, and researcher. In S.W. Freedman (Ed.), *The acquisition of written language: Revision and response* (pp. 3-32). Norwood, NJ: Ablex.

Hecht, B. (1983). *Situations and language: Children's use of plural allomorphs on familiar and unfamiliar settings.* Unpublished doctoral dissertation, Stanford University, Stanford, CA.

Henner-Stanchina, C. (1986). Teaching strategies for listening comprehension. Paper presented at the LaGuardia Conference on Learning Strategies, LaGuardia Community College, New York.

Henzl, V. (1973). Linguistic register of foreign language instruction. *Language Learning, 23,* 207-222.

Henzl, V. (1979). Foreigner talk in the classroom. *IRAL, 17,* 157-167.

Herskovits, M. (1948). *Man and his works.* New York: Knopf.

Higgs, T., & Clifford, R. (1982). The push toward communication. In T. Higgs (Ed.), *Curriculum, competence, and the foreign language teacher* (pp. 57-79). Skokie, IL: National Textbook Company.

Hillocks, G. (1986). *Research on written composition: New directions for teaching.* Urbana-Champaign, IL: ERIC Clearinghouse on Reading and Communication Skills and the National Council of Teachers of English.

Hinds, J. (1987). Reader versus writer responsibility: A new typology. In U. Connor & R. Kaplan (Eds.), *Writing across languages: Analysis of L2 text* (pp. 141-152). Reading, MA: Addison-Wesley.

Hoetker, J., & Ahlbrand, W. (1969). The persistence of recitation. *American Educational Research Journal, 6*, 145-167.

Holden, J. (1981). *Drama in language teaching.* London: Longman.

Horowitz, D. (1986). What professors actually require: Academic tasks for the ESL classroom. *TESOL Quarterly, 20*, 445-462.

Horwitz, E. (1990). Attending to the affective domain in foreign language learning. In S. S. Magnan (Ed.), *Shifting the instructional focus to the learner* (pp. 15-33). Middlebury, VT: Northeast Conference on the Teaching of Foreign Languages.

Horwitz, E. K., & Young, D. J. (1990). *Language anxiety.* Englewood Cliffs, NJ: Prentice Hall.

Hosenfeld, C. (1979). Cindy: A learner in today's foreign language classroom. In W.C. Born (Ed.), *The foreign language learner in today's classroom environment* (pp. 53-75). Middlebury, VT: Northeast Conference on the Teaching of Foreign Languages.

Hosenfeld, C. et al. (1981). Second language reading: A curricular sequence for teaching reading strategies. *Foreign Language Annals, 14*, 415-422.

Huebner, T. (1983). *A longitudinal analysis of the acquisition of English.* Ann Arbor, MI: Karoma.

Hughey, J. B., Wormuth, D., Hartfiel, F., & Jacobs, H. (1983). *Teaching ESL composition: Principles and techniques.* Rowley, MA: Newbury House.

Hymes, D. (1972). On communicative competence. In J. B. Pride & J. Holmes (Eds.), *Sociolinguistics: Selected readings* (pp. 269-293). Baltimore: Penguin.

Hymes, D. (1974). *Foundations in sociolinguistics: An ethnographic approach.* Philadelphia: University of Pennsylvania Press.

Hymes, D. (1986). Discourse: Scope without depth. *International Journal of the Sociology of Language, 57*, 49-89.

James, C. (1980). *Contrastive analysis.* London: Longman.

Jenkins, S., & Hinds, J. (1987). Business letter writing: English, French and Japanese. *TESOL Quarterly, 21*(2), 327-343.

Johns, A. (1986). Coherence and academic writing: Some definitions and suggestions for teaching. *TESOL Quarterly, 20*(2), 247-266.

Johnson, D. M., & Roen, D. H. (Eds.). (1989). *Richness in writing: Empowering language minority students.* New York: Longman.

Johnson, D. W., Johnson, R., & Holubec, E. (Eds.). (1986). *Circles of learning: Cooperation in the classroom.* (Rev. ed.). Edina, MN: Interaction Book Company.

Johnson, K., & Morrow, K. (Eds.). (1981). *Communication in the classroom: Applications and methods for a communicative approach.* Essex: Longman.

Joiner, E. (1986). Listening in the foreign language. In B. H. Wing (Ed.), *Listening, reading, and writing: Analysis and application* (pp. 43-70). Middlebury, VT: Northeast Conference on the Teaching of Foreign Languages.

Jones, K. (1982). *Simulations in language teaching.* Cambridge: Cambridge University Press.

Jones, S., & Tetroe, J. (1987). Composing in a second language. In A. Matsuhashi (Ed.), *Writing in real time: Modeling production processes.* Norwood, NJ: Ablex.

Jorstad, H. L. (1981). Inservice teacher education: Content and process. In D. L. Lange & C. Linder (Eds.), *Proceedings of the National Conference on Professional Priorities.* Hastings-on-Hudson, New York: ACTFL Materials Center.

Kagan, S. (1986). Cooperative learning and sociocultural factors in schooling. In *Beyond language: Social and cultural factors in schooling language minority students* (pp. 231-290). Sacramento: Bilingual Education Office, California State Department of Education.

Kagan, S. (1989). *Cooperative learning: Resources for teachers.* San Juan Capistrano, CA: Resources for Teachers.

Kaplan, R. (Ed.). (1983). *Annual Review of Applied Linguistics.* Rowley, MA: Newbury House.

Kasper, G. (1985). Repair in foreign language teaching. *Studies in Second Language Acquisition, 7,* 200-215.

Keller, E., & Warner, S. (1979). *Gambits 1: Openers; Gambits 2: Links; Gambits 3: Responders, Closers and Inventory.* Hull, P. Q., Canada: Public Service Commission of Canada.

Kellerman, E., Ammerlaan, T., Bongaerts, T., & Poulisee, N. (1990). Lexical gaps, and the cyclic nature of compensatory strategies in second language performance. In R. Scarcella, E. S. Andersen, & S. D. Krashen (Eds.), *Developing communicative competence in a second language* (pp. 163-178). New York: Newbury House/Harper & Row.

Klima, E., & Bellugi, V. (1966). Syntactic regularities in the speech of children. In J. Lyons & R. Wales (Eds.), *Psycholinguistic papers.* Edinburgh: Edinburgh University Press.

Klippel, G. (1984). *Keep talking.* Cambridge: Cambridge University Press.

Kohn, A. (1987, October). It's hard to get out of a pair — Profile: David and Roger Johnson. *Psychology Today* 53-57.

Kramsch, C. (1990). Discourse and culture. Keynote presentation at the annual meeting of the Alabama Association of Foreign Language Teachers, Birmingham.

Krashen, S. D. (1980). The theoretical and practical relevance of simple codes in second language acquisition. In R. Scarcella & S. D. Krashen (Eds.), *Research in Second Language Acquisition* (pp. 7-18). Rowley, MA: Newbury House.

Krashen, S. D. (1981). *Second language acquisition and second language learning.* Oxford: Pergamon.

Krashen, S. (1982). *Principles and practice in second language acquisition.* Oxford: Pergamon.

Krashen, S. D. (1984). *Writing: Research, theory, and applications.* New York: Alemany.

Krashen, S. D. (1985a). *The input hypothesis: Issues and implications.* New York: Longman.

Krashen, S. D. (1985b). *Insights and inquiries.* Hayward, CA: Alemany Press.

Krashen, S. D., Long, M., & Scarcella, R. (1982). Age, rate, and eventual attainment in second language acquisition. In S.D. Krashen, R. Scarcella, & M. Long (Eds.)., *Child-adult differences in second language acquisition* (pp. 175-201). Rowley, MA: Newbury House.

Krashen, S., Scarcella, R., & Long, M. (Eds.). (1982). *Child-adult differences in second language acquisition.* Rowley, MA: Newbury House.

Krashen, S. D, & Terrell, T. (1983). *The Natural Approach: Language acquisition in the classroom.* Oxford: Pergamon.

Kroll, B. (1991). *Second language writing: Research insights from the classroom.* Cambridge: Cambridge University Press.

Kumaravadivelu, B. (1989). *Task-based language learning.* Special issue of *Papers in Applied Linguistics, 1.*

Labov, W. (1963). Social motivation of a sound change. *Word, 19,* 273-309.

Labov, W. (1966). The social stratification of English in New York City. Washington, DC: Center for Applied Linguistics.

Labov, W. (1970). The study of language in its social context. *Studium Generale, 20,* 30-87.

Labov, W. (1972). *Sociolinguistic patterns.* Philadelphia: University of Pennsylvania Press.

Lapp, R. E. (1984). The process approach to writing: Toward a curriculum for international students. *University of Hawaii Working Papers in ESL.*

Larsen-Freeman, D. (1980). *Discourse analysis in second language research.* Rowley, MA: Newbury House.

Larsen-Freeman, D. (1991). Teaching grammar. In Celce-Murcia, M. (Ed.), *Teaching English as a second or foreign language* (2nd ed.). New York: Harper & Row/Newbury House.

Larsen-Freeman, D., & Long, M. H. (1991). *An introduction to second language acquisition research.* London: Longman.

Lavine, R. Z. (Forthcoming). Task-based activities in the foreign language laboratory.

Lavine, R. Z., & Oxford, R. L. (1990). Addressing affective issues in the second and foreign language classroom. Paper presented at the annual meeting of the Modern Language Association, Chicago.

Lavine, R. Z., & Oxford, R. L. (Forthcoming). Language learning diaries: Let the learners tell us.

Lebauer, R. (1988). *Learn to listen: Listen to learn - An advanced ESL/EFL lecture comprehension and note-taking textbook.* Englewood Cliffs, New Jersey: Prentice Hall.

Lebauer, R. (1991). Personal communication.

Lebauer, R., & Scarcella, R. (1992). *React: Multicultural reading-based writing modules.* Englewood Cliffs, NJ: Prentice Hall.

Lee, D. (1991). Personal communication.

Lee, D., & Larson, D. (1991). *Tapestry: Guiding principles.* Commissioned manuscript, Heinle & Heinle, Boston.

Lewis, G. (1974). *Linguistics and second language pedagogy: A theoretical study.* The Hague: Mouton.

Levenston, E. A. (1978). Error analysis of free compositions: The theory and the practice. *Indian Journal of Applied Linguistics, 4*(1), 1-11.

Lindfors, J. (1987). *Children's language and language learning* (2nd ed.). Englewood Cliffs, NJ: Prentice Hall.

Littlejohn, A., & Hicks, D. (1986). Task-centred writing activities. In C. N. Candlin & D. Murphy (Eds.), *Lancaster Practical Papers in English Language Education, 7.* Oxford: Pergamon.

Littlewood, W. (1981). *Communicative language teaching: An introduction.* Cambridge: Cambridge University Press.

Long, M. H. (1976). Group work and communicative competence in the ESOL classroom. In M. Burt & H. Dulay (Eds.), *On TESOL '75*. Washington, DC: TESOL.

Long, M. H. (1980). *Input, interaction, and second language acquisition.* Unpublished doctoral dissertation, University of California at Los Angeles.

Long, M. H. (1981). Input, interaction and second language acquisition. In H. Winitz (Ed.), *Native Language and Foreign language acquisition. Annals of the New York Academy of Sciences, 379,* 259-278.

Long, M. H. (1983a). Does second language instruction make a difference? A review of the research. *TESOL Quarterly, 14,* 378-390.

Long, M. H. (1983b). Linguistic and conversational adjustments to non-native speakers. *Studies in Second Language Acquisition, 5,* 177-249.

Long, M. H. (1985). Input and second language acquisition theory. In S. M. Gass & C. G. Madden (Eds.), *Input and second language acquisition* (pp. 377-393). Rowley, MA: Newbury House.

Long, M. H. (1988). Instructed interlanguage development. In L.M. Beebe (Ed.), *Issues in second language acquisition: Multiple perspectives* (pp. 115-141). New York: Newbury House/ Harper & Row.

Long, M. H., Adams, L., McLean, M., & Castaños, F. (1976). Doing things with words — verbal interaction in lockstep and small group classroom situations. In J. Fanselow & R. Crymes (Eds.), On *TESOL '76* (pp. 137-153). Washington, DC: TESOL.

Long, M.H., & Crookes, G. (1986). Intervention points in second language classroom processes. Paper presented at RELC Seminar, Singapore.

Long, M. H., & Porter, P. A. (1985). Group work, interlanguage talk and second language acquisition. *TESOL Quarterly, 19*(2), 207-228.

Long, M. H., & Sato, C. (1983). Classroom foreigner talk discourse: Forms and functions of teacher questions. In H. W. Seliger & M. H. Long (Eds.), *Classsroom-oriented research in second language acquisition* (pp. 268-285). Rowley, MA: Newbury House.

Macias, J. (1987). The hidden curriculum of Papago teachers: American Indian strategies for mitigating cultural discontinuity in early schooling. In G. Spindler & L. Spindler (Eds.), *Interpretive ethnography of education at home and abroad* (pp. 363-360). Hillsdale, NJ: Erlbaum.

Maculaitis, J., & Scheraga, M. (1990). *The complete ESL/EFL resource book: Strategies, activities, and units for the classroom.* Lincolnwood, IL: National Textbook Company.

Maley, A. (1987). Poetry and song as effective language-learning activities. In W. M. Rivers (Ed.), *Interactive language teaching* (pp. 93-109). Cambridge: Cambridge University Press.

Maley, A., & Duff, A. (1982). *Drama techniques in language learning* (2nd ed.). Cambridge: Cambridge University Press.

Mangelsdorf, K. (1989). Parallels between speaking and writing in second language acquisition. In D. M. Johnson & D. H. Roen (Eds.), *Richness in writing: Empowering language minority students* (pp. 134-145). New York: Longman.

Mayeroff, M. (1971). *On caring.* New York: Harper & Row.

McCombs, B. L. (1987). The role of affective variables in autonomous learning. Paper presented at the annual meeting of the American Educational Research Association, Washington, DC.

McKay, S. (Ed.). (1984). *Composing in a second language.* Rowley, MA: Newbury House.

McKay, S. (1989). Topic development and written discourse accent. In D. M. Johnson & D. H. Roen (Eds.), *Richness in writing: Empowering language minority students* (pp. 253-262). New York: Longman.

McLaughlin, B. (1978). The Monitor model: Some methodological considerations. *Language Learning, 28,* 309-332.

Mehrabian, A. (1971). *Silent messages.* Belmont, CA: Wadsworth.

Melvin, B., & Stout, D. F. (1987). Motivating language learners through authentic materials. In W. M. Rivers (Ed.), *Interactive language teaching* (pp. 44-56). Cambridge: Cambridge University Press.

Mendelsohn, D. J. (1984). There ARE strategies for listening. *TEAL Occasional Papers, 8,* 63-76.

Meyer, R. (1984). "Listen my children, and you shall hear . . ." *Foreign Language Annals, 17,* 343-344.

Mittan, R. (1989). The peer review process: Harnessing students' communicative power. In D. M. Johnson & D. H. Roen (Eds.), *Richness in writing: Empowering language minority students* (pp. 207-219). New York: Longman.

Moerk, E. L. (1983). *The Mother of Eve — as a first language teacher.* Norwood, NJ: Ablex.

Mohan, B. (1979). Language teaching and content teaching. *TESOL Quarterly, 13*(2), 171-182.

Mohan, B. (1986). *Content-based language instruction.* Reading, MA: Addison-Wesley.

Montgomery, C., & Eisenstein, M. (1985). Real reality revisited: An experimental course in ESL. *TESOL Quarterly, 19* (2), 317-334.

Morley, J. (1987). *Current perspectives on pronunciation: Practice anchored in theory.* Washington, DC: TESOL.

Morgan, J., & Rinvolucri, M. (1983). *Once upon a time: Using stories in the language classroom.* Cambridge: Cambridge University Press.

Munby, J. (1978). *Communicative syllabus design.* Cambridge: Cambridge University Press.

Murray, D. M. (1978). Internal revision: A process of discovery. In C. R. Cooper & L. Odell (Eds.), *Research on composing: Points of departure* (pp. 85-103). Urbana-Champaign, IL: National Council of Teachers of English.

Naiman, N., Fröhlich, M., Stern, H. H., & Todesco, A. (1978). *The good language learner. Research in Education Series, 7.* Ontario Institute for Studies in Education, Toronto.

Nemser, W. (1971). Approximative systems of foreign language learners. *IRAL, 9*(2), 115-123.

Newport, E. L. (1976). Motherese: The speech of mother to young children. In N. J. Castellan, D. B. Pisoni, & G. R. Potts (Eds), *Cognitive theory* (Vol. 2). Hillsdale, NJ: Erlbaum.

Nida, E. (1954). *Customs and cultures.* New York: Harper & Row.

Noddings, N. (1984). *Caring: A feminine approach to ethics and moral education.* Berkeley: University of California.

Nord, J. R. (1981). Three steps to listening fluency: A beginning. In H. Winitz (Eds), *The comprehension approach to foreign language instruction* (pp. 69-100). Rowley, MA: Newbury House.

Nunan, D. (1985). Using objective grids in planning language courses. *Prospect, 1*(2), 19-31.

Nunan, D. (1988). *Syllabus design.* Oxford: Oxford University Press.

Nunan, D. (1989). *Designing tasks for the communicative classroom.* Cambridge: Cambridge University Press.

Nyikos, M. (1987). *The use of color and imagery as associative strategies for the retention of lexical items in German.* Unpublished doctoral dissertation, Purdue University, West Lafayette, IN.

Ochs, E. (1983). Input: A socio-cultural perspective. In M. Hickman (Ed.), *Social and functional approaches to language and thought* (pp. 305-319). New York: Academic Press.

Ochs, E. (1989). *Culture and language development.* Cambridge: Cambridge University Press.

Ochs, E., & Schieffelin, B. (1984). Language acquisition and socialization: Three developmental stories and their implications. In R. Sweder & R. LeVine (Eds.), *Culture theory: Essays on mind, self and emotion* (pp. 251-272). Cambridge: Cambridge University Press.

Ochs-Keenan, E. (1974). Conversational competence in children. *Journal of Child Language, 1,* 163-183.

Ogbu, J., & Matute-Bianchi, M. E. (1986). Understanding sociocultural factors: Knowledge, identity and school adjustment. In *Beyond language: Social and cultural factors in schooling language minority students* (pp. 73-142). Bilingual Education Office, California State Department of Education.

Oller, J. W. (1981). Research on the measurement of affective variables: Some remaining questions. In R. W. Anderson (Ed.), *New dimensions in second language acquisition research* (pp. 114-127). Rowley, MA: Newbury House.

Olshtain, E. (1983). Sociolinguistic competence and language transfer: The case of apology. In S. Gass & L. Selinker (Eds.), *Language transfer in language learning* (pp. 232-249). Rowley, MA: Newbury House.

Olshtain, E., & Cohen, A. (1983). Apology: A speech act set. In N. Wolfson & E. Judd (Eds.), *Sociolinguistics and language acquisition.* Rowley, MA: Newbury House.

Olshtain, E., & Cohen, A. (1987). The learning of complex speech act behavior. Paper presented at the annual TESOL convention, Miami.

Omaggio, A. (1986). *Teaching language in context: Proficiency-oriented instruction.* Boston: Heinle & Heinle.

O'Malley, J. M., & Chamot, A. U. (1990). *Learning strategies in second language acquisition.* Cambridge: Cambridge University Press.

Oprandy, R. (1991). *Position statement for listening/speaking component of Tapestry.* Commissioned manuscript, Heinle & Heinle, Boston.

Oxford, R. (1990). *Language learning strategies: What every teacher should know.* New York: Newbury House/Harper & Row.

Oxford, R. (Forthcoming). Culture learning for language students: Encouraging initiative and interest through cooperative project work.

Oxford, R. L., & Cohen, A. D. (Forthcoming). Language learning strategies: Crucial issues in concept and definition.

Oxford, R., & Crookall, D. (1988). Language learning strategies. In J. Berko-Gleason (Ed.), *You CAN take it with you: Helping students maintain second language skills* (pp. 23-49). Englewood Cliffs, NJ: Prentice Hall.

Oxford, R. L., & Crookall, D. (1989). Language learning strategies: Methods, finding, and instructional implications. *Modern Language Journal, 73*, 404-419.

Oxford, R., & Ehrman, M. (1989). Psychological type and adult language learning strategies: A pilot study. *Journal of Psychological Type, 16*, 22-32.

Oxford, R., Ehrman, M., & Lavine, R. Z. (1991). Style wars: Teacher-student style conflicts in the language classroom. In S. S. Magnan (Ed.), *Challenges in the 1990's for college foreign language programs* (pp. 1-25). Boston, MA: Heinle & Heinle.

Oxford, R., & Nyikos, M. (1989). Variable affecting choice of language learning strategies by university students. *Modern Language Journal, 73*(3), 291-300.

Oxford, R. L., Talbott, V., & Halleck, G. (1989). Motivation, learning strategies, and other factors in a university intensive ESL program. Paper presented at the annual meeting of TESOL, San Francisco.

Oxford, R., Lee, D., Snow, A. M., & Scarcella, R. (Forthcoming). Integrating the four language skills: An empirical study of intensive ESL programs.

Paulston, C. B. (1975). Linguistic and communicative competence in the ESOL classroom. *TESOL Quarterly, 8*(4), 347-362.

Paulston, C. B., & Bruder, M. (1976). *Teaching English as a second language: Techniques and procedures.* Cambridge, MA: Winthrop.

Pavesi, M. (1986). Markedness, discoursal modes, and relative clause formation in a formal and an informal context. *Studies in Second Language Acquisition, 8*(1), 38-55.

Perl, S. (1979). The composing processes of unskilled college writers. *Research in the Teaching of English, 13*(4), 317-336.

Peters, A. (1983). *The units of language acquisition.* Cambridge: Cambridge University Press.

Peyton, J. K. (1990). *Students and teachers writing together: Perspectives on journal writing.* Alexandria, VA: TESOL.

Peyton, J. K., & Reed, R. (1990). *Dialogue journal writing with nonnative English speakers: A handbook for teachers.* Alexandria, VA: TESOL.

Philips, S. (1972). Participant structures and communicative competence: Warm Spring Indian children in community and classroom. In C. Cazden, D. Hymes, & J. P. Vera (Eds.), *Functions of language in the classroom* (pp. 370-394). New York: Teachers College Press.

Philips, S. U. (1983). *The invisible culture: Communication in classroom and community on the Warm Spring Indian Reservation.* New York: Teachers College Press.

Pica, T. (1983). Adult acquisition of English as a second language under different conditions of exposure. *Language Learning, 33*(4), 465-497.

Pica, T. (1987). Second language acquisition, social interaction, and the classroom. *Applied Linguistics, 7,* 1-25.

Pica, T. (1988a). Interlanguage adjustments as an outcome of NS-NNS negotiated interaction. *Language Learning, 38*(1), 45-73.

Pica, T. (1988b). Negotiated input as an aid to learner output. *Language Learning, 37*, 471-493.

Pica, T., Barnes, G. A., & Finger, A. G. (1990). *Teaching matters: Skills and strategies for international teaching assistants*. New York: Newbury House/Harper & Row.

Pica, T., Doughty, C., & Young, R. (1986). Making input comprehensible: Do interactional modifications help? *ITL Review of Applied Linguistics, 72,* 1-25.

Pica, T., Holliday, L., Lewis, N., & Morgenthaler, L. (1989). Comprehensible output as an outcome of linguistic demands on the learner. *Studies in Second Language Acquisition, 11*(1), 63-90.

Pica, T., & Long, M. H. (1986). The linguistic and conversational performance of experienced and inexperienced teachers. In R. R. Day (Ed.), *Talking to learn: Conversation in second language acquisition* (pp. 85-98). Rowley, MA: Newbury House.

Pica, T., Young, R., & Doughty, C. (1987). The impact of interaction on comprehension. *TESOL Quarterly, 21*(4), 737-758.

Pienemann, M. (1984). Psychological constraints on the teachability of languages. *Studies in Second Language Acquisition, 6*(2), 186-214.

Povey, J. (1979). The teaching of literature in advanced ESL classes. In M. Celce-Murcia & L. McIntosh (Eds.), *Teaching English as a second language.* Rowley, MA: Newbury House.

Purves, A. (Ed.). (1988). *Writing across Languages and cultures: Issues in contrastive rhetoric.* Newbury Park, CA: Sage.

Reber, A., Kassin, S., Lewis, S., & Cantor, G. (1980). On the relationship between implicit and explicit modes in the learning of a complex rules structure. *Journal of Experimental Psychology: Human Learning and Memory, 6*, 492-509.

Reid, J. M. (1987). The learning style preferences of ESL students. *TESOL Quarterly, 21*, 87-111.

Reid, J. M., (1989). English as a second language composition in higher education: The expectation of the academic audience. In D. M. Johnson & D. H. Roen (Eds.), *Richness in writing: Empowering language minority students* (pp. 220-234). New York: Longman.

Reid, T. B. W. (1956). Linguistics, structuralism and philology. *Archivum Linguisticum, 8,* 28-37.

Ricento, T. (1987). *Aspects of coherence in English and Japanese expository prose.* Unpublished doctoral dissertation, University of California at Los Angeles.

Richard-Amato, P. A. (1988). *Making it happen: Interaction in the second language classroom: From theory to practice.* New York: Longman.

Richards, J. (Ed.). (1974). *Error analysis.* London: Longman.

Richards, J. (1985). *The context of language teaching.* Cambridge: Cambridge University Press.

Richards, J. (1990). *The language teaching matrix.* Cambridge: Cambridge University Press.

Richards, J., & Schmidt, R. W. (Eds.). (1983). *Language and communication.* London: Longman.

Rigg, P. (1981). Beginning to read in English the LEA way. In C.W. Twyford, W. Diehl, & K. Feathers (Eds.), *Reading in English as a second language: Moving from theory. School of Education Monographs, 4* (pp. 81-90). Bloomington, IN: Indiana University.

Rivers, W. M. (1987). *Interactive language teaching.* Cambridge: Cambridge University Press.

Robinett, B. W., & Schachter, J. (1983). *Second language learning: Contrastive analysis, error analysis and related aspects.* Ann Arbor, MI: The University of Michigan Press.

Romaine, S. (1986). *The language of children and adolescents: The acquisition of communicative competence.* Oxford: Basil Blackwell.

Rubin, J. (1981). Study of cognitive processes in second language learning. *Applied Linguistics, 11*, 118-131.

Rutherford, W., & Sharwood Smith, M. (Eds.). (1988). *Grammar and second language teaching: A book of readings.* New York: Newbury House/Harper & Row.

Sachs, J. (1977). Adaptive significance of input to infants. In C. Snow & C. Ferguson (Eds.), *Talking to children: Language input and language acquisition* (pp. 51-61). Cambridge: Cambridge University Press.

Sacks, H., Schegeloff, E., & Jefferson, G. (1974). A simplest systematics for the organization of turn-taking in conversations. *Language, 50*, 696-735.

Sato, C. (1982). Ethnic styles in classroom discourse. In M. Hines & W. Rutherford (Eds.), *On TESOL '81* (pp. 11-24). Washington, DC: TESOL.

Savignon, S. (1971). *A study of the effect of training in communicative skills as part of a beginning college French course on student attitude and achievement in linguistic and communicative competence.* Unpublished doctoral dissertation, University of Illinois, Urbana-Champaign.

Savignon, S. (1983). *Communicative competence: Theory and classroom practice.* Reading, MA: Addison-Wesley.

Scarcella, R. (1983a). Developmental trends in the acquisition of conversational competence by adult second language learners. In N. Wolfson & E. Judd (Eds.), *Sociolinguistics and language acquisition* (pp. 175-183). Rowley, MA: Newbury House.

Scarcella, R. (1983b). Discourse accent in second language performance. In L. Selinker & S. Gass (Eds.), *Language transfer in language learning* (pp. 306-326). Rowley, MA: Newbury House.

Scarcella, R. (1983c). Socio-drama for social interaction. In J. Oller & P. A. Richard-Amato (Eds.), *Methods that work* (pp. 239-245). Rowley, MA: Newbury House. Also (1978). *TESOL Quarterly, 12*(1), 41-46.

Scarcella, R. (1990). *Teaching language minority students in the multicultural classroom.* Englewood Cliffs, NJ: Prentice Hall.

Scarcella, R., Andersen, E., & Krashen, S. D. (1990). *Developing communicative competence in a second language.* New York: Newbury House/Harper & Row.

Scarcella, R., & Brunak, J. (1981). On speaking politely in a second language. *International Journal of the Sociology of Language, 30,* 59-75.

Scarcella, R., & Higa, C. (1981). Input, negotiation, and age differences in second language acquisition. *Language Learning, 32*(2), 409-437.

Scarcella, R., & Stern, S. (1990). Reading, writing, and literature: Integrating language skills. In D. Crookall & R. Oxford (Eds.), *Simulation, gaming, and language learning* (pp. 119-124). New York: Newbury House/Harper & Row.

Schachter, J. (1984). A universal input condition. In W. Rutherford (Ed.), *Universals and second language acquisition* (pp.167-183). Amsterdam: John Benjamins.

Schachter, J. (1986). Three approaches to the study of input. *Language Learning, 36*, 211-226.

Schegloff, E., Jefferson, G., & Sacks, H. (1977). The preference for self-correction in the organization of repair in conversation. *Language, 53*, 361-382.

Schmidt, R. (1990). The role of consciousness in second language learning. *Applied Linguistics, 11*(2), 129-158.

Schmidt, R., & Frota, S. (1986). Developing basic conversational ability in a second language: A case study of an adult learner of Portuguese. In R. Day (Ed.), *Talking to Learn: Conversation in second language acquisition* (pp. 237-320). Rowley, MA: Newbury House.

Schmidt, R. (1983). Interaction, acculturation, and acquisition of communicative. In N. Wolfson & E. Judd (Eds.), *Sociolinguistics and second language acquisition* (pp. 137-174). Rowley, MA: Newbury House.

Schumann, J. H. (1978). The acculturation model for second language acquisition. In R. C. Gingras (Ed.), *Second language acquisition and foreign language teaching* (pp. 27-50). Washington, DC: Center for Applied Linguistics.

Schumann, J. H. (1986). Research on the acculturation model for second language acquisition. *Journal of Multilingual and Multicultural Development, 7*(5), 379-392.

Scollon, R. (1974). *Conversations with a one year old.* Unpublished doctoral dissertation, University of Hawaii.

Scovel, T. (1978). The effect of affect on foreign language learning: A review of the anxiety research. *Language Learning, 28*, 129-142.

Scovel, T. (1988). *A time to speak: A psycholinguistic inquiry into the critical period for human speech.* New York: Newbury House/Harper & Row.

Scovel, T. Personal communication, 1991.

Scovel, T. (1991). *The role of culture in second language pedagogy.* Commissioned manuscript, Heinle & Heinle, Boston.

Searle, J. (1969). *Speech acts: An essay in the philosophy of language.* Cambridge: Cambridge University Press.

Seelye, H. N. (1987). *Teaching culture: Strategies for intercultural communication.* Lincolnwood, IL: National Textbook Company.

Seliger, H. W. (1983). Learner interaction in the classroom and its effect on language acquisition. In H. W. Seliger & M. H. Long (Eds.), *Classroom-oriented research in second language acquisition* (pp. 246-267). Rowley, MA: Newbury House.

Selinker, L. (1972). Interlanguage. *IRAL, 10*, 209-230.

Selinker, L. (Forthcoming). *Rediscovering interlanguage.* London: Longman.

Selinker, L., & Douglas, D. (1985). Wrestling with "context" in "interlanguage theory". *Applied Linguistics, 6*(2), 190-204.

Selinker, L., & Douglas, D. (1989). Research methodology in contextually-based second language research. *Second Language Research, 5*, 1-34.

Selinker, L., & Lamendella, J. T. (1981). Updating the interlanguage hypothesis. *Studies in Second Language Acquisition, 3*(2), 201-220.

Shavelson, R., & Stern, S. (1981). Research on teachers' pedagogical thoughts, judgments, and behavior. *Review of Educational Research, 51* (4), 455-498.

Shaw, P. (1982). *Fluency and the ESL writing skill.* Unpublished Master's thesis, University of Southern California.

Short, D. (1991). *How to integrate language and content instruction: A training manual* (2nd ed.). Washington, DC: Center for Applied Linguistics.

Sinclair, J., & Brazil, D. (1982). *Teacher talk.* Oxford: Oxford University Press.

Sinclair, J., & Coulthard, M. (1975). *Towards an analysis of discourse.* Oxford: Oxford University Press.

Singleton, D. (1989). *Language acquisition: The age factor.* Clevedon, Avon: Multilingual Matters.

Slavin, R. (1981). Synthesis of research on cooperative learning. *Educational Leadership,* 655-660.

Slavin, R. (1983). *Cooperative learning.* New York: Longman.

Slavin, R. (1989, December; 1990, January). Research on cooperative learning. Consensus and controversy. *Educational Leadership, 47*(4), 52-55.

Slobin, D. I. (1973). Cognitive prerequisites for the development of grammar. In C. Fillmore & D. I. Slobin (Eds.), *Studies of child language development* (pp. 175-208). New York: Holt, Rinehart & Winston.

Smith, S. M. (1984). *The theater arts and the teaching of second languages.* Reading, MA: Addison-Wesley.

Snow, C. (1972). Mothers' speech to children learning language. *Child Development, 43,* 549-565.

Snow, C. (1977). Mothers' speech research. From input to interaction. In C. E. Snow & C. Ferguson (Eds.), *Talking to children: Language input and acquisition.* Cambridge: Cambridge University Press.

Snow, C. E., & Ferguson, C. (Eds.). (1977). *Talking to children: Language input and acquisition.* Cambridge: Cambridge University Press.

Snow, M. A. (1991). *Themes and tasks position statement.* Commissioned manuscript, Heinle & Heinle, Boston.

Snow, M. A., Met, M., & Genesee, F. (1989). A conceptual framework for the integration of language and content in second/foreign language instruction. *TESOL Quarterly, 23,* 201-217.

Spack, R., & Sadow, C. (1983). Student-teacher working journals in ESL freshman composition. *TESOL Quarterly, 17*(4), 575-593.

Staton, J. (1984). *Acquiring practical reasoning through teacher-student interactions in dialogue journals.* Unpublished doctoral dissertation, University of California at Los Angeles.

Steinbeck, J. (1947). *The pearl.* New York: Viking.

Stern, S. (1985). *Teaching literature in ESL/EFL: An integrated approach.* Unpublished doctoral dissertation, University of California at Los Angeles.

Stern, S. L. (1991). An integrated approach to literature in ESL/EFL. In M. Celce-Murcia (Ed.), *Teaching English as a second or foreign language.* New York: Newbury House/Harper & Row.

Stevick, E. (1963). *A workbook in language teaching.* New York: Abington.

Stevick, E. W. (1976). *Memory, meaning, and method: Some psychological perspectives on language learning.* Rowley, MA: Newbury House.

Stevick, E. (1980). The Levertov machine. In R. Scarcella & S. D. Krashen (Eds.), *Research in second language acquisition.* Rowley, MA: Newbury House.

Stewart, E. C. (1972). *American cultural patterns: A cross-cultural perspective.* Yarmouth, ME: Intercultural Press.

Stoller, F. (1986). Reading lab: Developing low level reading skills. In F. Dubin, D. E. Eskey, & W. Grabe (Eds.), *Teaching second language reading for academic purposes* (pp. 51-76). Reading, MA: Addison-Wesley.

Street, B. V. (1984). *Literacy in theory and practice.* Cambridge: Cambridge University Press.

Strevens, P. (1988). Interaction outside the classroom: Using the community. In W. Rivers (Ed.), *Interactive language teaching* (pp. 170-176). Cambridge: Cambridge University Press.

Swain, M. (1984). Large-scale communicative language testing: A case study. In S. J. Savignon & M. S. Berns (Eds.), *Initiatives in communicative language teaching: A book of readings.* Reading, MA: Addison-Wesley.

Swain, M. (1985). Communicative competence; Some roles of comprehensible input and comprehensible output in its development. In S. M. Gass & C. G. Madden (Eds.), *Input in second language acquisition* (pp. 235-253). Rowley, MA: Newbury House.

Swales, J. (1987). Utilizing the literatures in teaching the research paper. *TESOL Quarterly, 21*(1), 41-68.

Swales, J. (1990). *Genre analysis.* Cambridge: Cambridge University Press.

Talbott, V., & Oxford, R. L. (1991). Creating a video variety show: Student-generated simulations. *Simulation/Games for Learning, 20* (4). 378-397.

Tannen, D. (1990). *You just don't understand: Women and men in conversation.* New York: Ballentine Books.

Tarone, E. (1978). Conscious communication strategies in interlanguage: A progress report. In H. Brown, C. Yorio, & R. Crymes (Eds.), *On TESOL '77* (pp. 194-203). Washington DC.: TESOL.

Tarone, E. (1981). Some thoughts on the notion of communication strategy. *TESOL Quarterly, 15*(3), 285-295.

Tarone, E. (1988). *Variation in interlanguage.* London: Edward Arnold.

Taylor, S. E. (1964). *Listening: What research says to the teacher.* Washington, DC: National Education Association.

Tharp, R. G., & Gallimore, R. (1988). *Rousing minds to life: Teaching, learning and schooling in social context.* Cambridge: Cambridge University Press.

Tharp, R. G., & Gallimore, R. (1989). Rousing schools to life. *American Educator, 13*(2), 20-25.

Tucker, G. R., Hamayan, E., & Genesee, F. H. (1976). Affective, cognitive, and social factors in second language acquisition. *Canadian Modern Language Review, 32*, 214-226.

Ur, P. (1981). *Discussions that work.* Cambridge: Cambridge University Press.

Ur, P. (1984). *Teaching listening comprehension.* Cambridge: Cambridge University Press.

Van Ek, J. A. (1976). *The threshold level for modern language learning in schools.* Strasbourg: Committee for General and Technical Education, Council of Europe.

Van Ek, J., & Alexander, L. (1980). *Threshold level English.* Oxford: Pergamon.

Van Lier, L. A. W. (1988). *The classroom and the language learner.* London: Longman.

Varonis, E., & Gass, S. (1982). The comprehensibility of non-native speech. *Studies in Second Language Acquisition, 4*, 41-52.

Varonis, E., & Gass, S. (1985a). Miscommunication in native/non-native conversation. *Language in Society, 14*, 327-343.

Varonis, E., & Gass, S. (1985b). Non-native/non-native conversation: A model of negotiation of meaning. *Applied Linguistics, 6*, 71-90.

Via, R. A. (1976). *English in three acts.* Honolulu: University Press of Hawaii.

Via, R. A. (1987). "The magic if" of theater: Enhancing language learning through drama. In W. M. Rivers (Ed.), *Interactive language teaching* (pp. 110-123). Cambridge: Cambridge University Press.

Vygotsky, L. S. (1956). *Izbrannie psichologicheskie issledovania (Selected psychological research).* Moscow: Izdatel'stvo Akademii Pedagogicheskikh Nauk.

Vygotsky, L. S. (1978). *Mind in society: The development of higher psychological processes.* M. Cole, V. John-Steiner, S. Scribner, & E. Souberman (Eds. & Trans.). Cambridge, MA: Harvard University Press.

Vygotsky, L. S. (1987). *Collected works.* R. W. Rieber & A. S. Carton (Eds.), N. Minick (Trans.). New York: Plenum.

Wallace, C. (1988). *Learning to read in a multicultural society: The social context of second language literacy.* London: Prentice Hall.

Wenden, A., & Rubin, J. (1987). *Learner strategies in language learning.* Englewood Cliffs, NJ: Prentice Hall.

Weslander, D., & Stephany, G. (1983). Evaluation of English as a second language program for Southeast Asian students. *TESOL Quarterly, 17*(3), 473-480.

White, L. (1985). The acquisition of parameterized grammars: Subjacency in second language acquisition. *Second Language Research, 1,* 1-17.

White, L. (1987). Against comprehensible input: The input hypothesis and the development of second language competence. *Applied Linguistics, 8*(2), 95-110.

White, R. H. (1959). Motivation reconsidered. *Psychology Review, 66*(5), 297-333.

White, R. V. (1980). *Teaching written English.* London: George Allen & Unwin.

White, R. V. (1981). Approaches to writing. *Guideline, 6,* 1-11. Reprinted in M. H. Long & J. C. Richards (Eds.). (1987). *Methodology in TESOL: A book of readings* (pp. 298-304). New York: Newbury House/Harper & Row.

Whorf, B. (1956). *Language, thought, and reality.* Cambridge, MA: MIT Press.

Wilkins, D. A. (1976). *Notional syllabuses.* Oxford: Oxford University Press.

Williams, J. D., & Capizzi Snipper, G. (1990). *Literacy and bilingualism.* New York: Longman.

Wing, B. H. (Ed.). (1986). *Listening, reading, and writing: Analysis and application.* Middlebury, VT: Northeast Conference on the Teaching of Foreign Languages.

Wipf, J. A. (1984). Strategies for teaching second language listening comprehension. *Foreign Language Annals, 17,* 345-348.

Wolfson, N. (1981). Compliments in cross-cultural perspective. *TESOL Quarterly, 15*(2), 117-124.

Wolfson, N. (1989). *Perspectives: Sociolinguistics and TESOL.* New York: Newbury House/Harper & Row.

Wolfson, N., & Judd, E. (Eds.). (1983). *Sociolinguistics and language acquisition.* Rowley, MA: Newbury House.

Wolvin, A. D., & Coakley, C. G. (1985). *Listening* (2nd ed.). Dubuque, IA: William C. Brown.

Wong, R. (1987). *Teaching pronunciation: Focus on English rhythm and intonation.* Englewood Cliffs, NJ: Prentice Hall.

Wong Fillmore, L. (1985). Second language learning in children: A proposed model. *Issues in language development.* Rosslyn, VA: National Clearinghouse on Bilingual Education.

Wong Fillmore, L. (1986). Research currents: Equity or excellence? *Language Arts, 63,* 474-481.

Yule, G., & Tarone, E. (1990). On the role of communication strategies in second language performance. In R. Scarcella, E. S. Andersen, & S. D. Krashen (Eds.), *Developing communicative competence in a second language* (pp. 179-194). New York: Newbury House/Harper & Row.

Zamel, V. (1987). Recent research on writing pedagogy. *TESOL Quarterly, 21*(4), 687-716.

Zimmerman, C., & West, C. (1975). Sex roles, interruptions, and silence in conversation. In B. Thorne & N. Henley (Eds.), *Language and sex: Difference and dominance* (pp. 130-151). Rowley, MA: Newbury House.

INDEX